the series on school reform

Patricia A. Wasley
Bank Street College of Education

Ann Lieberman
NCREST

Joseph P. McDonald
New York University

SERIES EDITORS

This series also incorporates earlier titles in the Professional Development and Practice Series

TEACHING IN COMMON

Challenges to Joint Work in Classrooms and Schools

Anne DiPardo

**National Council
of Teachers of English**
Urbana, Illinois

**Teachers College
Columbia University
New York and London**

for Megan Engelfried Rich

Published by Teachers College Press, 1234 Amsterdam Avenue, New York, NY 10027

Copyright © 1999 by Teachers College, Columbia University

Library of Congress Cataloging-in-Publication Data

DiPardo, Anne, 1953–
    Teaching in common : challenges to joint work in classrooms and schools / Anne DiPardo.
        p.   cm. — (The series on school reform)
    Includes bibliographical references and index.
    ISBN 0-8077-3764-X. — ISBN 0-8077-3763-1 (pbk.)
    1. Group work in education—United States—Case studies.   2. Inter-school cooperation—United States—Case studies.   3. Team learning approach in education—United States—Case studies.   4. Effective teaching—United States—Case studies.   5. Educational change—United States—Case studies.   I. Title.   II. Series.
    LB1032.D52   1998
    371.39'5—DC21   98-28699

ISBN 0-8077-3763-1 (paper)
ISBN 0-8077-3764-X (cloth)
NCTE stock number 50683

Printed on acid-free paper
Manufactured in the United States of America

05   04   03   02   01   00   99   98   8   7   6   5   4   3   2   1

Contents

Acknowledgments

This work was funded by a National Academy of Education Spencer Post-Doctoral fellowship and a grant from the NCTE Research Foundation. The University of Iowa offered additional assistance, including an Old Gold Summer Fellowship and grants from the College of Education Dean's Fund and the Graduate College. Thanks to all who provided generous support over several years of data collection and writing.

There is a basic irony in a single-authored book about collaboration. I knew my share of isolation in this work—hours on the road, then alone at my desk, expanding field notes and drafting chapters. But the years I spent working on *Teaching in Common* were full of wonderful company, too, people who have sustained me with their kind encouragement and sage guidance. I am particularly indebted to Renee Clift, Mike DiPardo, Russel Durst, Sarah Warshauer Freedman, David Wallace, and Helena Worthen, each of whom read an earlier version of this manuscript with insightful care, offering feedback that showed me how to correct flaws and make my purpose clearer. I was blessed, too, with a host of supportive friends and colleagues, each providing just the right kind of help when it was most needed. Thanks to Betsy Altmaier, David Bills, Ursula Delworth, Caroline Heller, Bill Lyons, Jim Marshall, Theresa Mitchell, Meg Rich, Mike Rose, and Leslie Schrier.

I am grateful to the teachers who let me in on their relationships, classrooms, and lives. I stayed a long time, contributed little to the needs of the moment, asked lots of nosy questions, and took years moving my observations into print. I am a better person for having known them, and hope I can offer here some small portion of what they gave me.

Chapter 1

Introduction

Collaboration is hardly a new idea in education or anywhere else—indeed, the search for substantive, productive company has a way of pervading our individual and collective histories alike. Most of us can remember the slogan "two heads are better than one" from our earliest years on the planet, long before "distributed cognition" entered our professional vocabulary. We live amidst reciprocal influences, shaping and being shaped by the people and places around us. This is no less true for those who teach, although the rules and rituals of the profession may tend to make us think so: frenetic scheduling, days spent in what Dan Lortie (1975) called "egg-crate architecture," a long cultural tradition that casts effective teaching as solitary performance. Schools often furnish little incentive to collaborate, offering insufficient time, resources, or rewards for doing so (Little, 1990). The obstacles are familiar, even as teacher collaboration continues to be highlighted as a key feature of effectively restructured schools (Quellmalz, Shields, Knapp, & Bamburg, 1995), its benefits described as plentiful and varied.

ONE WORD, MANY THINGS

The current enthusiasm for teacher collaboration is enmeshed in a number of broader trends. Many are coming to believe that schools should more closely resemble collaborative workplaces in the world outside (Myers, 1996; New London Group, 1996; Siegel & Byrne, 1994; Wirth, 1992), and that a greater share of school decision making should emerge from conversations among teachers (Fullan & Hargreaves, 1996; Lieberman, 1995; Sizer, 1992; Wilson & Daviss, 1994). More broadly still, talk of "community" and "interdependence" has come to pervade the wider arena, whether in political campaigns or newsmagazines, or sprinkled across the pages of best-selling books (e.g., Bellah, Madsen, Sullivan, Swidler, & Tipton, 1985, 1991; Covey, 1989; Csikszentmihalyi, 1993; Etzioni, 1993; Peck, 1987). These arguments are sometimes vaguely nostalgic, infused with a longing for better times, before the cogs of technocratic bureaucracy began moving at full speed (Merz & Furman, 1997). As our thoughts turn to the common good, schools may well seem, as they did for John Dewey nearly a century ago, a logical place to start.

Researchers have repeatedly argued that isolated teachers are unduly limited in imagination and reach—narrowly conservative in their pedagogic thinking and approaches (e.g., Johnson, 1990; Lortie, 1975), unable to track students' continuing growth (Rosenholtz, 1985, 1989), given to feelings of powerlessness (Ashton & Webb, 1986) and professional loneliness (Fullan & Hargreaves, 1996; Lightfoot, 1986). Effective-schools researchers have repeatedly made the case for closer collegial relations (see Purkey & Smith, 1983), as have those working from a more ecological perspective (e.g., Lieberman, 1992; Lieberman & Miller, 1984, 1991; Lightfoot, 1983)—arguing that enhanced opportunities for collaboration will ease newcomers' anxieties, keep some of our best veteran teachers in the classroom (Little, 1987), and better support student learning (Rosenholtz, 1989). Collaborative work may provide opportunities to examine critically the process by which decisions are made and knowledge is constructed; in addition to exploring new perspectives, collaborating teachers may be moved to take on new roles, including leadership responsibilities (Clift, Johnson, Holland, & Veal, 1992; Clift, Veal, Holland, Johnson, & McCarthy, 1995). In a diverse democracy where students must learn to find places to stand among competing points of view, classrooms might best be seen as places for weighing this perspective against that, for facilitating awareness of one's own and others' intellectual constructions (Clift et al., 1995, p. 5). By modeling such a process in their own work—exploring differences, sharing strengths, and locating common ground—teachers can model the social nature of learning for their students.

Meanwhile, others emphasize the moral and affective aspects of teacher collaboration. In contrast to empirical work on school effectiveness, these perspectives are associated with a philosophical literature arguing the importance of warm, "caring" relationships in schools (e.g., Noddings, 1988, 1992; Sergiovanni, 1994). While such bonds may promote pedagogic innovation, they are also said to enhance teachers' lives in more complexly human ways, promoting a richer mode of being for both individuals and groups (Greene, 1991). For Clandinin and Connelly (1995), collaboration allows possibilities to listen receptively to one another's stories, to forge relationships, and to "think again" (pp. 155–156). In related work, Clandinin (1993) argues that shared storytelling can help teachers make "new sense of practice," while also encouraging them to live "more moral lives" as they negotiate among "many ways of knowing, many ways of making sense, and many institutional stories" (p. 12). Such perspectives echo Robert

Coles's (1989) arguments for the healing power of story, and its potential for helping us understand our individual narratives in light of the larger human experience.

Although multiple claims have been made for the benefits of teacher collaboration, we know relatively little about the various forms such activities can take, or their implications for school reform. Collaboration is, as Dewey once said of society, "one word, but many things" (1916/1944, p. 81)—including efforts both far-reaching and superficial, both teacher-owned and administratively mandated, each scenario holding potential pitfalls all its own. Collaborative relationships raise questions of power, of who initiates, guides, and gauges. Commonly bundled under the "teacher collaboration" rubric are programs such as "peer coaching," where teachers visit one another's classrooms, usually at administrators' urgings, for the purpose of providing evaluative feedback (Joyce & Showers, 1982; critiqued by Hargreaves, 1994). Meanwhile, others have argued that teachers must have the authority to set their own goals and projects (Rudduck, 1988; Schwartz, 1991; Thiessen, 1992), as well as ample time to generate ideas, plan instruction, and build trust (Maeroff, 1993). Andy Hargreaves cautions that where policymakers regard collaboration as an unmitigated good, teachers may be nudged into "contrived collegiality," required to share their work even where they prefer, perhaps for quite principled and compelling reasons, to maintain autonomy (Hargreaves, 1993, 1994). The fact of people joining together does not necessarily mean looking to the wider good, together embracing an inclusive ethic of mutual care; indeed, groups of any kind can become mere cliques, providing a sense of membership even as they undermine efforts at productive change (Dewey, 1916/1944; Hargreaves, 1994; Little, 1993a). Rather than offering useful challenges and fresh perspectives, collaboration can conceivably serve to reinforce "poorly informed habit" (Little, 1990, p. 525).

Calling teacher collaboration "conceptually amorphous and ideologically sanguine," Judith Warren Little (1990, p. 509) acknowledges the need for more fine-grained terminology to distinguish among these various categories of meaning. To describe substantive collaborations that allow teachers an active voice, she proposes the term "joint work," defined as "interdependent professional activity involving conscious structuring of time and task, as well as teacher leadership and initiative" (p. 519). The definition is useful, shaving away more superficial or tightly controlled efforts, gesturing toward a territory that remains both wide and varied. Here rest lots of issues, questions even more fundamental than how to assess the effectiveness or goodness of such work. The American penchant for individualism has been played out with something of a vengeance in the profession of teaching, and any attempt to reverse historic precedent is sure to be fraught with complication. Before we can begin to wonder what such joint work can do, perhaps we need to ask more basic questions concerning some of the things it is or might be.

TOWARD A SOCIAL-CULTURAL PERSPECTIVE

Collaboration is increasingly seen as key to learning at any age, whether the learners be fourth-graders, college freshmen, or veteran teachers. While it may bring to mind Deweyan social constructivism (1916/1944), the collaborative-learning movement has been more overtly grounded in the theories of Lev Vygotsky (1978, 1986), the Russian cognitive psychologist whose writings date back to the early decades of this century. For Vygotsky, all learning occurs in what he calls the "zone of proximal development," wherein an "expert or more capable peer" helps learners perform tasks just outside their independent mastery. In this zone lie "functions that could be termed the 'buds' or 'flowers' of development rather than the 'fruits' of development," those abilities "that have not yet matured but are in the process of maturation, functions that will mature tomorrow but are currently in an embryonic state" (1978, p. 86). In other words, here are things one cannot do alone, but might do with help—help that is gradually withdrawn as the learner "internalizes" the assistance made available through supportive interaction (Applebee & Langer, 1983; Bruner, 1978).

Transplanted to a different place and time, Vygotsky's provocative, somewhat sketchy theories have been invoked to defend a range of classroom practices here in the States, including essentially traditional strategies in cosmetically altered form (Cazden, in press). These appropriations have raised a host of issues, and so too has the theory itself. Sometimes learning does not occur in dyads, for instance, but in interactive, participatory groups wherein zones of proximal development overlap and intertwine (Moll & Whitmore, 1993; Rogoff, 1994). Problematic, too, is Vygotsky's "expert" or "more capable peer" bringing the neophyte along (1978, p. 86)—roles that are a good bit more fluid in actual teaching–learning interactions (Hatano, 1993; Stone, 1993). Finally, issues of power come into play, questions of who decides the how, when, and what of collaboration (Palincsar, Brown, & Campione, 1993).

A number of theorists have argued the need to build beyond Vygotsky's contributions, toward a more comprehensive social-cultural theory that might better inform both research and practice. Wertsch (1991), for instance, incorporates the theories of Vygotsky's contemporary Mikhail Bakhtin (1981, 1986) in suggesting the need to locate educational events within wider cultural, institutional, and historic contexts. Freedman (1994a) observes that as provocative as such constructs may be, they provide little by way of specific guides to concrete situations; rather, she argues, researchers need to engage in the theory-building enterprise of observing the "continuum of involvement and the kind of social space necessary to promote high levels of involvement" (p. 91). Such spaces occur not only between particular people, but across the ecologies of larger groups and whole institutions as well, moving us to reconceptualize the nature of learning and places where it happens. According to Forman, Minick, and Stone (1993), we are only beginning to sort through the ramifications of these new perspectives:

> To say that social interaction and cognition develops as part of an integral system in connection with motivation, affect, and values does not merely imply the need for an addendum to earlier theoretical formulations. A fundamental reconceptualization of mind and its development in social practice is implied . . . this reconceptualization has profound theoretical, methodological, and pragmatic implications that we are only just beginning to understand and address. (pp. 6–7)

Seen from this perspective, teacher collaboration is an element of a social-cultural dynamic encompassing self and setting, cognition and spirit. These notions are consonant with recent attention to the ecological nature of reform (e.g., Sarason, 1971/1996), the idea that schools are systems characterized by reciprocal influences across sectors and levels. If we regard collaboration among teachers and collaboration among students as organically linked, then efforts to promote either will be enhanced by attention to both. If we hope to see learners actively engaged in argument, reflection, and the co-construction of new understandings, then it makes good sense to create similar opportunities for teachers (Clift et al., 1995; Kohn, 1996; Little 1993a; Maeroff, 1993; Meier, 1995; Sarason, 1972, 1990, 1971/1996; Tharp, 1993). If students internalize cultures for teaching and learning as well as particular bits of content, then we might best promote human environments that favor authentic "instructional conversations" (Chang-Wells & Wells, 1993, p. 85), opening spaces where an array of collaborative activities can take root. Collegial relations help influence environments for learning, but so too are they shaped by the policies, issues, and group dynamics that characterize whole schools and school districts (Merz & Furman, 1997).

This study explores the nature of joint work as seen from different angles of vision, particularly the teachers' own. I also observe varied contexts for collaboration, considering issues at the levels of teams, departments, schools, and districts. In each case teachers face a defining set of challenges—concerns that, taken together, comprise a list of some of the key dilemmas before educators today. They run the gamut, from de-tracking to gender discrimination, from managing crises in the lives of at-risk students to school restructuring. These portraits of human relation-ships are also portraits of places, of the institutional cultures that set the terms and shape the issues.

PLACES AND PARTNERSHIPS

My four sites are all in the heart of the midwestern United States, a place known for its commitment to quality education and penchant for pedagogic innovation (Sutton, 1991). I began an 18-month process of data collection in August of 1993, at the conclusion of a summer of disastrous flooding widely reported in the national media. Watching months of volun-teer sandbagging and cleanup, one West Coast journalist observed that these images of community spirit rest oddly beside the region's reputation for "conformity," "conservative politics," and "low-grade xenophobia." "The challenge may be collective—a swollen river, a closed factory," she wrote. "Or individual—a family illness, a burned-out house. Either way, people instinctively come to the rescue and demand, 'What do you need?'" (Salter, 1993).

Educators who advocate professional collaboration here find the ground in many ways well prepared. Certainly officials in all four districts I visited were avidly in favor of promoting more collaboration among teach-ers; but meanwhile, teachers lobbied for conditions that would better sup-port their joint work, including increased time and authority (Sutton, 1991). In a report to the general public, one midwestern teachers' organization put it this way:

> One reason schools are inflexible is that teachers lack authority over profes-sional functions. We are ready to build trust by working cooperatively; to interact with one another collegially; and to build meaningful goals and com-mitments for schools. But we are blocked by obsolete, undemocratic notions of authority and bureaucracy. To do our jobs, we need a clear definition of our authority. (Sutton, 1991, p. 4)

While these teachers faced many of the same roadblocks confronting their colleagues across the nation, in other respects my four sites looked to be best-case scenarios, situated in a region known for educational excel-lence, public support for schools, and norms of cooperation. The teachers I followed had all experienced success as both individuals and teams; well-educated, worldly, and caring, they possessed as well a kind of off-handed neighborliness, carrying a sense of interdependence into their personal and professional lives alike. They were quintessential midwesterners, the kind of people who show up at potlucks carrying carefully prepared covered dishes, who give away home-grown produce, who serve as community volunteers. Born collaborators, perhaps—but challenged just the same, as each site presented its quietly troubling contours, each relationship its snags and stresses. Together these teachers provide opportunities to explore the dynamics of essentially successful collaborations, and invitations to reflect on ways that such work might be better supported.

Since I wanted to explore diverse instances of joint work across contrasting sites, I chose schools informed by a range of values, challenges, and traditions. The collaborations themselves were varied as well, including teachers newly engaged in such ventures and well-established partnerships between or among veteran teachers. In some cases these were full-fledged co-teaching situations where two teachers were present before a class at the same time; in other cases, they involved extensive co-planning and joint reflection. Since my own background is in literacy education, I elected to follow partnerships that included at least one English–language arts teacher. In two instances, these teachers worked with same-discipline colleagues; in the remaining two they negotiated the complexities of interdisciplinary collaboration, in one case involving colleagues from science and English, the other a middle-school "house" group comprised of science, social studies, reading, math, and language arts teachers. I looked for strong teachers who spoke highly of their collaborations, and for teams and schools that would present a provocative array of issues.

I stayed an instructional trimester at each site, listening to teachers plan, reflect, and argue; observing their classes; and interviewing them both individually and jointly. Since I was interested in gathering multiple perspectives on each of these collaborations and sites, I also talked to school and district administrators, teachers and staff members, and focal teachers' students. I looked to insiders to guide me to what was important, following themes and concerns that they repeatedly named as key, asking them to suggest other informants or events I might seek out. Later, as I sifted through my notes and transcripts for each site, I was able to draw from multiple perspectives, both in identifying significant strands and in illustrating with relevant quotes, narrative, and description (Bogdan & Biklen, 1982; Erickson, 1986; Goetz & Lecompte, 1984; Lincoln & Guba, 1985; Merriam, 1988). (I assigned all participants pseudonyms, and altered details in order to safeguard the confidentiality of research sites.)

These portraits are slices frozen in time, documenting individuals and institutions wrangling with various kinds of change. Readers may recognize something of their own stories here, and help, perhaps, in articulating issues, arguments, and questions. This is what qualitative researchers call "user" or "reader" generalizabilty (Merriam, 1988; Walker, 1980)—that is, to provide others an opportunity to "generalize personally to their own situations" (McCutcheon, 1981), to use these "images of the possible" (Shuman, 1986, p. 146) as an impetus to reflect on local contexts, to discover fresh directions of inquiry and discussion (see also Connelly, 1978; Connelly & Clandinin, 1990; Guba & Lincoln, 1989). As we continue to hear calls for greater collaboration among teachers, the time seems right to consider some of the different ways that real people experience it—how their joint work influences opportunities for their students, and how it is enmeshed in the wider ecologies of programs, schools, and communities (Sarason, 1971/1996).

WHAT'S AHEAD

In the coming chapters I depict teachers together confronting a range of challenges, tracing connections between individual lives, collaborative relationships, and the contexts of classrooms and schools. Chapter 2 takes us well off the beaten path, to a public alternative school called the "Self-Directed Learning Center" (SDLC). A place of hard and often urgent challenges, the SDLC was the least recognized, least prestigious of the schools I followed. It was also the site of the most widely based collaboration, a rippling network that encompassed teachers, administrators, resource people, and students alike. Here I followed Max and Bill, two veteran teachers co-teaching a workshop class devoted to producing a weekly magazine of student writing, joint work enmeshed in an array of related efforts to manage the diverse needs of the SDLC's students. Max and Bill underscore the importance of collaboration in working with troubled young people, while their small, tightly networked school provides a model of generative institutional support.

In Chapter 3 I turn to Hamilton High, the recipient of numerous state and national awards for academic excellence. The many plaques lining its central corridors told only half of the school's story, a history long entangled in issues of social class, ethnicity, and educational philosophy. Hamilton's students were primarily European Americans from the wealthiest areas of its city, and African Americans from its poorest, a great divide reflected in a tradition of academic tracking. Here I followed Ada and Lou, two controversial English teachers offering parallel sections of a nontracked 10th-grade language arts class. They taught in neighboring classrooms far from the school's center—out in the industrial arts wing, one flight above the auto shop—where they together grappled with the challenges of integration, and faced down colleagues' disapproval. Ada and Lou's work highlights the modest power of small-scale collaboration in stimulating innovation; meanwhile, their colleagues and administrators remind us that institutional politics can present significant opposition, especially where a collaboration threatens time-honored traditions.

In Chapter 4 I turn to Anspach Middle School, the recent recipient of a prestigious award for its new interdisciplinary "house" teams. Located in an affluent bedroom community and well known for educational excellence, Anspach was quietly beset by funding problems and a burgeoning student population. Here issues of time and overcrowding took center stage, as I watched a team of veteran teachers struggle to meet the needs of the 182 students each of them saw every day. They offered one another wry humor, warm collegiality, and mutual support—but also the sad recognition that their workload was overwhelming, that the realities they were facing belied the school image presented by their public-relations savvy principal. Their conversations reveal the inner workings of a house system, confirming some of the much-touted benefits, but also exploring ways that such efforts can be imperiled.

Chapter 5 details a collaboration between two beginning teachers, Jo and Jane, exploring the mutual support they provided through a series of challenging passages. Graduates of the same teacher-preparation program, they became fast friends when they began work nine months earlier at Pioneer Junior High, located in a well-funded rural district. The beneficiaries of careful mentoring, Jo and Jane offered one another what the official channels could not—an opportunity to talk frankly about sensitive issues, to confess their insecurities, to imagine curricula informed by their shared beliefs—and connection that extended well beyond school walls. Their partnership suggests how collaboration can support the professional growth and emotional well-being of young teachers, enhancing instruction while also providing comfort and friendship. Meanwhile, Jo and Jane's collaboration also strengthened their efforts to enter a wider collegial network, to assume increasing responsibilities in a school marked at once by pedagogic innovation and cultural conservatism.

To look closely at an instance of teacher collaboration is to consider as well what teachers are collaborating about, why, and what sorts of help or hindrance they encounter along the way. In a concluding chapter, I consider the implications of these collaborations and places, each marked by excellence and success, but also stymied by challenges and obstacles. Here I will explore the kinds of conditions that best support collaboration, and propose some new ways of imagining the relationship between teachers' joint work and school culture.

These cases are not scenarios easily transplanted or duplicated, for "collaboration" cannot mean the same thing for all teachers in all places. "Any social arrangement that remains vitally social, or vitally shared, is educative to those who participate in it," wrote Dewey (1916/1944); "only when it becomes cast in a mold and runs in a routine way does it lose its educative power" (p. 6). The teachers I write about here would be the last to offer formulas, but I hope they will remind you what a professional life vitally shared might be and do.

Chapter 2

Learning by Surviving: *Max and Bill*

He has too much shade; the corn won't amount to much. But a squash is ablaze with blossom—maybe he'll get something there. I recall a saying of the desert monks: "If a man settles in a certain place and does not bring forth the fruit of that place, the place itself casts him out."

(Norris, 1993, p. 182)

It is late August, the end of a season of rains the national press called biblical. People in this midwestern town talk of "the summer that wasn't," turning to the new school year with a collective sense of loss. But for now it finally feels like summer, the morning air heavy as I walk up the mossy steps of a public alternative school called the Self-Directed Learning Center (SDLC). Downstairs are the district's administrative offices, where the walls are cool white, the furniture oak, the temperature a perpetual 72 degrees, the student art work professionally framed and placed behind glass. Upstairs and to the left, the SDLC's walls are a riot of colorful murals, the moist heat densely oppressive, the cast-off furniture carved by years of hard use. In both places, people plan a new beginning, there with official decorum, here with animated zeal, sitting on mismatched chairs that squeak.

A MUNDANE-FREE ZONE

The SDLC's nine teachers gather around a big table, together for the first time in 10 weeks. "So what did you do over summer vacation?" asks their principal, an avuncular man named Bob. The others smile, but one by one they tell of their time away—at a Trappist monastery, on a cross-country bike trip, pumping water out of basements, visiting the Vietnam memorial. A reading teacher named Lana wears a T-shirt bearing an image of an attaché-carrying couple, the international "no" symbol superimposed, the slogan reading "Mundane-free zone." She's the SDLC's resident internet enthusiast, and tells of correspondents from around the world converging on her soggy home. Next is the school's art teacher, a painter, published writer, and former physician. Everyone has trouble remembering how many languages he speaks or all his life has encompassed, but his face bears the scars of years spent working as a United Nations surgeon in war zones. He speaks now of a summer spent not far from his boyhood home, of walking the streets of Jerusalem with his ailing mother on his arm, worrying as much about random street violence as the progression of doctors' verdicts. In his pocket he carried a loaded gun, his hand always on it. And at night, there on the flickering TV was his more recent home, half a world away, besieged by surging water. In one of the more violent places on earth, he tells us, the disaster news was of midwestern states beginning with "I," the footage including glimpses of people boating down streets but a short distance from the SDLC. He carries great sadness through much of the story, but when he reaches this turn his dark eyes dance, and everybody laughs.

And then the whirl of collaborative work begins, as the principal recedes to the sidelines and the teachers brainstorm what to do before school begins in a scant four days. Lana jumps to her feet, chalk in hand, and begins making a list as the others generate items: a new orientation system, plans for an upcoming accreditation review, revising the graduation process, a schedule of courses for the new semester. I slowly realize that they have yet to decide who will teach what or when, but the teachers seem to feel none of my alarm. Max, the school's science teacher, moves to the board as Lana sits down, fitting course titles into the grid he draws, erasing and rearranging as the others hammer out possibilities. The art and English teachers propose a course called "literary illustration" that will bring published authors to the school to talk about their work and engage students in critical reading and artistic response. A new teacher wants to offer a student-taught course in conflict resolution, but Max wonders: Might the other kids see the peer leaders as an elite? Another teacher notes the growing number of junior-high kids the SDLC is bringing in this year, and frowns as she scans the emerging schedule for appropriate courses. There seem to be many untied ends, but the teachers are on a roll.

Gene, the math teacher, offers to take a van of kids to do flood cleanup next week. He is a shy man who glances down as he speaks, hesitating now and then, but when he smiles his eyes light up, and his face has the washed look of someone uncommonly good and kind. The others like to brag about Gene's election as president of the state's alternative schools association, and whenever it comes up today there is playful genuflecting and remarks about lofty position. Gene is quietly watchful, and he is attentive when everyone else seems to have forgotten my presence. "When I taught in traditional schools," he whispers to me, "I knew what I'd be teaching in April, even what *students* I'd have." His grin says that he likes the spontaneity of today's meeting, but he wonders what I might be making of it, and acknowledges that it can seem disconcerting. He talks of how much he values his colleagues' collaborative work, how he walks away from these meetings amazed at the fruits of their labors. He wears his own accomplishments lightly—the grant writing, the time at state leadership meetings, the footwork on creative new programs. "What a staff," he says, nodding toward the group.

It all seems tacitly choreographed: No one is asked to take notes on the spirited conversation, but someone always does, a different someone every half hour or so. As they plot the fall schedule, the conversation turns rhythmically now and then to particular kids—who was spotted at a shopping mall or county fair over the summer, who called from out of state to say they wouldn't be back, who was down in the flood plains, filling sandbags day after day. Their talk is warmly affectionate, full of references to "our kids," and praise of those helping with flood relief. But they talk also about one of the kids who seems permanently lost to them, a Native-American student who has quit school and joined a street gang. "You know, I feel like we really failed him," says Dave, the school counselor; "in some ways I feel like *I've* failed." No one blames the student, and no one tries to alleviate the general feeling that his fate is somehow the staff's fault. "The reason he's out there with them," says Max, "is because they're giving him what he needs, and we didn't. It's nonminority kids, too. We lose *a lot* of kids." The room is suddenly still. "The kids," says the principal, breaking the long silence, trying to bring the brightness back, "that's what we're all about—that's who we'll be talking about all year."

STARTING OVER AT A STEALTH SCHOOL

On Monday morning, business-suited visitors to the central offices are suddenly outnumbered by a raucous crowd of the SDLC's own, kids with tattoos, earrings in odd places, a flair for creative profanity, and inventive hairstyles. All the commotion makes it hard to believe, but only 66 students are present on this first day of classes. Bob estimates that total enrollment will peak at around 100 for the trimester, with lots of coming and going in the months ahead. He predicts that perhaps 30 or so will be with them all the way to June—but of these, some will stay on for a number of years, working closely with an advisor, becoming "almost like an extended family." One of the key goals of the school is to move students toward an understanding that learning can be "intrinsically rewarding," and while teachers offer feedback and credit for work produced, none of the courses are graded. Students fulfill a series of flexible requirements, call teachers by their first names, and, if all goes well, assume increasing responsibility. Only a handful graduate each year, but the ceremony is a cherished occasion, a public opportunity for students and teachers to talk about what they learned from one another. In watching the ceremony, notes the district superintendent, "You've got this sense that *all* of the people there are learners, not just the kids."

Teachers carefully avoid the deficit-oriented language that has long hounded many of these kids, but they acknowledge that if the SDLC is a family, it is a complicated one. According to the SDLC's mission statement, many of the school's students have experienced a "lack of success or ownership in the conventional school setting," and are seeking "personal relevance in their education that balances their present station in life with their ambitions and desires":

> Students enter the SDLC from various life situations and circumstances, e.g., group homes, teen-age parents, full-time employment, return from treatment or juvenile correction centers, independent living, foster care, disenfranchised from the family, high artistic creativity, etc. . . . In many cases students must get their lives in order before they can concentrate on the direction of their education. At SDLC, acceptance and acknowledgment of the real-life factors beyond the school door that have an impact on the student's performance are integrated into the student's educational plans.

Everyone seems painfully aware of the stigma surrounding the school—students speak angrily of hearing it called a "school for losers," and teachers say that many of their conventional-school colleagues regard the SDLC as a strategy of last resort. The school remains a relatively well kept secret, right down to its unmarked front entrance. When a teacher died a few years ago, his colleagues decided to grant his longtime wish of erecting a sign next to the building, "just like at any other school," as Dave puts it. After much wrangling, the sign went up—not beside the main door on a much-traveled street, but just off the parking lot, where only SDLC students and staff see it. "And yet, there's some advantages to being a stealth school, too," one teacher says. "We get away with being pretty creative."

This morning at 8:00 the staff gathers for its first before-school faculty meeting of the year, crowding into a sweltering conference room adjacent to the SDLC office. These meetings happen every morning, providing a chance to worry together about particular students, discuss a range of policy issues, and pin down last-minute logistics. Today there are many of those, but also a casual confidence that the details will settle into place, that the vans will arrive for flood cleanup, that someone will pick up bagels for the kids' morning break and find money to pay for them. Again Bob takes a back seat as teachers assume the lead in brainstorming an agenda for this morning's whole-school meeting. While Bob jots down what they want him to say, the staff passes around a fat stack of snapshots.

The photos are of a mural dedication just before the close of the last school year. Over that spring, the SDLC's art teacher and a group of students had been painting scenes of the town and its people on a wall in a downtown mini-mall. One of the artists, a 14-year-old boy who was fast becoming an SDLC success story, added a figure on a bike traveling in the midst of automobile traffic. Higher up, where the sky and clouds were supposed to be, he painted the grille of a car. Classmates argued that it seemed out of keeping with the mural's realism, but he just shrugged and said "my car's in heaven." Several days later he was struck and killed by a drunk driver as he pedaled his bicycle down a dark highway late at night, leaving a host of unanswered questions and a school in grief. The mural was dedicated to him last May in a ceremony attended by the whole SDLC community and a sprinkling of district administrators and friends. "The SDLC is really more like a family than a school," one student said to the assembled crowd, revealing a tenderness she usually kept hidden. Now, on this first day of a new year, the teachers pass around photos of this wild-haired young woman at the microphone, the mural an explosion of color behind her, remembering.

The meeting runs late, and this year's students are already crowding against the office door, ready to sign in for the day, one singing over and over a line from "New York, New York": "I want to be a part of it . . ." Meanwhile, Bill is ending the meeting on a note of alarm: The new orientation procedures they developed last week won't be in effect for several days, and he worries about the new kids. "We're throwing them to the wolves for a week!" he warns, his voice charged with caution. Already moving toward the doors, the others call out strategies to make sure everyone gets immediate advising and counseling. Bill's long, pale face still registers worry, but he's a man with an off-beat sense of humor and expansive love for this staff, and he walks away smiling, ready with wisecracks for the students waiting outside, bidding a temporary good-bye to the boss he calls "Uncle Bobby."

It is time for homeroom—called "Oasis" here—and I follow Bob down to the big multipurpose room where the whole-school meeting will be held afterward. We find Max's group there, since district administrators are using his regular room for a meeting. His students ask about the big, echoing space. Max diminishes a touchy issue, saying the school "didn't sign up for the other room in time." "That sucks," says a female student. "I like it down here," says another, "it's a lot more convenient for smokers." Max says he hates the acoustics, then settles down to business, interrupting himself a few minutes later as a girl comes in late. She holds her head down, looking painfully shy, but Max seems genuinely gleeful: "Awriight!" he exclaims in greeting, asking her to sign in for the "official count." "It's good to see you again," he adds.

Bob and I have a quiet conversation off to one side. He tells me that this room was a gymnasium back when the building housed an elementary school; when the SDLC first moved in, this was a space where kids could run off some energy, but now it is primarily reserved for school board meetings. Bob says he makes "no bones" about the SDLC's feeling crowded, but shrugs when asked about a new building, noting how many times a bond measure for a new elementary school has been defeated. Students are filing in early for the school meeting, and a pack of cigarettes in a boy's pocket catches his eye. Bob engages the student in warm conversation about family and mutual acquaintances, then tells him, gesturing toward the small box, to "keep those where I can't see 'em—'cause otherwise I'll have to cause trouble about it."

The decibel level rises as ragged students show up for the morning's all-school gathering, tossing aggressive banter across the now-crowded room. As Bob calls the meeting to order, he waits for help from students. "Settle down, be a little serious!" shouts one. "This is an alternative school—we're *supposed* to be rude!" yells another. Eventually it is quiet enough for Bob to be heard, and he explains that anyone interested in working on the school's home construction project should go see an advisor ("If you don't have an advisor," he adds, "it's my fault"). Anyone interested in signing up to receive the lunch meal should go to "Barb's office," he tells them—Barb being the school's secretary, this the office the two of them share. There is a brief announcement about an upcoming ice cream social, and a reminder to "tell your parents." The same question rings out from various corners of the room: "What if we don't *live* with our parents?" Then Bob steps aside, ending his leadership of school meetings for the duration of my stay. He was nervous today, he tells me later, and prefers to maintain a lower profile, letting the staff run the show. "The less he does to make it look like it's his school," a teacher adds, "the more it becomes *our* school."

A student holds the floor for awhile, maintaining that people in the district offices have a "bad opinion" of the SDLC because of the "poor attitude" exhibited by the smokers congregating outside during break times; "You need to show respect," she says firmly. Then the teachers each say who they are and what they teach, and I have a chance to describe my project. Finally, the kids introduce themselves: "My specialty is flunking," says one. A few pause long before speaking, and the others yell out, urging them to get on with things. When the crowd grows boisterous, a student shouts them down: "The sooner we do this, the sooner we can get out of here."

It is time for course sign-ups, and Bill takes the floor, assuming the pseudo-smooth voice of what he calls his "quiz-show host" persona. "We don't have a student newspaper here at the SDLC," he says, "we have— '*Zine*!" Bill explains that '*Zine* is a weekly magazine published all year, and that there's also a '*Zine* class, a writing workshop he co-facilitates with Max. While anyone can contribute to '*Zine*, he urges people who are especially interested to join them. He makes it sound inviting, and when sign-ups begin a few minutes later, two-thirds of the students present crowd around the '*Zine* table. It will be a big class by SDLC standards, maybe too big, but when kids are interested in something, these teachers are loath to set limits.

I already know a little about '*Zine*—that Max and Bill started it a year earlier, hoping to ease kids' fears of literacy, encourage more substantive writing, and teach some computer skills in the bargain. I will learn more about it as I watch Max and Bill move through the trimester, and more about them, too—who they are as individuals and a team, and how their joint work moves with the shape-shifting energy of the SDLC.

MEN AT WORK

Max

Max is a compact man of perhaps 50 or so with a drooping mustache and a voice that seems somehow larger than his physical presence. He has a way of drawing out vowels that lets you know he is still thinking, that his outspokenness comes with an invitation to take issue or help him along. One week '*Zine* would feature a student's cartoon of a monster named "Evil Max," a big devilish-looking thing with horned, bat-like wings and a spike growing out of his head. "Stop reading this picture and go to class," the words in the balloon sneered, "you *rodents*!" On the one hand, Max is a tough customer who calls himself the school's "enforcer," but he is also a guy who hesitates to censor perspectives of any kind, even if it means being playfully caricatured as some malevolent version of himself. Max's openness and lack of cynicism make him seem somehow younger than his years, and even when afire with anger, he comes across as deeply peaceable. This fall marks his 15th year at the SDLC, a record among the current staff, but Max is doing more than holding on: He is a vital, energetic force here, a resilient veteran who gives liberally, cares deeply, and knows how to maintain sanity.

Max grew up Quaker in a North Dakota college town, then moved around the country as he completed undergraduate and graduate studies in biology and limnology, the study of freshwater lakes and streams. He was a conscientious objector during the Vietnam War, and his alternative service involved working for two years in a residential school for troubled youth, an experience that shone a sort of light on his professional path. After that he worked a string of jobs that sound impossibly hard—as a house parent in a school for mentally retarded kids, at a boarding school for court-adjudicated juvenile delinquents. When he found himself out of a teaching job, he worked for awhile at a gas station, then as a stock man at J. C. Penney's, where he was eventually offered an administrative post with lots of responsibility and a big salary. "I went home and said, 'that's not what I want to do with my life,'" Max recalls, "'I don't want to be a regional manager making lots of money; what I want to do is work with kids.'"

It is hard to imagine Max doing anything else. He strikes me as a person more at home outdoors, but the SDLC allows opportunities for that, too, for engaging kids in hands-on learning about prairie restoration or the town's polluted river. Max is an activist citizen involved in a range of efforts beyond the SDLC—local politics, various youth organizations, the district's equity committee, efforts to promote bicycling to work, historic preservation, cleaning up his neighborhood creek—but his first calling is right here. "Our mission is to help these kids who won't make it otherwise," he says emphatically. "I have a burning passion to try and help these kids, because I think it's important for them as individuals, important for us as a society. If *we* lose them, they're *lost*." Max speaks of the need to "bowl kids over with your desire to teach them," but he draws a distinction between being a "rescuer" and a clear-headed "advocate for the person": "You can't have bleeding hearts here," he notes, "because they'll get consumed."

When Max talks to preservice teachers at a nearby university, he tells them that his job requires a "high tolerance for failure":

> We have more dropouts than anybody else in this school district by far, probably 10 times the drop-outs of the other schools. So that's one level, but also in just the little things. I mean every one of those one-on-one interactions where the kid shuts you right off, and you have to regroup and figure out what you're gonna *do* about that.

Teaching here is a tough job, and Max has learned to take small breaks, maintaining clear distinctions between what he calls the "professional me and the personal me," reminding himself that while his relationships with kids are "caring and compassionate, I have a life other than that." Physical exercise has long been a way both to reinforce these boundaries and tackle the tougher challenges of his work:

> Most of my existence here I have either ridden my bicycle or walked to school and done the same going home, and that's been a real physical separation and transition time. Exercise in my life is a kind of a release of some of the tensions I carry from here. I've frequently found myself riding my bicycle like hell out of town, thinking about a kid, and by the time I got out and came back I had some plans for that kid. I have very vivid memories of some of those experiences.

Talking with colleagues is another way Max frames problems and arrives at solutions, but he sees an even broader value to his network of co-workers. "Being stuck in a room by yourself all that time, that just kills you," he says with a shrug, calling collaboration a "longevity-promoting experience," a way to keep teachers from becoming "old fogies" before their time. At its best, collaboration has been for Max the "synergistic generation of power and product," the sort of back-and-forthing where

> both feel like it's theirs and it didn't come from one or the other, it really came out of that working together. Both people are contributing things and both people take strong roles—somebody'll be pushing to get done or somebody'll be shooting out ideas and somebody'll be writing 'em down.

Max remains eager to "change and hear and learn from a colleague about how to do a better job—I certainly don't think I have all the answers, and so the richness is exciting, and I think positive and energy-creating." He argues forcefully, but Max is always open to other points of view:

> When we've had a philosophical clash sometimes I'll spin on that some outside of school, and come back and say "well what about this and this and this," you know. And sometimes that'll be convincing and sometimes it won't. The growth that comes out of that is exciting personally for me, and it's got to be good for the kids, too—there isn't always one way that's right.

Max cautions that younger teachers may find this give-and-take tricky, especially given the system of top-down evaluation and threats to job security so endemic to the system. He says he taught "for 10 years, maybe more than that" before he no longer cared about "that external stuff," before "getting to a place where I felt confident enough that I was able to do what I thought was right and not worry about anything else." It was an "enormous release," Max recalls: "In my mind I'm untouchable. It doesn't mean I'm untouchably good, but I mean I know what I'm doing is good, and I can do it, and I don't have to worry, I don't have to second guess everything all the time." The opinions of his colleagues still matter, and he listens carefully to their counter-opinions; he let himself feel moved when the state's alternative-schools association honored him recently with a teacher-of-the-year award. Still, when you know and trust yourself, you learn to "float above" random grumbling, especially when it comes from higher-ups: "That's something that comes with kind of an age thing," says Max. But being confident doesn't mean knowing it all, and Max revises his thought midstream: "I mean not just age, but age and *experience*. It's one of those things that you really gain from having been around."

Bill

Bill is tall and thin, a tender, witty man whose face registers a changing spectrum of emotions. He loves the play of language—whether tossing off one-liners, explaining his philosophy of teaching, or turning his intense, respectful gaze to a student's writing. Just beneath the surface of Bill's every word rests a profound compassion for kids, a turn of spirit that sometimes places him in emotional jeopardy. When a crowd of TV reporters broke the news of last spring's tragedy to students returning from the SDLC's softball tournament, it was Bill who advised them not to answer questions and told the reporters to leave. "I stood out there," Bill recalls, "making sure they didn't do it any more. I just stood out there until they eventually left."

Bill's job takes its toll, but he is quick to point out its joys and benefits. He arrived in town 10 years ago with degrees in English education and theater, years of junior high experience, and a desire to find a way of teaching that better fit his fundamental beliefs. "I'm not really a traditional guy," he says now, "but I'd been trying to teach traditional material in a reasonably traditional method." Professional organizations helped him develop a workshop pedagogy that put him in the role of coach and gave his students lots of choice, but he was teaching at a mainstream junior high, and his kids didn't seem to want the freedom Bill was offering. "The last year I was there," Bill recalls, "was a terrible year, just horrible."

Then the district went through some changes, and Bill was transferred to the SDLC. The school's often aggressive students intimidated him at first, and he worried about working under colleagues' watchful eyes. Back then, he still thought of himself as a "closet failure"—but since coming to the SDLC, he adds with assurance, "I've proven to myself that that's not true." As he embarks on his fifth year, he calls it "the best job I ever had, bar none":

> I've learned how to teach since I've been here. You're creating your own curriculum, because no one's handing you a curriculum guide, you gotta create it. And you're dealing with other people, other teachers, you're team teaching with them, and you spend a lot of time talking about what's working and what isn't, what we'd like to do. You spend all of your time thinking about the most important aspects of education. And when you're thinking about what's best for each individual student and you have the time more or less to do that, then your thinking comes into line with the way that learning actually occurs.

Bill has learned to cut himself some slack, to realize that these kids' problems are often "so extreme" that no one person could be expected to come up with definitive solutions. Here, collaboration is more than just comforting or nice:

> There's gotta be a united front with our kids. So many of them know how to play the games—so many of them *invented* the games. You can't help them unless you hold them accountable, and you can't hold them accountable unless you work together on it. If you approached this job from the standpoint of *I* will decide what is best, *I* will run the show, *I* will do this, *I* will do that, you'd *die* here. You'd just die, because the powers that you're facing are so huge, so numerous, and so far-reaching, you can't possibly be a strong enough person to come up against everything that all of these kids face every day. It is so overwhelming, so overwhelming.

Bill loves the human intensity of the SDLC and its staff: When the faculty gets together, he says only half-facetiously, "there's tears, there's joy, there's tragedy, there's comedy." He remembers those pre-semester faculty meetings as a reentry into the generative fray: "Lights went on in my head, and I watched lights go on in everybody else's head, one at a time, and it didn't matter where the ideas came from, boom, problem solved." Collaboration, says Bill, is "just everywhere" at the SDLC:

> We have such a sharp staff here, people who realize that disciplines combined are much stronger than disciplines apart. Kids begin to

see how one area bleeds into the next, and that it's not all segre-
gated, there really is a *gestalt* to education. I get to work constantly
with some of the finest people I've ever worked with or known.
You're never alone here—there's always somebody to talk stuff
over with who knows exactly where you are, exactly what's going
on, because they're working with exactly the same kids. The energy
that people put into the place is cumulative, it's *more* than cumulative, it's logarithmic, you know, 2 + 2 + 2 = 50. It's just the energy
level and the level of innovation and commitment. This place is just
filled with people who have lots of ideas, and work really hard to
bring them into focus. Boy, it's hard not to do a good job here. It's
just contagious.

In this place where everybody is a potential leader, Bill and Max are
orchestrating an array of collaborative efforts, most notably an extended
description of school philosophy and curriculum for the November accreditation review. Bill seems amazed at the way he and Max can now communicate with a brief glance: "It's real helpful," he explains, "to have that
immediate feedback with somebody who you work with so much that you
don't have to talk it all out, it's just understood." But Bill is quick to admit
that his bond with Max has been hard won, their collaboration alternately
blocked and energized by conflict. "We've had numerous disagreements
in the past," Bill says with a laugh, recalling occasions when he temporarily
quit speaking to Max:

> I'd get ticked at him, and I wouldn't say anything, so I'd *stay* ticked,
> you know? And then finally I would get so mad I would *have* to
> talk. So I'd talk, and usually he'd say "Gosh, I wasn't aware there
> was any conflict." I was all upset and then I'd tell him what the
> problem was and he'd say "Oh, okay, I can see that, okay. All right,
> I'll watch for that." And he would. And he'd say, "You let me know
> if that's happening." And I'd tell him, and he'd say "Oh, I see that,"
> and it was like, you know, why didn't I do this six months ago?

Bill says that he and Max got "progressively tighter and tighter" over
the last year, prompted by necessity and encouraged by Max's penchant
for listening as well as arguing. "He is never one who shies away from
speaking his mind," Bill observes;

> he'll argue until he's blue in the face, and sometimes far past all
> reason, but he never shuts me off. He never attempts to say that
> what I have to say isn't valid, he just tries to change my mind if he

disagrees with me. Sometimes I get madder than hell at him and he probably gets fairly annoyed with me, too, but there's no problem in doing the arguing, that's just part of the game.

These days, Bill sees their differences as more complementary than conflictual, and he talks of how their joint work has helped him, especially in shaking loose old individualistic conceptions of teaching and learning. "There's not his space or my space," Bill explains; "it is *our* space, and we work that space together."

In many ways, what Bill is learning from his work with Max matches what he wants students to learn. Members of the SDLC community may get frustrated with one another, but to Bill this is all part of belonging here:

The kids who stay become part of the family. And you get exasperated, but you have patience. It's okay to get exasperated—and it's okay with *them* after they've been here awhile, because they know you'll still be there for them. They're used to getting exasperated and cutting ties, a lot of our kids are, that's how they deal with exasperation, frustration, anger. And over time, here they come to learn that that's not necessarily the way things have to be, that it's okay to disagree, that doesn't mean that you're going to lose this relationship.

HATCHING AN IDEA: 'ZINE

The SDLC had a school paper before 'Zine, but, as Bill admits, it was "pretty traditional, down-the-line." While Bill fretted about putting out a "polished" product that would reflect well on the school, so few students were submitting articles that the paper came out only once every several months. Meanwhile, the SDLC was acquiring an array of desktop computers, and Max was looking for new ways to teach kids to use them. Then one day he saw an article in the paper about a study of student magazines, and, as Bill recalls, "we hatched this idea. I don't know what came from whom, but we hatched this idea of having the publication come out every week no matter what was in it—two people, really excited about it, and here we are." Anyone could submit stories, but all last year a small band of regulars met in a regularly scheduled 'Zine class, some working on the computers scattered around the edges of the classroom, others gathered at two big conference tables in the center. Bill held writing conferences and got 'Zine ready for desktop publication, while Max helped kids generate ideas and work on "mastery of the machine." There would be no 'Zine without them both, observes a colleague: "Max doesn't write, and Bill doesn't do computers. They each bring expertise, aside from the fact that they're both very inventive, eclectic, caring-about-kids people."

This fall they will again distribute the weekly *'Zine* at the Monday-morning school meeting. Max and Bill like to keep it a strictly in-house publication to ease censorship pressures, although they routinely talk kids out of material that is sexist, racist, or homophobic. Occasionally Bill will ask a student to tone down sexual content, but he's open to negotiation—"Look," he'll say, "Bob's butt's gonna be on the line if you put this stuff out there, can you make some adaptations?" Students know they can bargain at such moments, that if they take one questionable passage out another can stay, and Bill will handle any flack. Meanwhile, *'Zine* has become something of an institution, and an instructional tool to boot: "More than any other place," Bill explains, "*'Zine* is a place where kids will come in and be concerned about what they're writing, and really have a legitimate stake in it, want it to be good, because it's gonna have their name on it and people are gonna read it." "You can't just put in total B.S.," says a veteran *'Zine* student; still, he adds, "It's a pretty big scale of things you can write on."

Max too has good things to say about last year's *'Zine* experience. While he had originally "thought of it as a vehicle that would allow kids to have a pragmatic application for computer skills," it took on "a real life of its own," becoming "a real communication medium":

> Adolescents have all kinds of stuff going on in their lives, and this is an outlet for all that. It's also a real positive outlet for a lot of energy that could be festering about petty problems, like, say, if Bob busts a kid for smoking. They can direct that into looking at the smoking rules, writing up a *'Zine* article, either an editorial or an analysis of the situation. It's a positive way to deal with problems, and for kids to sort themselves out some.

But while Max and Bill are pleased that kids have used *'Zine* for their own purposes, both long to see them branch out a bit—to do "a little more research," as Bill puts it, "be experimental and try out different kinds of things, go out into the community and write opinion pieces. Product-wise it's not as striking or effective or what I would have liked." Max, too, admits that he's been "a little disappointed":

> As a science teacher, I'd hoped that I'd get some kids into doing investigative reporting about science-related issues. This town's got a water mess, and I think there's a great potential to do research and write that up. I'd kind of hoped to see that happen, and

there've been a few little things, and maybe my vision is too grand or maybe it's too soon, but I'd like to see that kind of thing where some kids take on some pretty serious issues.

The fall group is big, and around half are new to the school, still unconvinced of a central SDLC tenet: "You don't have to be here," as Bill puts it, "but if you're here, you work." The 'Zine classroom cannot hold them all, and the only available overflow space is at the other end of the hall. "Major bummer," Max says of the space crunch; "major bummer," Bill echoes. But such is the life in this cramped upstairs school, and they walk to class on the first day of the new year determined to make it work.

DEALING WITH WHAT WE GOT

The 'Zine class meets in a light-filled classroom called the "Big Room," a center of activity for the school as a whole, but a permanent base for Max. The room is richly shared, host to cluttered shelves of computer manuals, a closet-turned-darkroom, the school's recycling center, and a telephone the SDLC's kids are welcome to use any time. It is also a place with many distractions, and Max and Bill are concerned about holding a large class here, especially with so many kids new to the SDLC. "We have to be careful," Max cautions, "not to have the chaos just flow everywhere." Max, who will take the lead in nudging kids to work, estimates that his challenge would be cut in half if only they could open up the vinyl room divider and use the adjacent space, needed just now by the social studies teacher. "Oh, well," Max says, "gotta deal with what we got."

Max and Bill eat lunch with the kids at a folding table out in the corridor, talking about everything and anything—families, politics, homelessness, reasons to quit smoking, Bill's fallen arches, and, when they can wedge it in, school or class plans. They also watch the clock, determined to begin class consistently on time. During this first week, they remind students that the 'Zine class meets from 12:30–2:00 every Monday, Wednesday, and Friday, and that latecomers will be locked out until the 1:15 mid-point. The lockout policy was Bill's idea, and while Max fought against it, as class opens today he is the one who firmly explains it to a restless new group. Many sit munching fastfood lunches, sipping Coke from huge paper cups, a greasy smell hanging heavy in the too-warm air. Max tells them they should eat lunch before they come into class or risk being asked to leave. "We'd rather you be here," Bill puts in.

They together generate a list of writing projects the kids might undertake: opinion pieces, advice columns, SDLC history, sports, interviews, poems, cartoons, political debates, short stories, reviews. Max explains about the vacant room down the hall: "I hope people don't use it as a place to gab it," he cautions. "You have to use it well," Bill adds, asking them not to make Max remind them of this. Then the group disperses, a few students settling to work at computers, others to conversation at the central tables, a cluster of new kids moving down the hall with instructions to sort through past issues of *'Zine* and decide on projects. Bill meets with small groups, and Max embarks on a long, steady effort to move everyone to work. Entering the overflow room, Max straddles a chair, gets nose-to-nose with a kid who moments before was chatting with a classmate about flood damage to this year's marijuana crop. "How are you doing?" Max asks. "Fine," says the kid. "How would I *know* that?" Max counters, a hard edge in his voice. "The bottom line is, I expect you to be *working* when you're here." The kid's bravado drops, and he slumps in his chair. Max moves on: "Is this a good place for you to be?" he asks another. "Yeah," the kid says with a grin. "No!" Max emphatically replies, kneeling beside the kid, making eye contact.

Meanwhile, Bill holds extended writing conferences, his interest respectful and warm. He keeps asking for more, pointing to particular places in students' drafts. "I want to see you blow this up," he says, "there must have been lots of things that happened in those seven hours. You want to zoom in on important moments, put in all the details, paint all the pictures." He grins at a rambunctious student who is steadily off task, a stocky guy in a baseball cap. Bill suggests that he try writing a poem called "cliché," making every line what the title suggests. They both smile now, but Bill means it, proud of this tidbit from his boundless store of off-the-wall writing suggestions. Bill wanders off, then returns a few minutes later, having overheard the kid reading his work aloud. "That's *terrible*," Bill says in mock horror. "But it's got *feeling*, Bill," protests the pretend-earnest student. "It's cool," Bill responds, jotting down credit for the day, giving in this time. He wears a "Road Kill Cafe" T-shirt, the slogan "you kill 'em, we grill 'em" on one side, a revolting menu on the other.

Max greets latecomers warmly, asking "Where ya been?", but signals firmly that he expects them to settle quickly to work. Often he talks to students about overall attendance habits, asking about an absence earlier in the day or week, poking through cagey denials. "How would I know you were here if you didn't see me?" Max asks on one such occasion. The student argues and explains, then heads for the door, muttering "It don't matter to me, so . . ." Max stops him. "Where were you supposed to be?" "Here," the student answers. "Why are you just getting here?" Max persists. There is some give and take about rides, buses, waking up. Max tries to get the kid to take responsibility for being late, but it proves to be uphill work. "I can't control what time I wake up," the kid says. "Yes," Max says, "you *can*. I can help you." "You can call me and wake me up every day?" the kid asks. "I didn't say I'd do that," Max replies; "I'll help you *learn* to do it." "Whatever," the kid says, sauntering out the door as Max turns to someone else.

"I see a lotta people who aren't doin' anything" becomes Max's opening mantra, a call to work that's never answered fully or for long. Away from the kids, Max describes himself as "frustrated" at the prospect of facing this "large group, probably 50% of them having no experience with this or this school. And so we're having to deal with a whole lot of side issues about attendance and, you know, 'do we have to work, can I sit in here and talk instead of work?'" Max continues to circulate during these early weeks, guiding kids through the processes of formatting disks and doing spell checks. At least once every class session, a student misplaces a file and explodes that Max has "fucking lost my shit!" Max's policing frees Bill to hold extended writing conferences, to pay close attention to the productive few, to mull over punctuation choices and stylistic options.

At the end of each class session, students hand Max their "blue books," passbook-like ledgers of time on task. Soon afterward, Max and Bill review their own assessments of each student's progress, talking of small successes, troubleshooting, and brainstorming. Together they keep hope afloat, coming up with strategies for the class as a whole, setting times to meet for extended conversation, and pushing forward the boundaries of the possible.

HONEYMOON'S OVER

Every academic year has its honeymoon period, Max and Bill say, and by late September it is clear that theirs has fled with the warm weather. The chill in early-morning staff meetings is both literal and figurative, the problems facing the SDLC's kids seeming more permanent, more serious than before. One morning Max brings up a "psycho-educational evaluation" he requested on one of his advisees, a *'Zine* rabble-rouser who draws pictures but refuses to write. "It doesn't tell us much we didn't already know," Max says—that the student is clinically hyperactive, artistically gifted but delayed in math and literacy development, challenged and not "lazy," as his parents believe. Max says he believes the kid tries hard but "something just isn't working for him." There is a brief argument about the many learning-disabled kids being referred to the SDLC, of the fact that these students are asked to sign away their rights to special-education assistance, which the staff of the SDLC, for all its caring attention, cannot provide. The meeting has already grown tense when Max reminds them that their preparations for the upcoming accreditation review have lagged behind, and there is edgy talk of timelines and things to do.

Over in 'Zine, Max and Bill have devised sensible new strategies, none of which have proven terribly successful. Max keeps bringing up the gathering problem, and Bill tries to be supportive: "I'll start this off," Bill tells the kids on one of the stern-reminder days, "because people are always sayin' 'Oh Bill, you're so nice and Max is such a hard butt.'" Max and Bill again review procedures for storing and retrieving work, this to raucous cries of "keep it in your drawers!" Students are now to have at least one back-up project in mind, insurance for stuck times, but many still need constant reminding.

Meanwhile, Max and Bill worry that many kids are using the survey option to avoid more substantive work. In a troubleshooting session, Bill tries to find a more positive angle:

> *Bill:* So I'm reticent to say let's squash it, but remember last year when the surveys got to be a real problem.
> *Max:* Right.
> *Bill:* 'Cause they were just doodly-squat, they were stupid?
> *Max:* Well, that's what *these* are.
> *Bill:* Right.
> *Max:* "Are you sexually active?"
> *Bill:* We took some time with the people who are going to do surveys and said "all right, if you're going to do a survey here's what you have to do." So I don't wanna, I don't wanna *not* do surveys.
> *Max:* Well, how do we do that?
> *Bill:* Just what you said, talking to people and saying that there's a lot of survey work going on and that's perfectly okay, but one of the things that we want people to learn is better skills as writers and that isn't happening through the venue of a survey. If you're going to do a survey we're gonna want to work with you on techniques, on reasons and on write-ups.
> *Max:* Yeah, because now basically what it is, somebody writes out a provocative question, takes it around and hands it to people, they don't even write their answers down, they just give it to 'em and have them, you know, talk about it. You know, so . . .
> *Bill:* Yeah. So let's get people together who want to do surveys . . .
> *Max:* Okay.
> *Bill:* I would rather attack it that way because then we're saying we want to make it . . .

Max: Well, see I think . . .
Bill: . . . more of a learning experience.
Max: Well, yeah. So it's maybe more positive.
Bill: In essence that's what we want to do . . .
Max: But the reality is the same thing will happen, I think.
Bill: Yeah.

Increasingly, teaching 'Zine looks like swimming in sand. These days Max gives an abbreviated version of his reminder to get back to work, saying students' names emphatically, calling them back to awareness that this is a class. His rhetorical ploys signal his support: "If you sit here, you might be tempted to talk," he often says, "so why don't you sit over there instead?" Occasionally he lets kids see his aggravation: "I'm feeling manipulated," he tells a student artfully adept at avoiding work. "I'm trying to help you, and you're doin', I don't know *what.*" After two warnings, they are gone for the day, sometimes trailing long strings of shouted profanity in their wake, sometimes acting heartbroken. "Max, there is a wound deep in my heart," a departing student says through tears; "I may never forgive you. And why the *hell* . . ." "Okay," responds Max to such protests, "how can we make it *not* be that way?" He doesn't ignore the quieter students, either: "Whatcha doin'?" he asks a boy who sits placidly at a vacant table. "Waitin'," comes the calm reply." "Waiting?" responds Max, incredulous. "Waiting for what?" "Waiting for class to end," says the kid, unmoved. "Why don't you leave?" asks Max. "I'm not giving credit for waiting, I give credit for *doing.*"

Meanwhile, Bill offers focused, extended attention to those who are actually writing—about child abuse, lost love, life in a distant galaxy, and matters scatological. "This is a time where I'm asking you to think more about the effect that your words have," Bill explains to students, "In any kind of writing you do with me, that's what I want you to be thinking about. What effect are you trying to create? What are you trying to do with those words and what's the best way to get it done?" Hunched at the keyboard, Bill talks earnestly about stylistic or mechanical issues, drawing students into discussions of word choice or punctuation that are playful, earnest, and marked by enormous tolerance. In unison, Bill and a student read aloud an opening passage: "This thing was so important that I actually motivated myself to write about it." When the "thing" in question turns out to be "silent farting," the student says slyly, "bet you weren't expecting that!" but Bill continues, fully absorbed in a problem with punctuation. He advises insertion of a comma before the "and" in a compound sentence: "Is it a moral imperative?" the student asks, "even if you don't *feel* it there?" "Yeah," responds Bill, "moral imperative for a compound. You're talking about bites, bites of a sandwich. That's a long sandwich. Try to take it in two bites 'cause it's two sentences." He suggests a dash to "grab you by the collar and shake you and say 'listen to this,'" or a period for a more stately, plain effect. "See?" says Bill, "punctuation is not a big puzzle. Punctuation is figuring out how you want something to be read and then writing it that way. That's all punctuation is." Bill continues to read aloud until he reaches the phrase "sick of everyones shit." "'Everyone' is possessive," he says, looking up, "and therefore, [hitting the apostrophe key] bingo." "Okay," says the student, leaning in for a better look.

Students often say that while they depend on Max for computer help, they will show drafts only to Bill. "He understands the way I write and he understands the things that I do," says a young woman. "He's open to anything you want to do. He always laughs at the funny parts—a lot of teachers don't get it, and he *always* laughs when it's funny. He doesn't try to, like, evaluate your life because of what you've written, but he just accepts it, and he doesn't make a big deal out of it." The young man who writes about farting calls Bill one of his "favorites": "We get along really good. We think the same stuff's funny and the same stuff's strange. I'm always shockin' Bill with my strange things that I write. And he says, 'God! Oh, I guess we can put that in the paper anyway.' So that works out really good." But the kids also say that they need both Max and Bill; 'Zine without either, observes a student, "would suck—yeah, it would suck." In any case, notes another, neither is a teacher in the traditional sense of the word, nor is 'Zine a usual class:

> They don't preach at us. It's more like we're all just there together and they help us, direct us in the way they want us to learn, bounce ideas off of. They're not standing up in front of us and just telling us stuff. They're, you know, *in* with us, which is sort of unusual.

Together they model ways of being: Bill showing kids that people who love language can be off-beat and caring, Max embodying ideals of accountability and self-control. They often tell me that the class involves more than putting out a weekly magazine of student writing, that with this many rowdy new kids, they are centrally involved in the work of orientation and acculturation as well. In the process, they let the kids see who they are, but they also maintain margins of privacy. For Bill this means remaining the consistently friendly reader with a strange sense of humor, hiding his gathering worry about all these kids in trouble. Meanwhile, despite long after-school hours helping the staff get ready for the accreditation review, Max is maintaining a vital life apart from his job, staying up late to squeeze in work on an environmentalist's city-council campaign. He too looks occasionally worn, but Max can brighten suddenly, seeming by a small effort of will to rouse himself. At a faculty meeting on the morning of the school's open house, Bob cautions the staff to get the evening's introductions over quickly so the entertainment can begin. "What?" protests Max, grinning mischievously despite a deep cough, "you mean you don't think I'm *entertaining*?" He strolls down to his classroom a few moments later, cheerfully greeting a waiting student. "I'm having a bad day," she responds. "Why?" Max asks, sounding amazed. "You can *control* it."

Max and Bill present balanced resources, but progress is unsteady even on the best of days, their challenges like something out of a casebook of hard dilemmas. One Friday in early October, Max moves through 'Zine with uncharacteristic heaviness, pausing now and then to gaze around the room. Meanwhile Bill reads a young woman's work, his face intense with concentration, his lips moving slightly. Each time things settle this way, a student erupts suddenly in ear-splitting song, this to cries of "shut up!" from other students. A student across the room has changed the generic error boing on one of the computers to a loud burp, and he exclaims "Oh, shit!" in feigned alarm every time it sounds. "How do you change the log-in sound?" he asks Max, who responds that he doesn't remember so unconvincingly that the whole group erupts in laughter.

The room settles rather miraculously after each interruption, but then a tall, pale student with flowing brown hair is seized by a theatrical impulse. He is talking to another boy about women sexually harassing men, and Max looks up calmly, a bit bemused, and asks "Why aren't you writing about it?" The answer becomes plain as the student rises to his feet. "I can walk down the street, get my ass grabbed by a woman, that's not sexual harassment," he shouts, "but if I tell a woman she has nice breasts, it is!" Gesturing expansively now, playing to the whole room, he moves nearer the corner where Bill sits talking to a student. "If someone's offended or potentially offended by it, it's harassment," Bill tells him quietly. He listens to several more shouted proclamations, then offers a challenge: Write these thoughts for 'Zine, and he'll personally compose a rebuttal. "This is a *challenge*," Bill says with mock-macho emphasis, playing to the crowd now, too, "and I *will* be successful!" The kid keeps talking, but Bill refuses to take any more in: "Don't you *want* to," he asks, "because you can't argue as well on *paper*?" Bill turns back to the piece he was reading: "I'm going to talk to this young man here, who *has* written something," he says dismissively. The student charges out, but soon he returns with a promise: "Okay, I'm gonna write this bitchin', burnin' thing!" Then again a few minutes later: "I'll have the *whole weekend*, Bill! Will you be *ready*?"

On Monday I tell Bill that I was impressed by his deft Friday-afternoon response. He looks up from his lunch, looking tired: "He won't do it," he says. "I won't see a thing from him." Bill adds that he has grown cynical about books and articles chronicling classroom successes: "On a good day," he says, "I reach maybe 30%. The people who write that stuff would *die* if they only reached 30% on a good day." Down the table, Max has been engaging students in talk of world affairs, about ethnic separatism proliferating across Europe, about intercultural relations here in the States, about humanity's propensity for war. But Max is adept at carrying on one conversation while monitoring several others, and he glances up: "30%?" he shoots back. "You'd be lucky! It'd be a *real* good day."

TAKING CARE OF EACH OTHER

'Zine is looking impossible by most measures, but Max and Bill still wonder how to make it better. At times, even Max lets his sterner persona go: "What are you doing?" he asks a girl fidgeting with an audio headset. "I'm *trying*," she replies indignantly, "to find my *song*." Max and Bill catch one another's eyes and, before issuing the inevitable reminders, laugh through their frustration like affectionate parents.

For a brief moment in mid-October 'Zine seems to be improving a bit: a new six-week session has begun, there are markedly fewer students, and one afternoon Max and Bill are able to make productive contact with all of them. They are exuberant afterward, exclaiming that the "numbers have made all the difference," engaging in extended conversation about particular kids' needs. The challenges still sound arduous, but they find courage today to tackle it all, promise that all their caring and creativity may yet yield rewards. But the high is momentary: At the next class and the one after that, 'Zine is the same old zoo, full of kids artfully resisting the invitation to write, still using the surveys as an excuse to visit. Bill says he knows this is because "it's so terribly hard for them," but Max is frustrated with his job of policing, aching to see some excitement grab hold.

During the next Monday's faculty meeting, Bill brings out a list of students from his "Arguing for Non-Writers" course who habitually fail to hand in work. This is the hardest day of the week for Bill, who lets his frustration and then his sadness show. Soon he is impassioned, almost shouting: "This writing thing's too loaded for them," he says, wondering how much he can ask of kids who "run away" when it comes time to put pen to paper. "But you had a hard group," Max says gently, scanning the list. They talk about the various clinical labels these kids have been given, wondering if some will ever be functionally literate. These students' needs have not been met at mainstream schools, says Dave, "and the buck stops at the SDLC." "So be it," says the music teacher. "I'm asking for some *help* here,"

Bill persists, "what do I *do*?" Advisors agree to lean on their kids a bit, but Bill's question leads to a charged discussion of illiteracy, and Bob finally says, struggling to move them peaceably into the new day, "We're not gonna settle this thing this morning."

During their 'Zine debriefing session later that afternoon, it's Max's turn to let discouragement show. "How ya doin' chief?" Bill asks. "Mediocre," comes the heavy reply. Max goes down the list, noting that too many students signed out early after a lackluster appearance. "Let's see what comes out of it," Bill responds. "If good stuff comes out of it, we don't mind. It's all right." But both look weary, and even Max seems low today. They go through the motions a bit mechanically, Max untangling a paper jam when a student cries out that the printer's "fucked up," signing students' blue books as a lingerer sings, in a mock-operatic voice, "If that won't do, smoke a joint or two."

And then things take a worse turn. As the day darkens into a crisp fall evening, three of the SDLC's students slip into an alleyway across town. They are inhaling fumes from butane lighter fluid, a practice known among them as "huffing," when one breathes in some of the fluid itself, freezing his lungs. Seized by fear, one of the boys runs away; the one who stays is a current 'Zine student, a kid Max and Bill have been fretting about, a kid Bill talked about in this morning's faculty meeting. As the boy flags down a passing car, his friend is panicking, crying, unable to breath, on a long slide into unconsciousness. Death comes later at a local hospital, the second tragedy to beset the SDLC in less than five months. The boy was only 16, and like the still-younger classmate who died last May, he looked by all accounts to be one of the SDLC's success stories, a kid with whom they'd recently "turned a corner."

First thing in the morning Bob gathers the school together, confirms the news that most have already heard, and introduces the district's new crisis team, a half-dozen strangers who will be present throughout the day. Students get together to write poetry or draw pictures, and the teachers keep fine-grained track of the absent ones, finding private places for one-on-one conversation, encouraging everyone to accept their own reactions and be tolerant of others', encouraging kids to connect in their homeroom groups. In the late afternoon they finally gather as a staff, the crisis team still present, to check in with one another. Max is among the first to speak, his voice almost as steady as on an ordinary day: "I'm okay personally," he reports, going on to list students he is concerned about, kids he has talked to, kids he needs to talk to more, asking the staff to help keep an eye out. Others follow suit, worrying about how students already on the edge are affected. "Oh, jeez," someone says now and then, but there is little open grieving here, just on-task urgency. One kid who has been at the school through multiple tragedies commented today that he thinks about being somewhere else every May and October, the months when disasters have recurrently struck. A crisis team member makes a joke: "If only it were that easy," she comments, "we'd close everything down and then the whole world would be safe." There is scattered laughter, but not from the teachers.

From time to time the crisis team makes suggestions, usually about the staff tending to its own needs. The teachers listen politely, then continue to throw out names: How did this kid take it? What about that kid? What kind of support can we arrange? What can we do? There are lots of swollen eyes and blotchy faces that look a decade older. Bill, usually at the center of meetings, is silent. Both this boy and the student killed in May were Gene's advisees, and he is silent too, his head down even when Dave places an arm around his shoulders. "The only thing I'm hurtin' for," Max finally says, "is I wish our staff had some time together." Then, looking at the crisis team: "I appreciate you all bein' here, but we need some time to talk among us." As Bill told me later,

> We were just thinking just "get out of here so we can talk." And I guess they didn't finally leave until a quarter of three, three o'clock. And that's when we were able to start talking. Just talk a lot. I never fully realized the ramifications of how alone the typical classroom teacher is. Could not deal with the things that happen here being that kind of alone. I mean it's obviously a reason for people to shut themselves off from kids. It's obviously a reason, because you are out there alone.

The dead boy's mother holds a press conference in her living room, hoping to alert others to the dangers of inhalant abuse, and the evening news includes footage of 'Zine students sobbing in her arms. It is said that the boy was burdened, his father away in prison, his younger brother about to be sent to a facility for troubled kids. There are shots of the alleyway, and then of reporters, their polish incongruous beside the entrance to the SDLC, noting that it has been a "hard year" for the school, this being a second loss. Students and staff avoid the cameras, savvy to the presence of inquisitive reporters.

A few kids are relatively unaffected, but many are badly shaken, and the teachers worry that a few already troubled kids may be shifting closer to the edge. There are three days left before the funeral, and the staff makes the decision to keep the school up and running. The boy died on Monday night; Tuesday is devoted to crisis intervention, and Wednesday 'Zine is back in session. The staff has encouraged me to continue my usual visits, flicking aside my urge to disappear. "This is part of what we do together,"

Max tells me, "and if you're studying collaboration, you need to see it."
During the Wednesday lunch hour I find him sitting at the principal's desk,
helping field stray phone calls and chatting amicably with students. Tufts
of his gray-and-brown hair stick out at funny angles and his eyes betray a
serious lack of sleep, but everything in his manner otherwise announces
that Max is open for business. Bill comes down just moments before class,
still somber and remote, but he's soon conferencing with the handful of
students present, settling to the task at hand.

A pair of students who have shown up today seem even giddier than
usual, passing the time with off-color humor, sending one another into
giggly spasms. Max has given them a CD ROM encyclopedia to browse,
and one screams when they come on a photo of a nude Roman statue:
"*Penis!*" he shouts. "Put a *leaf* over it!" Later the computer develops a
malfunction and Max puts it off limits, but even this fails to stop them. One
of the boys records a wildly obscene message that repeats every time sometime touches the keyboard. Bill somehow finds energy to move across the
room, calmly explaining that perhaps they should consider the embarrass-
ment of someone coming in to use the machine. Across the room, Max
joshes with a student about lame excuses for being late. "Best one I've
heard," Max says, "is 'my hair's wet.'" Then the daily litany: "How much
time?" "How can we make this more productive for you?" Max seems
exhausted despite the persistent effort at normalcy, and Bill rushes out at
the end of class, mumbling good-byes.

As the room clears I find myself alone with Max, and I ask him how
he is, if he is taking care of himself. My questions sound clumsy and clichéd,
like the questions the crisis team was asking the other day, questions that
pinged off the surface while the staff longed for time alone. Max is kind,
showing a face of suffering, but gently brushes aside these individualistic
notions of grief. "More or less," he responds, redirecting the focus to a friend
and colleague more profoundly affected. He tells me that last Sunday Gene
gave a talk at his church about the integration of his spiritual and professional lives—strands that he sees as increasingly intertwined, he explained.
"He used his work with this kid as an example," Max says, "and two days
later, this kid he's talking about is dead." For a moment Max seems as much
amazed as grieved, but he is careworn, affected in a quieter way than the
others. I say something about how good it is that the staff pulls together,
everyone worrying about Gene. "Yeah," says Max with a sigh, "we're pretty
good about that around here." But "it hurts," he adds, and "there's just no
way you can take that away."

The funeral will begin just after the close of school on Friday, but only
three students are present for 'Zine, and most are here to play video games.
"Okay, it's time!" Max calls out at 12:30, but it soon becomes clear that this

won't be anything like a usual class. Despite the warm day, Max's winter coat hangs beside his desk: "It was kinda chilly when I rode by bike down here last night," he tells me. I slowly realize that Max has been here since before dawn, that he and Gene are working even now on the past-due accreditation materials. Gene moves among the classroom computers, and I tell him to kick me out if I get in his way. "I'm holdin' okay," he says, looking me full in the face, calm and fully present. And Bill's here, too, alternately writing and chatting, suddenly calling out to me from across the room. "That's another thing," he says, as if continuing a conversation, "trust. Trust is a big deal here. We trust our students." I move closer as Bill continues, and we talk for awhile about trust, then about our own childhoods, the costs of trying so hard to be good. The 'Zine kid who has become famous for bathroom humor and strange error messages is sitting nearby, listening in as he leafs through computer magazines. "Yeah," he says, looking up, "I was always that way in school, too." Bill and Gene gaze at him, hesitating. But after a few moments the kid can no longer keep a straight face, and we all laugh.

Then the teachers gather into groups, hastily deciding who will ride with whom. Bill rises slowly, sighing. "I don't even believe in the American way of death," he says to no one in particular, "and here I am going to another funeral. I believe in parties!" Gene rides his bike to school even in the depths of winter, and Bill wants to give him a ride: "Don't leave without me," he says, adding his voice to the chorus of people wanting to be with Gene. Meanwhile Max bustles about, trying to figure out if he should stay behind and mind the school, deciding to go with the others only after he learns that someone else will be here. He is matter-of-fact and brisk, wondering, as usual, where help is most needed.

As I watch them go, I ponder the unspoken understandings that knit these people together. I once asked Bill if he and Max put conscious energy into managing their relationship. He paused a long while before responding, his answer referencing not just him and Max, but the whole of the staff. "At this place," Bill said, "people are careful about people that they love and respect, very careful that those people remain okay and with their head above water. But I don't consider that 'working on the relationship,' I just consider that people taking care of each other."

NOT THE SEASON YOU PLANNED

Dave, the school counselor, had tried to warn me a few weeks earlier: "At some point this year," he predicted, "we will have a catastrophe, or some sort of a tragedy that'll affect all of us. Every year we do. I mean, whether it's someone cutting their wrists in the bathroom or a death or a rape—all those things happen because our kids are very much at risk, and because they live in danger." What had struck me as a shade exaggerated then seems ponderously present now, as grief-stricken kids return to school enveloped in an air of danger. Their teachers are stricken, too, but they turn their collective energies outward, together scanning the close horizon and wondering what to do next.

The district's substance-abuse prevention specialist comes to Monday's faculty meeting, explaining the dangers of inhalant abuse and pointing out that the relapse rate is high. Then they go down the list of known abusers among the SDLC's kids, and Max takes the lead in brainstorming plans for a peer-support group. Bill is taking the day off, many of the other teachers are still grappling with fresh grief, and the information is ominous, reinforcing everyone's fears of a domino effect. As they discuss the kids most at risk, Max shakes his head. "And these are *little* kids we're talking about," he says. The youngest is actually 16, and all are tough, troubled kids, kids I have forgotten to think of as little. But I see now that this is the way Max thinks of them, as children in need of a guiding hand, children who must be saved. Max observes that all are from low-income homes, too, unable to afford costly treatment programs. There are moments of palpable desperation, but Max stays afterward, still talking strategy with Dave.

When the staff meets to talk about accreditation materials two days later, they do their best to return to the old routines, joking around, weaving an elaborate analogy between Oz and the SDLC. Bill is taking the lead again, but he stays out of the joking, and now and then grief demands a voice. He notes that they are more behind than ever, reminds them of something scheduled for completion last week; Dave remarks quietly, "Last week was a hell of a week." "So it was," Bill responds, and there is a small silence. Then Gene, with a light smile: "Maybe we need to keep moving." Lana remarks that it can't hurt her anymore than it already has, and someone else says something about how they can't just forget. Then the group is back on task, turning a few moments later to more giggly diversion.

Everything that was running off course before is surging out of bounds now, and 'Zine is no exception. Max still nudges and Bill still talks stylistic fine points, but here, too, are scattered moments when the ongoing crisis can no longer be held at bay. Two 'Zine students who were especially close to the boy who died become the focus of schoolwide concern. The old problems continue, but now Max and Bill's first desire is that these kids just come to school every day. When they show up for 'Zine, Max zeroes in, utterly focused on engaging, on keeping them here. When asked how things are going, Max's reply makes inevitable connection back to these two boys—a good day becomes a time when they are present, a bad one when they fail to show entirely. If they come late, Max rushes over to capture their attention; if they move to leave, he follows them out to the hall, reaching out his hands, fairly begging them to stay, his face knotted with worry as he turns away. Max continues to work on the accreditation materials, but he snaps at colleagues that they're stalling, "dribbling, dribbling, dribbling," and I often find him quietly cursing as he sits working at a computer.

His first focus is on kids, but Max cares about the staff, too, even as he wonders how much he has to offer a deeply emotional colleague like Bill. Max tells me that he has a "high tolerance" for pain, but worries about the down side, those "parts of me that aren't as sensitized as others":

> I go on very matter of factly, and that's nice because I'm able, I mean in this place I'm able to function very well, but at the same time I think it can be seen as callused. I don't have a way of offering a whole lot of support, that's not in my repertoire, and so sometimes I feel like, in those situations, I feel like I should be doing more than I had inside me. I mean I couldn't really do any more, so I didn't.

Bill looks to the wider network for emotional support, but he is counting on Max too—on his steadiness, his work ethic, his quiet strength. Bill has been hit hard, describing his grief as "still very close to the surface" a couple of weeks after the student's death. He turns especially to Lana, who listens and talks and tries to put things in perspective. She helps, Bill says, but this remains a hard time, and there is so much to be done between now and Thanksgiving. "I think that what I do is the most important and moral thing that a person can do," Bill tells me, his voice breaking. "I can't imagine myself not teaching, but when things are really stressful like they are now, there's a part of me every morning that doesn't want to get up."

In 'Zine, Bill is his old self, laughing appreciatively at students' jokes, doing the "grammatical two-step," suggesting ideas and more ideas. For extended periods, he is "doin' okay, talkin' to the same kids, talkin' about the same possibilities, workin' over the same ground over and over and over again." But things keep happening—kids tune out, disappear, and Bill suddenly finds himself bereft, his reserves already shot. "It is my nature to be open to children," he explains:

> I often wish that it was less. It's a hard balance for me—I would be more effective in my job if there was less. If I could feel as under control as I sometimes seem. A lot of my kids are just losin' it, you know? I do the insomnia thing, I will wake up in the middle of the

night worrying about things and of course I'm tired the next day,
which makes it worse, which makes me wake up in the middle of
the night and worry about things. Been having bouts of that
throughout the fall.

Even a few days after the funeral, there are moments when 'Zine is an
unchanged set of struggles. Sending a clear message that he will not lighten
up, Max kicks kids out, challenges those who exaggerate the amount of
time spent working, reminds everyone that now is a good time to get productive. A week after the tragedy, Max and Bill meet once again to tackle
the 'Zine problem. They talk about the kids who are good at appearing busy,
they worry that the class period may be too long, they work out ways to
enlist the support and counsel of kids' advisors. Max is concerned that none
of it will be enough, and Bill suggests that he run "the policeman budda-
hudda." "But what happens if they're *not* productive," Max asks, "and
we've run the policeman thing?" Max looks like the tough cop, but at heart
he always searches for ways to keep kids in class, and he grimaces at Bill's
suggestion that "maybe this will be a massive kick-out." What happens at
the next meeting comes as something of a relief: Max is unusually stern in
his opening warning ("I'm sick and tired of this group not gettin' anything
done! One warning and you're gone!"), and the class is a bit more on task
than usual. Afterward Max admits his frustration—"me more than Bill,"
he says. Lowering his voice, he explains that some of the "higher functioning" kids aren't in 'Zine anymore, that they now have lots of kids with
serious learning problems, that they aren't sure how to motivate them, how
to persuade them to produce.
    Then, just a week later, blunt student complaints erupt at the Monday-
morning school meeting: "Why isn't 'Zine worth reading anymore?" the
kids want to know. "Why was it so much better *last* year?" Later that morning Max and Bill meet again, this time acknowledging that perhaps the only
thing to do is, as Bill says, "put it to bed for six weeks and then start out
fresh." But Max has one last idea: "Let's show 'em this and see what happens," he says, pointing to the pile of unclaimed 'Zines. As they walk into
class that day, Bill holds the stack aloft, then slowly counts them, telling
the kids "these are the 'Zines that no one wanted to read." Max asks what's
up, and what they want to do about it.
    And then something magical and unhoped-for happens, a rare mo-
ment when the power of the peer dynamic suddenly begins functioning in
'Zine's favor. For the next 45 minutes, the kids berate their own work habits,
a number of them confessing "I haven't done anything for weeks," a chorus of "me too" breaking out across the room. "Bang, they were off," Bill
recalls later. "Max and I had to say very little. We kinda steered conversa-

tions sometimes and threw in a few ideas here and there, wrote ideas down, helped 'em to facilitate." It was, he says, "the best thing—sittin' and listenin' to those kids go to town. They raked themselves over the coals and then built the program back up."

Despite the enduring sorrows of the first trimester, the 'Zine recovery proves as substantive as it was unlikely, lending Max and Bill a much-needed cause for celebration. They are still euphoric a couple of weeks later, excited about the audience-aware work kids are doing now, shaking their heads at this unexpected good fortune:

> *Max:* I was real frustrated with that kind of down we had there, and it was one of those wonderful moments when they fixed it that day. It was really neat.
>
> *Bill:* And we'd been saying the same things for weeks, but it wasn't until they really bottomed out and we held up that four-page *'Zine* where three-quarters of them were not picked up. They bottomed out and said "this cannot go on." Which was, you know we were just sittin' there lookin' at each other goin' "whoa!" [laughs]. 'Cause five minutes before class we'd been in there talkin' about, "Well, maybe we shouldn't do it the next six weeks. Maybe we should just shut it down because it's not happenin'" and all of a sudden pow, pow, pow [snaps fingers] and it's right back, you know it's back as good as it's ever been over the last two years.
>
> *Max:* Yeah, I think so too. Real thorough and . . .
>
> *Bill:* Good stuff.
>
> *Max:* Good stuff.
>
> *Bill:* Lots of learning about writing and about how to create something, kids go into more depth than they've gone into before . . .
>
> *Max:* Much more depth, not this superficial stuff which really . . .
>
> *Bill:* Really looking for something . . .
>
> *Max:* . . . which really pleases me.

As hard as they work to create inviting circumstances, Max and Bill acknowledge that only the students could decide whether to engage or turn away, that teaching these kids involves both holding on and watching for the proper moment to let go. They see their collaboration as connected to a whole tangle of relationships, among students and the wider net of colleagues alike, a web that moves in its happier moments toward what Max calls "a synergistic generation of power and product." In the end, they emphasize, the power to set 'Zine right rested with the students alone:

Bill: We had been nudging for a long time. If the kids had not
wanted to do it we wouldn't have had 'Zine this next six
weeks, I don't think. Because we talked to them, we cajoled
them, we'd been kicking kids out. We worked individual
people, we did everything we could think of. And nothing
worked.

Max: Yeah. In fact, I think it just got worse. It kept gettin' worse
and worse and worse.

Bill: Yeah, it kept getting worse because of course we were the
authority figures coming down and that just made them dig
their heels in. *They* had to see it. You know the only way
something like 'Zine works is if the kids really have a vested
interest in it, *they* want to do it and *they* want it to work well.

Max: Well I think that vested interest also comes from outside of
the 'Zine class. They get reinforcement from their peers and
stuff like that. And they weren't gettin' that.

Bill sees a patterned lesson in all this, a maxim to take away: "Give
kids an excuse to do the right thing, and they'll do the right thing. If you
don't give 'em that excuse for doing the right thing, then they won't do it.
And this time they gave themselves the excuse—'we have to live up to last
year.' They didn't have to live up to Max or Bill, they didn't even have to
live up to themselves, they had to live up to *last year*." But for Max, the
'Zine turnaround is just another example of the need to take the long view,
to expect the unexpected, to honor the wider ecology. "We sow seeds all
the time," he says with a laugh, "and they just germinate at different times.
It's not the season that you necessarily planned, you know it's at *their own*
time."

LIKE A BIG OLD DINNER TABLE

The close of fall trimester coincides with Thanksgiving week, and I do
a final interview with Max and Bill just after the school's autumn potluck.
Every table the school owns is covered with white paper and crowded with
dishes donated by parents and staff. The place is packed, mostly with wild-
haired students in tattered clothes. There are lots of parents, too, people
who look worn and struggling, who brighten when teachers exclaim over
their offerings—cherry pie, Watergate salad, boiled beans with bacon bits.
Sprinkled among the crowd are members of the school board and the
superintendent, mostly sticking together, exchanging a few polite pleasan-
tries now and then with staff. A boy with flowing brown hair breezes down

the hall. "Just remember," he shouts, "the first word in funeral is *fun*! That's going to be the first line in my eulogy—the first word in funeral is *fun*! And I'm going to have Guy Smiley do it!" I help Bill wash dishes afterward, kids crowded around him like a favorite uncle, offering an ongoing stream of news and conversation.

Bill and Max are in a celebratory mood as we sit down to talk, still exuberant over the 'Zine turnaround, savoring their relationship, their workplace, their work. They laugh uproariously as they recall times when Bill got quietly angry at Max and quit speaking to him. In the beginning, Max allows, their collaboration "felt more like conflict." "Oh yeah," Bill says with a smile, "the biggest changes had to come from me." Bill remembers his days in traditional schools: "I never got to work with somebody, and so you didn't tell 'em what you didn't like. You just shut up about it because they weren't in your room anyway." "It was a little bumpy at first," Max says of their collaboration, describing the "good working rule" of the SDLC: "If there's a conflict, you go right to the source and deal with it— that makes for little rough edges, but there's never anything that boils up from behind you here." "It took me a long time to get used to that," Bill admits; then, pointing to Max, "*He* taught me—Max has helped me to be more of what I am." In traditional schools, says Bill, there is pressure to conform, but here is freedom to disagree, to develop one's individual style even in the context of joint work. "I can say the same thing for most of the people here," Bill adds, "but for some reason Max and I work really well together."

"I'm flattered that you say I've taught you," Max says, his face registering surprise. Max has collaborated for years, sometimes with people who became close personal friends, and his relationship with Bill is neither his deepest nor his longest partnership, but he's pleased now, perhaps caught a bit off guard. "I've learned from workin' with you, too," he says. "Bill has exemplary relations with his advisees," Max tells me. "I think he does a great job of being able to hold a hard line with 'em when they need that, and yet have them understand that he's not the ogre, he's helping them grow. It's something I work at," he adds with a laugh. Often "uncomfortable" with the atmosphere of 'Zine, Max repeatedly went to Bill over the last 12 weeks to register concern and work out strategies. "We have a different standard," Max allows. "I come from a sort of scientific, mathematical perspective, and I expect on-task behavior to produce product. And Bill is more tolerant of the creative process, maybe taking some time to mull things over, and so there doesn't have to be product shown for every minute. And so that's an ongoing conflict between the two of us," Max explains; then, after a moment's pause: "Not conflict, but difference of perspective." "I'd say it's a *balance*," Bill puts in. "Yeah," Max says, his eyes alight. "A balance, that's right. And both of us recognize it." "Conflict and balance are often the same thing," Bill tells me. "I also think we a little bit compensate for each other," Max adds with a smile. "When mom's in a bad mood, dad will take over a little bit more—I think we both do that with each other."

Much of their collaboration, Bill explains, is "almost kinesthetic by now"—there is less need to talk all the time, their mutual responsibilities and interpersonal snags worked out months before I met them, a moment's eye contact now serving as an adequate check for shared understanding. Students know that Bill offers feedback on writing and Max helps with the computers, but there is more, too, different versions of what it means to be caring and responsible. Bill is warm and inviting, a funny man who laughs at their jokes, who moves them to care about punctuation and grammar in the interests of getting a message across, of being seen and understood. Max loves kids in ways that inevitably involve challenge—whether issuing yet another of his anti-smoking lectures, getting eyeball-to-eyeball with the 'Zine dawdlers, or pressing them to consider issues before the wider world. As I sat at Max's desk one day during 'Zine, a kid with a bad cold walked over, rifling through drawers looking for a tissue. "All right," he said grimly, pulling out a tan box, "Max's special John Wayne brand, recycled tree bark." Max's way of caring involves taking students' wrath and jests alike, but he never seems to mind. When asked to describe himself in five words or less for a 'Zine survey, Max offered "caring, hard-working, persistent, patient, and involved."

Despite their lowered student-teacher ratio and scheduling flexibility, these teachers face monumental challenges each day. Sometimes they chisel out planning periods, but more often they make time for "kitchen conferences," a quick word in the almost-private alcove that houses the school's refrigerator. But there is scant pettiness here, just the slow steady hum of teachers struggling to serve kids better, teachers who trust in one another's concern, who find strength in the knowledge that they can reach their own decisions and carry them through. Bill remembers times back in his traditional school when "the word would come down, 'We're going to do something collaboratively, now the district really wants your input'— and everybody's first reaction was 'Yeah, right.'" Now, Bill says, "when Max wants my input, I *know* he wants my input. And whether he acts on what I say or not, he's gonna think about what I say, he's gonna take it into consideration. And I know that when we're doin' a class together it's gonna be *our* class—not his or mine, but it's gonna be *our* class."

For all its joys, theirs is an intense, sometimes punishing workplace, and Bill and Max acknowledge their need for time away, for time outside with their real families. But while they seldom see one another beyond the walls of school, their weekday lunches are free-for-alls at the hallway table, time spent talking to students about everything and anything. I tell them that these conversations often seemed like a really good class, and I mention Nanci Atwell's (1987) dinner-table metaphor. "Yup, this place is a lot like a big dinner table," Bill remarks, "When classes are running well, they're like big old dinner tables, you know? And when they aren't running—well, they're like big old *P.E.* classes." "That's right," Max seconds. "Eighty kids and a whistle," said Bill. "And the whistle doesn't *work*," adds Max. "Those are the bad days," Bill observes. "You blow really hard and the little thing pops out of the whistle and you go 'O God, what do I do now?'"

WE WERE ALL ALIVE

Dave, the SDLC's counselor, remarks that "teaching here is risky business." "We build up a lot of frustration," Bob adds; "every time a student leaves or doesn't make it for one reason or another, that bothers you. You can try to be thick-skinned and ignore it and all that, but the tension's still there." Gene remembers once going to hear Ted Sizer speak: "One of the comments he made was, 'I can always tell alternative-school teachers. They're the ones that in October look like a teacher is supposed to look in May. They just *always* look that way. They just keep going and don't quit.'" Sometimes Gene finds himself thinking in the evening about things that happened that day at school—"which could be a positive or a negative, depending upon whom you ask." Things feel less settled here, lots of challenges and questions he never faced at other schools, but he has no interest in returning to the mainstream: "It would bore me to death," he suspects, "because of the lack of collaboration."

Working together here is more than a way to ease the burden. At the SDLC, Lana says, "collegiality seems to be a way of survival," a mode of being that is pervasive, enduring, and, given the hard uncertainties of the challenges, profoundly necessary. At the center is an abiding concern for students: "I don't think anybody's team-teaching or working together for any other reason," says Bob. "I'm not saying that they're not stronger for it personally, but I think their motivation is legitimately what's best for students, how to help students." As Bill points out, helping these students can be an elusive goal, and the staff is always engaged in a search for "better ways":

You have this wonderful ability to talk with people that you don't get [in traditional schools]. Being able to talk with people, and talking with people who are not only in the room, but are actually working *with* you. I mean, that's teeth, you can do something with that, you can *bite* something.

Collaboration here is always part of a larger flow of participation and mutual assistance. This year the school has a new social studies teacher, a man who has taught for many years but never in an alternative setting, who describes himself as "awestruck" by all the joint work going on at the SDLC. More is involved than particular people or even partnerships, he explains—there is the opportunity to know the kids for a long time, to meet daily as a staff, to hammer out "common goals," and, perhaps most of all, "the key to success—ownership." Though Bill and Max groaned over the accreditation review, by trimester's end this, too, has become cause for celebration: It was, Bill says, "one of the most exhilarating experiences I've ever been through in my educational career—because it was *alive,* we were *all* alive, we were talking about life-and-death educational matters, really important stuff that would affect students in positive ways."

Bill and his colleagues know that "when we decide something, that's what we're going to do, and we can start tomorrow." But this knowing and doing does not preclude the play of individual opinions—in this, as in all else, they enjoy "elasticity," Bill explains. People may not always agree initially, Max observes, but once they reach consensus no one ever goes out to "snipe at it from the outside—that doesn't *ever* happen here." Teachers say that Bob's role as principal is that of "a great smoother of the waters," someone who honors the spirit of this "great debate society" while working to quiet an occasional flare of tempers. These people do not try to hide their opinions, and they get angry sometimes. "We sit and we argue," says the art teacher,

and say, "Oh, no, what you're saying is bullshit. That's wrong. I don't accept that." When you go to any other setting, the principal is in charge, the teachers are like pupils, like kids. Nobody's uttering a word. Be political. Be nice to others. Be smiling. Don't show your real face. Don't show your real feeling. Here you don't see that. We come inside this room, we cut each other into pieces and we leave this room friends. If we are all just one stereotypical character following our principal, the victim will be the student in the end.

Conflict is seen here as an integral part of joint work: "Of course we collaborate all the time," one teacher said to me early on, "haven't you seen the way we *fight?*" "There'll be conflicts," Bill says, "and we have to learn to talk them out. It's okay not to agree as long as you keep talking, keep listening, keep working to find the middle ground. We understand that change does not occur without conflict, and that learning how to *work* together—student-faculty, faculty-faculty, whatever—doesn't occur without conflict."

OUR SCHOOL

Max and Bill's task was made difficult even before the school year opened, even before the new kids passed into 'Zine and began testing the waters. Most arrive deeply discouraged, long cast as behavioral or academic problems, not quite knowing what to make of all these teachers who like them as people and believe in them as learners. Life at the SDLC carries a sense of daily urgency, the human stakes always high, the outcomes always uncertain, no matter how inspired and caring the teachers.

Pedagogically, the SDLC resembles what Barbara Rogoff has called a "community of learners" (Rogoff, 1994), a collaborative network that invites participatory problem solving, provides an array of roles, and offers opportunities for expert-apprenticeship coaching (Brown, Collins, & Duguid, 1989; Lave, 1988). Max and Bill's joint work makes possible such participation, grounded in a school culture that encourages risk-taking, frankness, respect for others, and responsibility. Recognizing that a diversity of strengths is needed, they watch for opportunities to extend the collaborative net farther still—to include joint work with parents, expert resources, and local business people. No one has to have it all under control, their collaboration says to students; no one has to present all the possibilities. This, too, is part of what these teachers model for students—that stumbling need not be a reason to give up, that the big challenges of life are often plagued by uncertainty, that we are all half-awkward works in progress. Max and Bill show kids that toughness can be part of caring, that conflict can be part of collaboration, that teachers can be catalysts who stimulate and support, then watch for opportunities to step back. They are, in other words, human models as well as instructional resources, caring adults as well as demanding teachers.

Meanwhile, the SDLC's school district increasingly wants harder evidence that kids are better off for attending here. School is ultimately about academics, after all, and the SDLC's graduation rate, a prime index for policymakers, remains low. Teachers resist the temptation to hike up percentages by lowering expectations, and so the issue persists. The arguments are familiar ones in school districts across the country: If kids drop out of such schools, why bother? Maybe closely knit small schools are a good thing—but why invest extra money in programs that serve a troubled few?

Might these schools become academic ghettos, places with lowered standards and dangerous peer dynamics? Perhaps, some suggest, too much in
these kids' lives has already undermined their motivation, the pattern is
already set.

Too often lost in such discussions is appreciation of the day-to-day
experience inside schools like the SDLC. Kids arrive with lots of troubles,
baggage that rests in long educational histories and lives outside. Dramatic
turnarounds are long shots, but the SDLC opens the possibility, beginning
with relationships of mutual care and trust, with establishing an uncommon sense of belonging to an educational enterprise. Students graduate
once their records show an accumulation of individual accomplishments,
but when teachers and kids talk about the SDLC, it is in collective terms—
"our staff," "our school." Even for those who do not graduate, perhaps this
turn of language represents a small sign of hope. For all our educational
jargon, we lack precise ways to describe the benefits of this cooperative
vision of life in schools or the job of teaching. If places like the SDLC are to
survive and prosper, we need to find such words, ensuring that the work
of teachers like Max and Bill becomes part of what we talk about when we
talk about school success.

Chapter 3

Boundary Crossings:
Ada and Lou

While a passionate age storms ahead setting up new things and tearing down old, raising and demolishing as it goes, a reflective and passionless age does exactly the contrary: it hinders and stifles all action; it levels.

(Kierkegaard, 1846/1962, p. 51)

I drive through a city done up in wintry shades of grey—a wan sky, dirty snow piled street-side, skyscrapers following the curve of a frozen river. A spice factory rests beside the downtown riverfront, and an aroma reminiscent of pumpkin pie wafts through the chill, signaling an early start to the new workday. I turn briefly onto the "business loop" and past a parade of commercial clutter—a bright McDonald's, a mortuary occupying a grand old home, a billboard commemorating mention of the city's symphony in *Time* magazine. At 8:00 A.M. the light is still pale, headlamps ablaze on yellow school buses advancing down the wide avenue.

The surrounding countryside is plotted out in square grids, a checkerboard of farms defined by neatly spaced county roads. This urban environment is imprinted with perpendicular lines, too, its main thoroughfares segmenting the city into distinct neighborhoods. The conservative high school on the northeast side serves the kids of blue-collar families; the south is newer and more affluent, a place of high-tech industry and forward-thinking pedagogy. On the northwest side is Hamilton High, described by one administrator as "the closest thing this city has to an inner-city school." He shrugs, acknowledging the claim's apparent silliness. The school is a mile or two from the heart of downtown, but it is also nestled within an enclave of old wealth, of manicured mansions passed from generation to generation, monuments to fortunes made in meat packing and the city's old starch works. Winter robs these streets of their lush foliage, but the skeletal trees remain stately, the homes shining monuments untouched by the pall of the season. Just a block or two north of the city's commercial jumble I reach this sedate and protected place, and here I find Hamilton High.

EXCELLENCE IN THE "INNER CITY"

Lines of buses converge on the central breezeway, but the student parking lot is already full, a Mercedes or Lexus scattered here and there among a sea of well-used sedans and trucks. The walk to the front door seems long in the cold morning air, past the sprawling auditorium, past a large sign proclaiming Hamilton High "Home of the Chargers," up to the glass doors that open into the main lobby. From the outside, the school is a monotonous bunker of tan brick, but inside is color and light. The entryway's track lighting is turned up a shade brighter during this passing period, a grim-faced vice-principal standing guard, but the bustle is orderly. Soon students deposit themselves in classrooms, the buzzer sounds, and lights dim on an empty expanse of lobby and corridor.

Just before I moved to the Midwest from the West Coast, my local newspaper ran a series of articles about a family that had come to this city so their kids could go to strong schools; I have recently learned that these kids are here, attending *this* school. As I walk Hamilton's main corridors I can't help thinking of that family, of what any parent might think visiting this building for the first time. Along virtually every inch of wall are award displays, shelf after shelf filled with carefully arranged plaques and citations. Most prominently displayed are a pair of national awards, emblazoned with the inscription "Excellence in Education" and "E Pluribus Unum." Here, too, are photos of various state ceremonies, the school's administrators seated on a raised dais next to the conservative governor.

Even beside a face transposed from the evening news, Hamilton's distinguished principal holds his own. Jack Graham is a tall presence around here, respected and liked by just about everyone I will meet. Staff say their principal is a good listener, that they feel heard even when they fail to change his mind. He steps back from curricular decisions, deferring to teachers and honoring diverse philosophies. But Jack keeps a watchful eye on just about every aspect of the school's functioning, carefully tending its glowing public reputation, representing the school in meetings with community members and state leaders. When Hamilton receives one of its frequent awards, Dr. Jack Graham is there to accept it, his face and name again in the papers, more good news to post in this proud corridor.

Just beyond the school awards, displays chronicle the scholastic achievements of individual students: honor roll, Academic Decathlon champions, highest grade-point averages, highest scores on the Iowa Test of Educational Development or ACT. The "Citizenship Society" recognizes "Service to Hamilton, Outstanding Attitude, Noteworthy Cooperation, Unusual Initiative, or Unique Contribution to Campus Life," often honoring kids not featured in the other displays. Teachers' nomination forms include written statements, and these are posted beside the smiling faces of Citizenship Society inductees. Here are students who have "shown positive attitude and perseverance in the face of academic adversity," who are "pleasant," "happy go lucky," "a pleasure," "cheerful," "conscientious," "dedicated," "cooperative," and "positive."

The school is its own museum, every available niche devoted to an ongoing chronicle of its success. Even the artwork in the sun-washed cafeteria celebrates achievement—I study a piece made of wooden tiles, each carved with the name of a school honor, prize-winning student organization, or various renditions of the Charger insignia. Further away from the main corridor the awards tend to descend in prestige value, but it seems that no honor escapes hallway notice, from the social studies "Dollars for Scholars" recipients to virtually every athletic award dating back nearly 40 years. I keep noticing an oft-posted list of "Hamilton High School Behavior Expectations," introduced with the line "Hamilton High insists upon a positive campus atmosphere." In a school this large someone must get into trouble sometime, but it is hard to imagine these kids being terribly negative. In classroom after classroom, rows of blue-jeaned young people sit silently in rows, sleepy but obliging.

Eighty percent of Hamilton's 1,500 students are European-American; of the remaining 20%, only half are African-American, but when people talk of diversity at the school, it is generally a black–white dividing line they have in mind. Most of the faces in the awards displays are white, while the demographics of the Citizenship Society more closely match those in the corridors. Hamilton is an ethnically diverse school by statewide standards, but its staff quietly acknowledge that diversity here encompasses socioeconomic status as much as race. These are patterns that overlap and intertwine, entangling white and black alike, for poverty affects more than one small group here. "I would say that between a quarter and a third of our students are genuinely poor and qualify for federal lunch assistance," Jack Graham tells me. The notion seems at odds with the air of affluence and ambition that pervades the public image of this place, recently cited for excellence by a national magazine.

But two miles to the north is an abruptly different world. It is easy to imagine some of the homes there more closely resembling the ones nearer Hamilton, with their expansive porticos and carefully tended gardens. A short bus ride from the school is an area of formerly prosperous homes peeling to raw silvery grey; no foundation plantings, lots of scrubby brown grass, plastic taped to windows in a fragile attempt to block out winter. It is a neighborhood much in the news this season, plagued by a rash of drive-by shootings, random muggings, and carjackings. It is also a place of high unemployment, where lots of people have nothing to do, where idle tempers periodically flare. People in the surrounding areas know the district well, warning newcomers not to buy houses there, describing it as "the closest thing we have to a ghetto." There is pride here, too, summertime efforts to repair and renew, close-knit families, students who work hard at school. But everyone I ask can name the boundaries, tracing the lines that quietly define a less-public side of Hamilton High.

A TRADITION OF TRACKING

Hamilton's social divide is reflected in a system of tracking—called "leveling" here—a tradition that has persevered despite gentle pressure from district headquarters. Ninth- and 10th-graders are placed in "skills-," "middle-," or "upper-" level courses, and teachers commonly refer to particular students by these tags, seemingly as well bounded as nearby neighborhoods. Eleventh- and 12th-graders are not tracked "on paper," the English department chair tells me, "but generally speaking the brighter students will choose to take AP English." "We have been reluctant to join the trend toward eliminating all leveling," notes the principal; "*I* have been reluctant. The other schools have eliminated more leveling than we have. Not because I don't think it's a worthy ideal, but because I think there are cases where it isn't practical."

A vocal majority of Hamilton's English faculty agree that untracking would ill serve low and high achievers alike. "I hate to see some of our kids who are really low-ability achievers thrown in with those that practically need no guidance to achieve," says one member of the department; "I just don't see where this benefits the low achiever—the high achiever will do it anyway." When I ask if he could see himself teaching an untracked course, his response is decisive. "I'd resign first," he answers. One of his long-time colleagues concurs:

> I'm pro-leveling, OK? Always have been. I've always felt that the
> disruptive have still been disruptive, and often the disruptive are
> the lower levels. I could not fathom—could you?—an AP class
> being unleveled. You'd have little mini-groups reading different
> selections. But then I don't know how you would quite handle that
> with *Hamlet* or, you know, something like that. I would think some

of those low-level students, low-intellect students would certainly
not be college-placement.

A number of their colleagues agree that untracked classes are hard to
teach well. "Theoretically, it could be done," says a teacher with background in special education, "but in actuality, one teacher cannot do it.
You're not just dealing with educational levels, you're dealing with emotional levels and so many other things." An English teacher who teaches
both skills- and upper-level courses says ninth-graders often tell him they
were "frustrated" with the lack of tracking at their middle schools; in his
leveled classes, he maintains, the bright kids finally feel challenged, while
the less bright finally feel successful. He sees the present system as simply
better for students: "Not that I'm too old, it's too hard, it's too different or
anything of that sort," he explains, "but I know that I cannot successfully
meet all the needs of 30 to 34 kids in my room by myself in an integrated
setting nearly as well as I can the way it is now. I would like to feel I'm a
very good teacher, but I know where my strengths are, and I don't think
that's one of them."

For a majority of Hamilton's English faculty, competition for upper-
track courses is both accepted and expected. A teacher who serves as advisor to the school's student newspaper and the Academic Decathlon team
notes an added incentive: Teaching upper-track courses is not only enjoy-
able, but also an ideal way to recruit "top-level people" for these prize-
winning efforts. Meanwhile, a first-year teacher bemoans the fact that as
the "new kid on the block, I kind of have to take what I can get." He sees
competition for "top-level kids" as natural: "Top-level kids are great to
work with—everybody wants to teach the great kids, you know, they want
their classrooms to be productive. They don't want to have to put up with
the headaches."

According to Hamilton's principal, support for tracking extends into
the more influential segments of the community. He is especially concerned
that affluent parents of upper-tier students would protest any blanket plan
to untrack: "If we eliminated all top-level language arts here," he explains,
"I'd have to *deal* with that—there would definitely be a political response
to that, without any doubt." Along with many of the teachers, he worries
that untracked classes would also complicate the task of teaching:

There's a wide gap here between the most capable and motivated
student in the freshman class and the least capable and motivated
student who's not in special education. There's a wide gap. And to
put them all in the same room creates some real instructional
problems that not all teachers know how to cope with.

Ironically, one of the only English teachers to try a nontracked language-arts course did so not by design, but by administrative mishap, a "glaring error": "They had top-level and skills kids all scheduled into one class," he recalls, "and it was *my* class." The mistake went undetected until two weeks into the semester, and by that time the administration was hesitant to reshuffle assignments. The teacher said "fine" somewhat reluctantly, only to be amazed by what he watched unfold:

> We went through the whole year all together and it was one of the best classes I ever had. And I'd thought "this has a lot of problems"—*could* have a lot of problems—the skills kids being very intimidated by the people who had never known a B in their lives, and these kids who had never *seen* a B in their lives. I saw it working just the opposite to that. The kids who didn't have a lot of study skills were all of a sudden being tutored by these guys. It was not "here, go tutor them"—they just did it automatically. And they became good friends, probably with some kids they would never have sought out while they were here—both ways. And some of the kids that were involved in theater got these kids involved in theater, and they're still involved in theater today. So from that aspect, I thought it was very, very good.

He acknowledges a few rough spots, but sees these as situated in the wider school context rather than the class per se:

> The problem with it was that we weren't set up to do it at that point. There were no materials that crossed all of these lines. I just had to put it all together as we went. [Another] problem I saw was that they were going to go right back that following year, and that's exactly what happened—they got tracked again. I've always thought that integrating classes was the way to go, but I know the biggest problem of that is teachers—"this is my level, I put in my time," that's a problem here, too.

Tracking, writes Goodlad (1984, p. 297) is a "retreat rather than a strategy," and a much-maligned retreat at that. The evidence has long been accumulating, layer after layer suggesting the same story: that minority and lower-SES kids are found in disproportionate numbers in the lower tracks, where Citizenship Society virtues of punctuality, cooperation, and obedience are valued over creativity, critical thinking, and self-direction (Goodlad, 1984; Oakes, 1985). Researchers observe that while tracking results in no significant achievement gains for any group (Slavin, 1988), it creates a rigid hierarchy that restricts friendship networks and promotes a sense of boundaries between "us" and "them" (Hallinan & Sorensen, 1985; Hallinan & Williams, 1989). It exacts an especially heavy toll on lower-track students, who suffer in terms of self-esteem, intellectual development, and options for the future (Gamoran & Berends, 1987; Gamoran & Mare, 1989; Oakes, 1985).

And yet the tradition of tracking persists, perhaps most emphatically at places like Hamilton, where academic boundaries reinforce socioeconomic and ethnic divisions (Oakes, 1992; Wells & Serna, 1996). But quietly, almost surreptitiously, another model is under construction here, if in a remote, little-noticed enclave. Two English teachers, Ada Finch and Lou Russell, are venturing an experiment, drawing a small cadre of interested parents and students. Theirs is a small effort, wildly at odds with most of the values and practices that surround them. Can they succeed without much support from the school as a whole? Might their work be the start of a bigger trend? How to risk and explore in a department dominated by a vocal pro-tracking faction? These are among the questions Ada and Lou often ask themselves, questions that guide their collaboration and shape its implications for school change.

INNOVATION OVER THE AUTOSHOP

Ada and Lou say that the long walk out to their classrooms is good for students, providing needed transition time. I need careful directions: down a long central corridor, past a seemingly endless succession of awards displays, beyond the sunlit cafeteria with its heavy aroma of fried food, out to the industrial arts wing—where the walls are white-enameled cement blocks, where the ceilings are high and steel-beamed, where the kids seem at first to belong to a different school entirely. This is also where special education is housed, and the students who congregate in the hallways are strikingly varied, a real contrast to the bustling, preppy crowd in the main lobby. Ada and Lou's neighboring classrooms are up a narrow metal staircase, one flight above the auto shop—far from the English department's central corridor, and far away in spirit, too.

They jokingly refer to one another as "frog" and "toad," after the two friends in Arnold Lobel's (1970) children's book. Both veteran teachers in their early 50s, they have grown progressively closer over the last several years, looking to one another through a host of challenges—encouraging peer collaboration, incorporating multicultural literature, brainstorming ways to meet the needs of culturally diverse students. They often volunteer for skills-level courses, and recently had an opportunity to teach a section jointly. Somewhere in that experience, somewhere in their conversations with one another and a few like-minded friends, they set on the idea of offering a 10th-grade language arts class that would not be tracked, a sanctioned version of their colleague's happy-accident course. I would follow Ada and Lou over the second trimester of the experiment, sitting in their parallel sections of the "integrated" class.

Lou says that while many teachers "aren't willing to admit that what they do doesn't always work," she and Ada continually talk about failures, "hammering out those issues." Together they worry and wonder—about the kids they fail to reach, and about ethnic tensions in the school and the city. Crime statistics in the nearby African-American neighborhood continue to climb, and several times recently, Ada and Lou have seen former students on the evening news, kids they care about hauled off in patrol cars. They spend a lot of time talking about these students' fortunes, about the combination of hopelessness and macho posturing that lands these young men in jail. They worry, too, about the ethnocentrism of many of the school's affluent European Americans. They want connection across sometimes highly charged boundaries, a tall order anywhere.

They have a planning period in common second hour each day, and they often manage time to sit and chat. Lou's room has a bank of windows that look out over a snow-covered soccer field, and a small coffee pot she switches on at 9:00 every morning, serving up steaming cups of gourmet brew in handmade cups. Their English Department colleagues over in the central corridor don't see them much, talking of Ada and Lou as if they were one entity, a sort of renegade faction. But people who know both see them as two quite different people holding basic principles in common. Their friendship springs partly from a mutual recognition of all they share, and partly from their own ability to cross boundaries, to find in one another's differences a source of challenge and delight.

Ada

The pseudonym "Ada" came as a gift from an admiring student. One day in her class I'd mentioned my need to come up with fitting pseudonyms, and later that hour a girl passed me a note. She had written her teacher's real name, then drawn an arrow to "Ada Finch," noting that she'd derived it from "Atticus Finch in *To Kill a Mockingbird*" (Lee, 1960): "Atticus is a warm, guiding individual that respects people for who they are—not where they live, their color, what they own, or family lineage." Kids see Ada's kindness and gentleness, but they also see her quiet strength. As Ada likes to say, students know who we are not only by what we say, but by how we act and by the effects we manage to have.

Ada is physically small, her salt-and-peppery hair clipped close, her voice so soft that students must listen closely to track the careful flow of her words. She wears sensible midwestern clothes, an assortment of cotton turtlenecks, denim jumpers, wooly dirndl skirts, and huge furry snowboots that seem at first off-scale, a half-comical concession to the season. Like Lou, she is fighting off a series of viruses this winter, but her ready smile is radiant. Ada moves through these months with sturdy cheer and understated serenity, an attitude that seems natural to her year-round. From time to time she offers reminders of her life outside Hamilton, that she is also a caring wife, mother, and citizen, but when she walks into her classroom, she belongs entirely to her students.

Ada grew up in a tiny midwestern farm town, then attended a small liberal-arts college, a campus her parents hoped would feel less jarring than a larger, more prestigious place. But she went on for a master's degree at a bustling public university, where she worked in a lab school and supervised student teachers. It was a happy time—the student teachers were "great, just great," Ada remembers, and the collegial company stimulating. After graduating she went to work at a high school across town, but went on extended leave a few years later when her husband became seriously ill. Ada was gone from her classroom for 3 years, but she volunteered during that time at a community preschool, working with a group of women who loved children but lacked formal training. "I realized that there is so much to teaching that doesn't have to do with stuff you've learned in books," Ada recalls; "those people were just so wonderful and warm. And we connected with the parents—we had parents' meetings, there was just this wonderful family kind of thing." Ada remembers conversations that centered on "real genuine teaching":

> The best part about it was nobody was getting paid. And so the rewards had nothing to do with money, and had to do with our really wanting to be there and work with those kids, and it was really informal in that nobody had any sort of power plays. And I realized that, you know, there is that potential for real communication and collaborative teaching.

When Ada returned to high school teaching it was at Hamilton, where she served for a time as English department chair. There was an influx of new teachers in those days, and she was given two free periods to mentor them, time to talk and to visit their classes. "We learned so much from each other," she recalls, "just talking." Ada believes that collaboration involves mutual learning regardless of any asymmetry in experience or knowledge, but that it must be grounded in trust, in "really listening and respecting and asking for help, and yet so much caring that you can share that kind of faltering." She worries that trust is too often eroded in the public-school workplace, with its system of top-down evaluation and norms of competition. To Ada, really collaborating means not only a different way of working, but a different way of being. "It's not one teaching another person," she explains,

> it's that sharing of everything, whether it's the successes or the parts that didn't work so well. And then sometimes you talk about the individual kids involved, too, and then you see how things worked with one kid and didn't with another one. The whole thing sort of deals with generosity. And generosity comes, I think, from confidence and from realizing that each individual is worth something. And so if you find something that works that's good, then the best thing to do with it is to share it rather than keep it for yourself. It has to do with connections with people. It has to do with that whole way of living, where people care about each other because they respect each other enough to value them. And those kinds of lessons you don't really say out loud. You just have to convey them through the way you live.

Ada's collaboration with Lou is a natural outgrowth of this way of thinking and being. "It just clicked," she says of their early friendship; "I'm sort of a natural at some of those things, and I don't really know exactly where they come from." Ada remembers the "isolation and tension" of teaching a skills course abating a bit when she and Lou did it together. Ada describes herself as "quieter in a relationship," but she quickly adds that she never feels dominated by Lou, that theirs is a relationship of give-and-take. "The people who are really into collaboration aren't going to be the power people," Ada muses, "people who feel as if they are absolutely the right ones and everybody should follow them." Ada links this to a "whole philosophy of teaching" that she calls "wide-awake," where teachers are open to kids, open to change, refusing to see themselves as lone authorities.

While they don't often visit outside of school—"she has a busy life and I have a busy life," Ada explains—their companionship at work is a daily treat, if an all-too-sparse one. Eager to spend more time with her family, Ada decided to work part-time several years ago, and she is now here only between 9:00 and 2:00. She particularly misses winding down after school, laughing with Lou about the day, imagining what they might do differently tomorrow. Even now, being free to talk during their planning period often means getting up at 5:00 in the morning to prepare her classes, but Ada is loath to complain. She feels for her colleagues with five classes and two or three different preparations. Teachers need to be "respected as professionals," she says firmly, "and they need professional time—they should have *relaxed* time, not this *hectic* time."

Ada's relationship with Lou has ripened over a period of years, but their joint efforts are not entirely free of complication. They have taught the nontracked language arts course for a trimester, and both are feeling a little unsettled. "It's not been the greatest class for either of us," Ada admits, longing for time to "work out how it's going to go," and to explore the sometimes different approaches each is trying out. "It's not perfect by any means," she allows; then, with one of her warming smiles, "I even said that in class yesterday—I said, 'You were better today. Not *perfect*, but better.' And one of the kids said, 'Well, wouldn't it be boring to be *perfect*?'"

Lou

Amid the jumble of student projects and professional resources, Lou has found spaces in her homey classroom for bits of whimsy. Students like to pass around her big plastic frog, a sly reference to the nicknames she and Ada have given themselves. A big cartoon image stands atop a file cabinet: Above a stern little girl with a dogged frown, the conversation bubble reads "Snap out of it!" It is easy to imagine Lou saying just those words with just that expression, to grasp that, like the bright green frog, the image represents the alter ego of a woman who is by turns playful, affectionate, and formidable.

Where Ada is soft-spoken and understated, Lou is all drama and panache. She is physically larger, and her voice is bigger, too, her talk pressing and emphatic, her laugh expansive and gusty. Lou is outspoken, whether talking through first thoughts or expressing opinions, her pitch registering gathering intensity. She adjusts her oversized glasses and runs her fingers through her helmet of glossy dark hair, pausing but never falling silent for long. "Because I am blunt sometimes, I think I have a real reputation for being bitchy," she says, seeming resigned to the idea. She dresses in uncluttered cotton knits, but the colors are often eye-catching and direct—sparkling white with pure black, a touch of clear red, often a flash of polished silver. Lou's favorite jewelry is a small clay pin, a likeness of a John Deere tractor. It used to belong to a friend and colleague downstairs, a woman named Jan whom Lou calls a mentor. "Growing up on the farm," Lou told her one day, "I *drove* a tractor just like that." The pin arrived a few days later wrapped as a gift, Jan explaining to Lou, "It just needs to belong to you." The clay tractor would become one of Lou's treasures, an emblem of friendship and a springboard to many stories.

Lou worked hard on her parents' South Dakota farm; there were no sons, and she often tells students that she performed what was more commonly considered "man's work." She went to college a Nixon Republican planning to become a missionary, and graduated a few years later a Democrat, atheist, and feminist. She married, earned a teaching certificate and a master's in English, and found herself riddled with professional doubts by the time she was pregnant with the first of her daughters. Lou describes her student teaching experience as "horrid," and her first regular post as "a killer job in a district that was really falling apart." Her supervisor used to pull misbehaving kids out of her class "and practically took them out in the hall and beat them up." Lou worried a lot about the damage school can do to kids; after 2 years, she felt "really uncomfortable," and by the time her first daughter was born, she found herself wondering if she would "ever teach in a school again."

But as her children approached school age, she found herself volunteering full-time at a public alternative school organized by a group of like-minded parents ("we were all really hippies, you know"). "A lot of my ideas about education really came out of that alternative experience," Lou explains, although at the time she would have called this work "maternal rather than professional." An administrator at the school—a man who now happens to be district superintendent—finally pulled Lou aside. "Lou," she remembers him saying, "you've got to get back in a classroom. It's ridiculous for you not to be teaching. You've *got* to get up in a classroom." Still Lou hesitated—until, that is, one of her now young-adolescent daughters came home upset about put-downs from a sarcastic language arts teacher. "It was just awful," Lou recalls, still angered. "The messages were just horrid! And so I thought, 'Well, I'm going to substitute and I'm going to find out what the hell's going on.'"

That led to full-time substituting for three years at the city's alternative secondary school, a richly collaborative place that Lou "just loved." But when a full-time language arts position went to a teacher reassigned from another school, she was for a time "really bereft, like something that I valued had been taken away." Again a friend offered the necessary push, nudging her to apply for a vacancy at one of the city's comprehensive high schools. She was hired, and soon found herself struggling "like a first-year teacher" with rough-edged kids and tradition-minded staff. Then Jack Graham called; he knew Lou from her alternative-school stint, was now Hamilton's principal, and wanted her to come on board as a full-time replacement while a woman named Ada Finch went on extended leave. Ada was teaching some tough "skills" classes back then, lots of rebellious kids who needed steadiness and sensitivity. Lou initially resisted but was eventually talked into it, finishing a term at one school as she found time to meet the woman she was hired to replace.

"Ada and I just clicked," Lou recalls, her words echoing Ada's. "It was sort of like I felt, I've just met this person I've kind of known all my life. You know? It was just amazing." During the decade that has since passed, Lou was hired as a permanent full-timer, while Ada came back part-time, assigned to far-flung classrooms in all corners of the school. Then two years ago, Ada was given a permanent classroom right next door to Lou's, and they were finally as close physically as they had long been philosophically. Time is still an issue—Lou estimates that they talk no more than 90 minutes in a typical week—but she sees it as a big improvement just the same.

Describing Ada as a very "tender person," Lou acknowledges that she sometimes feels brusque by comparison. "I've snapped at her," Lou admits; "I think part of how our collaboration works is that we have a lot of really high expectations for each other—and tolerance. So she lets me snap at her sometimes, and she almost never does, you know?" But theirs is clearly not a relationship that weathers storms with ease. Lou recalls that just last spring, they "reached kind of a crisis" when one of their skills-level kids plagiarized a paper:

> Ada sort of jumped in to save him and I felt he shouldn't have been saved. That was the wrong message. And that was hard. I think that was hard for both of us. I think it was hard for me to be angry with her, and it was hard for her to feel my anger, and I felt guilty about it.

These days, they note a bit more distance in their relationship, a focus on "survival," as Lou puts it, "on just figuring out how to teach this new curriculum together and just sharing materials and sharing ideas, making it work, keeping positive about it." Both feel dissatisfied with the way the class went when they tried it last term, and in these dark days of winter, morale is a serious consideration, especially for Lou. "That's the thing I always love about Ada," Lou says, "She doesn't let things get her down. I'll be really depressed about how something went and she'll say, 'Well, now, look. You're not thinking about this aspect, or maybe you need to talk about that or, you know, maybe you can go back and do it *this* way.' And I certainly appreciate that, you know."

Despite her strong presence, Lou, too, is tender in her way, needing these boosts of reassurance and advice. She is trying new things, things not often attempted at Hamilton, and she counts on this like-minded companionship. Perhaps their partnership requires special care, but she regards it as a rare gift. Lou estimates that there are only two or three other people in the building with whom she might collaborate the way she and Ada do, and she is eager to play down the relationship's challenges, to emphasize its many blessings. "The way that we differ has to do more with superficial kinds of things," Lou says. What they hold in common, she adds with assurance, feels more like bedrock: "a real respect for kids," a belief "that kids can learn and that you build from their strengths."

LESS A GHETTO: AN "INTEGRATED" CLASS

Ada and Lou originally developed plans for a series of nonleveled language arts courses with a colleague who teaches ninth grade. Hoping for a 2-year sequence of "integrated" courses, they read extensively, formulated a rationale, and wrote up a proposal. The three teachers asked Jack Graham for four sections to be split equally between the 9th and 10th grades, each including roughly balanced numbers of students designated "skills," "top," and "average." Arguing that students learn better in unleveled classrooms, their proposal detailed a pedagogy as well, suggesting strategies such as cooperative learning (Goodlad & Oakes, 1988), opportunities to exhibit multiple intelligences (Gardner, 1983), "personalized learning tasks," use of "open-ended/higher-level thinking strategies," and portfolio assessment. Then they listed the advantages of their proposed courses, positing a vision of teaching and learning that challenged a number of Hamilton traditions:

- All students will have exposure to a wider variety of people/less a ghetto of abilities and socioeconomic class.
- Classroom population will reflect the real diversity of ability and social class at Hamilton.
- All students will have a better chance to develop leadership.
- Students are accustomed to integrated grouping in middle school.
- All students will experience a richer mix of people.
- Broader range will encourage more risk-taking in the classroom.
- No stigma will be attached to not being in a top-level class or being stuck in a low-level one.
- Higher expectations for all students.
- More opportunity for divergent thinking.

Meanwhile, their brief list of "disadvantages" emphasized minor logistical matters, with a brief nod here and there to more substantive issues: "We will have to cope with a wider range of abilities," they admitted. And perhaps of even greater concern to Hamilton's image-minded administration: "There may be a public relations problem."

Lou recalls that while their principal was reluctant to experiment across the two grades, he agreed to provide 10th-graders a choice, and, at least initially, to let Ada and Lou speak about the new option to students in various level courses. What happened next is shrouded in mystery, but Jack made it clear that strong concerns were raised, and that the invitation to talk about the proposal—especially to top-level students—was no longer open. Jack honored his commitment to send a letter home detailing the new option for parents, but he asked that Ada and Lou discuss it only if directly asked. Publicity was scant and support covert, so it came as a bit of a surprise when sufficient students came forth to comprise two sections of the 10th-grade course. "I think it absolutely blew Jack's mind that we had two sections," Lou says with a smile.

Though insisting that "eliminating leveling in high schools is just pretty naive," Jack acknowledges that language arts may be an area more amenable to integration than some. Most of all, he wants to support Ada and Lou:

> I think Ada and Lou are both very egalitarian by nature, and so they wanted to try it, and our feeling generally is that if a teacher wants to try something, if it's not absolutely bizarre, we'd like to do what we can to support that to keep them fresh and interested. And so that's it. It was their idea, and they wanted to do it. It's not a super-high priority for me, but keeping those two happy and teaching here *is* a very high priority for me, so we've got to support them. That's about it.

The assistant principal echoes Jack's sentiments. He, too, sidesteps advocacy of the nonleveled approach, but is quick to endorse "allowing teachers to try things," and explains how he helps with scheduling concerns, making sure that the "kids they've identified can take it."

This is a school with much to lose, and administrators move quickly to quell controversy. When a staff committee recently reported that 25% of girls at Hamilton had experienced some form of sexual harassment, Jack had a private word with the group's chair. Lou, who serves on the committee, recalls his comments with a wry smile: "This is great work you're doing, but can't we make it sound more positive?" Now, with a storm brewing around academic tracking, Jack again looks for ways to minimize any bad news. Neither enthusiastic nor oppositional, he privately suggests that the courses have few top-level kids, that these classes closely resemble those called "average" under the traditional system—in other words, that this is not a real experiment in untracking at all. Not so, Ada and Lou remark, pointing out that Jack has not yet visited the classes. Nor do Ada and Lou's

English department colleagues pay much notice; one firmly denies that nonleveled classes are being offered, and none can comment on their substance. Most have little time to go exploring, and even potential sympathizers hold back, reluctant to stir the waters. Geography, scheduling, and philosophy conspire to divide the department. While colleagues in the central corridor comprise its tradition-minded core, Ada and Lou are out in the industrial arts wing, quietly confronting the complexities of a wish come true.

DIFFERENT BACKGROUNDS

I visit Lou's 8:00 integrated class for the first time on a dark morning in early December. Still getting over the flu that kept her home all last week, she is managing fatigue, marking time until the upcoming winter break. In this delicate dance of effort and conservation, the hard work of getting through the season, Lou's clothes stand in cheerful defiance—a faded denim shirt today, blue jeans, red shoes, dangling earrings. The day is chilly, thin sheets of ice coating the insides of her classroom windows, but the winter's record-breaking lows are still a few weeks off. What makes waking up so hard today is the lack of light, this beginning in the dark. Lou's students arrive on time, but they sit sleepily, passively, and a few make desktop nests of their winter coats, letting their heads drop now and then into makeshift pillows.

Like Ada, Lou is determined to include international literature in the curriculum, and her students are about to be handed well-thumbed photocopies of excerpts from *The Ramayana* (Narayan, 1972). Lou wants to make sure that they know a little about Hinduism before they commence reading, and she asks them to "group up for just a second" to review the terms written on the board: "Karma," "dharma," "Universal spirit," "caste system," and "lord of the dance." There will be a quiz tomorrow, but the students are slow to supply definitions, yawns outnumbering responses. Lou is gently persistent, but the East seems far indeed just now, and the next 15 minutes long. She shows a brief filmstrip about Hinduism, but no one heeds her note-taking advice, and several struggle to stay awake.

As the filmstrip ends, Lou asks them to "take a few minutes to pull it together for yourself—what was interesting or what was important." A few students write, but most sit and stare, and an occasional head goes down. After several minutes Lou asks what they noticed; then, to the silence, "Lauren, what did *you* notice?" "Uh, nothing," comes the flat reply. Lou persists: "Just things you already knew about?" but no response. Then again to the silent group, "Other things you noticed?" and another long pause.

"Well what about things you wondered about? Questions?" Brightening, Lou turns to *The Ramayana*. "Oh, my god," a boy groans. "How *long* might this book be?" a girl asks with rising alarm, Lou offering firm assurance that she can handle it. Another complains that Lou is "too lenient," and Lou asks with a smile what she might suggest, "stringing students up," perhaps? The girl counters with an extended description of a point system that would penalize students who hand in work late; the others seem too weary to take up sides.

The bells have for some reason been shut off, and the students seem surprised when their class time is finally up. "No bells today," Lou remarks, letting them go. "Kinda nice." The kids who crowd out her door are immaculately groomed, dressed in androgynous jeans, sweatshirts, baseball caps, sneakers. There are a few African Americans and Southeast Asians, but most are European American. Lou confesses that she wonders—she doesn't think the top-level kids are bored, but she worries about losing the others, and asks what I think. I want to blame it on the sleepiness that goes with dark cold, but remark instead that I have yet to figure out who the top, middle, and skills kids are. Lou smiles broadly. "This is good," she says, "this is the whole idea."

This is second hour, the planning period Lou and Ada hold in common. A just-arrived Ada comes in beaming, wrapped in a furry winter coat, her arms full of books. Lou puts on a pot of coffee, and the hour becomes an oasis, a time to touch down in doubts, to generate new ideas, to gather fortification for the long day still ahead. Lou tells Ada that she and her first-hour class reached "our lowest point today," that the kids are really worn, that she looks forward to moving on to fresh turf. Ada murmurs understanding, a receptive, supportive friend, and suddenly the room seems inviting and energized.

Lou starts with her concerns around grading. A first-hour student approached her several days ago to say that she must have an A, demanding that Lou spell out grading requirements and let her know when she falls short. The girl is the "kind of kid who doesn't have real good insight, and she can't pull things together very well," Lou says now. "What jars me," she adds, "is that she wants *me* to set the hoops." Still, Lou wonders at her reluctance to award an A for hard work alone. "I think I need to get over that," she remarks, and Ada quickly agrees. "There are some kids that are going to go in an organized, drone-like way that maybe *deserve* an A," Ada argues. "Sometimes those kids end up making breakthroughs and real connections," Lou replies, "and I'm a real sucker for that person." "Me too," Ada admits. But together they worry about students who seem intent on simply producing what teachers want, and Lou half-jokingly suggests that those kids should never get more than a C. Ada argues that if she and Lou articulate too explicitly what constitutes a B or an A, "we lose half of what we're trying to do in there, which is evaluate one kid in one way and one kid in another way, and give them the chance to go way beyond." For Ada, the central concern is how to make sure that kids "are really pushing themselves, whether they are really thinking of something in a new way." Like Lou, who wants to "open windows, to help kids learn about themselves and about the world," Ada longs to see "important changes take place, and not just on an intellectual plane—that you're a different person for having mixed it up somehow in this class."

Lou pushes for resolution, a strategy. She wonders if time is the key factor, if they might have students keep track of hours spent reading and writing. Ada says she plans to talk about time with her integrated class later in the morning, but she wants to communicate that she looks for other things, too—a willingness to take risks, intellectual eagerness, an ability to locate something of themselves in the lives of literary characters. Her class has been reading a book about an African village called *The Wrestling Match* (Emecheta, 1980), and Ada has been pleased to find kids "talking about the characters as if they're real people." She briefly describes the 14 reflective pieces she will ask her students to write, what sorts of analysis and synthesis she hopes to provoke, how hard it all is with such big classes, so many new students.

The hour is almost gone, and they crowd in bits of loosely linked news. Lou worries that she responded too harshly when a student remarked first hour today that Hindus are "really uncivilized." This somehow reminds Ada of an article in this morning's paper that she hopes to use in class, something about a housing development going up in an area of Native-American burial mounds, the sort of connection she hopes students will make between the multicultural emphasis of her class and local events. Meanwhile, the drama department is putting on a production of *Midsummer Night's Dream*, and Ada reminds Lou that they need to think about reading it in the integrated classes. Neither is particularly enthusiastic, agreeing that recent interracial productions of *A Raisin in the Sun* and *To Kill a Mockingbird* were more meaningful. The bells have been turned back on, marking the end of their time together as if by closing punctuation. Ada bids a warm farewell, and Lou turns to her rowdy third-hour Brit-lit class with renewed verve.

Later that morning, after a brief lunch with Lou, Ada teaches her midday section of the integrated course. There is little apparent link to Lou's class earlier in the day—here, Ada invites some kids to go off to the library to work on research projects, while others sit in small groups, making notes in their "reading reflection" logs about the first chapters of *The Wrestling Match*. Ada explains that writers have to be self-disciplined, and points with a grin toward me, scribbling through the hour in the back row. She plans to check each Monday to make sure everyone is doing the required 2 hours of weekly writing—"It's like playing a sport or staying on a diet," she says, "you have to be regular." Ada speaks in her gentle, steady voice for a full 20 minutes, but her students are awake, listening attentively. They might consider writing for an audience wider than the class, Ada explains, a letter to their mothers as a holiday gift, or "a special book to delight a child." In a few weeks, just before winter break, she has scheduled a "writers' festival" in which they'll share a favorite piece with the whole group. She speaks of their writing as a vital offering, a tonic: "Judy Blume says that she had lots of health problems until she started writing," Ada says, the creases around her eyes deepening with her smile, "so do your language arts assignment, and you won't have to take Vitamin C."

Ada turns to the first two chapters of *The Wrestling Match*, asking the students to help supply elements of the plot, checking to see if they recall the African names of the story's main characters. The chemistry here is quite different from Lou's sleepy early-morning class; Ada's noontime students are awake, clearly up to date with their reading, volunteering answers to her questions. After a few minutes Ada nudges them beyond factual recall, beginning the long steady work of encouraging connections to their own lives and communities. "Now how does it strike you," Ada asks of a conflict-resolution strategy employed in the book, "that the adults are going to mix things up so the *kids* have to solve the problem?" The invitation is friendly, the first question to which Ada does not have an answer, and she waits out a small silence. Then several students say that they think the adults in the book acted wisely, and complain that their own parents assume too much control, stepping in too readily to pressure or punish. As she said earlier to Lou, Ada is pleased when her students make these kinds of connections, wondering about characters in a book as if they were kids across street. All are African, Ada remarks, but it is important to realize that they come from different backgrounds. "Kinda like us," a student says before Ada has a chance, "*we're* all from different backgrounds." Ada nods enthusiastically, her arms outstretched in a gesture of inclusion. "Kinda like you," she repeats softly.

OBSTACLES

For Ada and Lou, authentic teaching is all about promoting conversation across apparent boundaries. They tend to assume blame where the boundaries win out, but there is much else that conspires to work against the ideals they embrace, obstacles that rest in the wider contexts of school and city. Even as they minimize the importance of tests and grades, for instance, Hamilton's principal offers continual reminders that such measures are to be regarded as important indeed. Jack Graham is on the PA in the days before an academic awards assembly, explaining where the award-winners and non-award-winners will sit ("we're very well-organized"), and encouraging the whole school to arrive promptly despite a forecast of heavy snow. On the morning that Hamilton's students are to take the Iowa Test of Educational Development, he appears on the TV monitors mounted in each classroom, urging students on as if before a big game: "When it comes to academic excellence, we are the district champion, the conference champion, and in many ways the *state* champion," he assures them. Just before winter break, he distributes a newsletter entitled "We're Proud of You!" that lists students with top grade-point averages, and offers his personal congratulations.

What Ada and Lou are trying to do pushes against powerful institutional norms, and they have much to talk about. But they also face a simple lack of time, many mornings when the need for photocopying or audiovisual scheduling preempts their planning-period chats. The clutter of their days does not allow time for closely coordinating curriculum; they teach the same things but not in tandem, and for weeks at a time their collaborative planning consists of little more than swapping lesson plans and offering brief greetings. In the absence of adequate time together, they welcome me as a potential collaborator, running through their perceptions and asking for mine ("How did it go? What do you think?").

When they do have time to talk, Ada and Lou celebrate successes only briefly, focusing for the most part on issues and frustrations. Sometimes these are concerns about how a particular class went—one day Ada's students "ended up with too many ideas, and not enough time to make the ideas their own," and a few mornings later Lou describes her exhaustion after an hour that went poorly. "It bothered me that it bothered me so much," she confesses; "Oh yes," Ada responds, "isn't that awful?" Each has stories that complement the other's, narratives that begin as empathy but soon move toward analysis and strategy-setting. Talk about curriculum comprises an essential part of these conversations, whether the focus is generating ways of getting a stalled class moving, or formulating a detailed grading policy emphasizing the ability to work cooperatively, to consider new ideas, and to think critically. Ada's students have been talking a great deal about their own families' rituals as they read the books she's assigned—*The Wrestling Match,* a novel about an Islamic girl called *Shabanu: Daughter of the Wind* (Fisher-Staples, 1989), and portions of *I, Rigoberto Menchu* (Menchu, 1984), a memoir of life in war-torn Guatemala. Her students bring up funny things, Ada tells Lou—people bringing food to funerals, the nervousness of mothers before weddings, quirky habits and customs. "Yeah," says Lou with a smile, recognizing names, "they're *neat* kids." Their students' stories somehow remind them of their own, and soon Ada and Lou are recounting childhood memories, finding their own connections across time and space.

Ada and Lou are teaching lots of international literature that they have not used before, and their students' responses are often as unpredictable as next week's lesson plans. Lou's kids complain of feeling "homesickness," and after consulting with Ada she decides to drop one of the books and spend a week doing *Rebel Without a Cause*. But most of all they wonder about particular students, like the mildly learning disabled boy who approached Lou one morning: "But Mrs. Russell," he said in a quavering voice, "you're expecting too much of me—I'm only a *skills* student." Ada thinks a lot about Tina, an African-American girl who lives in government-subsidized housing and hears gunshots in the night, who is personally acquainted with key players in a series of much-publicized crime incidents this winter. Ada is well aware that she asks something special of Tina when she encourages students to consider their own lives and locales in light of the novels and stories. Tina is gradually coming to trust Ada's sensitive eye, her availability for brief after-class chats, her careful listening. She writes a dryly humorous piece about her neighborhood ("You don't sit *outside* in the *projects*") and Ada writes back with gentle enthusiasm, whole paragraphs of Tina's prose etched in her memory.

But on a deeply cold day in January, I realize the dangers that surround Tina even in this environment, how fragile the safety Ada has created is. Students have been writing guidebook pieces about their city, imagining that a new student has arrived from another country who is eager to learn about local customs. Ada has accompanied her husband on a day-long series of medical checkups on a scheduled read-aloud day, leaving a nervous substitute and a brand new student teacher in charge. She has fostered habits of sensitive response, and even in her absence students listen attentively and clap politely. But it feels somehow more rushed, more playacted than when Ada is present, and when a boy begins reading a piece that makes Tina turn away, no one appears to notice or care.

He is a European-American kid who writes about how good his family is, how much his parents love him, how involved they are in his life, his voice sure and confident as he reads aloud. They have taught him "how to be well behaved," and "to work hard." He's lucky, he explains, for in this city is a "small section" with "horrifying violence," something he blames on a lack of "family values" among the people who live there. I watch Tina grimace, then cover her face with open hands. A few minutes later it is Tina's turn, and she looks up just long enough to ask the student teacher to read her piece for her. Tina's essay is about her enduring enthusiasm for Michael Jackson's music, especially her favorite song, "Black and White." As for allegations against him, she writes, "I think people forget there are two sides to every story." The sub offers vague praise, but Tina's face remains hidden.

During Monday morning's planning session I tell Ada and Lou of the boy's essay and Tina's response. "Oh, damn," Lou says, erupting briefly in anger. Ada says she saw an earlier version of the piece and encouraged the boy to tone it down: "You're talking about kids in our class," she remembers saying. "How do you think they're going to feel? Can you understand how this is going to come across? How is this going to feel to those other kids who live there, whose parents care too?" What Ada realizes now is that he deleted the names of particular places, but kept his original message basically intact. Ada explains that the boy lives in the transitional area between Hamilton's more affluent and impoverished neighborhoods, that perhaps his family eyes the rash of violence but a few blocks away with gathering fear. His mother recently called Ada to express concerns about the integrated class; her son had been designated middle-level previously, and she wondered if he were in the wrong class this time, "getting in with the wild kids." Today Ada seems disappointed that the others failed to be a bit *more* aggressive; "How did they let him get away with this?" she wonders. "Didn't anybody *say* anything?"

KEYED TO SOCIAL CLASS

Hamilton's great divide lives tenaciously on, supported by values that embrace habits of sorting and separation. Sometimes the chasm is evidenced in quiet, almost surreptitious ways, as in Ada and Lou's growing realization that virtually all students designated "upper level" have home computers, a few even bringing laptops to class, while perhaps half of the kids in their integrated classes still write the old-fashioned way. Hamilton is a school with abundant resources, but it is computer-poor, further severing options for kids unable to afford their own. Hamilton's lab has a collection of old IBMs, and kids go there only to convert first drafts to a more presentable form, using the machines like typewriters. Still, says Ada, "They feel like *real* writers when they're on the computers."

Ada's and Lou's classes tend to be meeting places for kids from different sectors, and while there are many moments of shared understanding, now and then a discussion flares into charged confrontation. Copies of the school's newspaper are distributed to Lou's students one cold grey morning, and moments later tempers unexpectedly erupt. A European-

American boy notices an article about minority-student mentoring, and suddenly angers flare: "Minorities get *everything*," he remarks. "Well, go create it for yourself, then," responds an African-American classmate. "Your people are *so stupid*," comes the response, and Lou is soon quieting raised voices, telling the one boy that there are limits to what she will tolerate, and acknowledging the other's patient forbearance.

It is a winter of insistent cold, of weeks when the temperature fails to climb above zero, and both Ada and Lou wonder how to make their classrooms places of warm engagement. They work to stimulate respectful but spirited discussion of tensions around town, often using newspaper articles as starting points. In February a series of articles on violence and youth appears that culminates in a town meeting, and Ada asks her students what they think about the issue. "There was a real spectrum of response," she explains, "all keyed to social class." The affluent kids in her upper-level section passed it off as having nothing to do with them, but "the integrated class felt that they were right in the middle of it." A few even admitted that they carry weapons, one boy half-joking that a future as a gun-toting Marine seemed to be among his few options.

When several of Lou's former students are arrested during four days of violence in the city's African-American community, she begins collecting articles about plans for a neighborhood park. In a piece she copies for class, kids and adult organizers contend that there would be less violence if the neighborhood's youth had something to do. "The city has 42 softball and baseball diamonds, and we can't find a place to play buckets," one "young basketballer" is quoted as saying. "Our neighborhood needs a place to play. We can't even find a place in the neighborhood to play hoops. This city couldn't care less about us. If it did care, it would put up a couple of baskets." Building the park would involve tearing down a storefront formerly occupied by Sam's Hangout, "seen by some as a vibrant neighborhood watering hole, but by others as a flashpoint for neighborhood violence." These days the building is occupied by "The House of Prayer," a combination soup kitchen and church run by a white man, the Reverend Cutter, a "70-year-old brimstone-hurling, harmonica-playing preacher, directed by God to open a church for street people and the homeless" (quoted in a local newspaper). Organizers want to buy his property and help him find another place, but he refuses. "If you build a park up there," he argues, "all you're doing is making another place for the gangs to hang out, another place for drug dealers to use, another place for kids to tear up, another expense to the taxpayers. I say one church will do more good than 19 parks."

Some of Lou's kids agree with the white preacher, others with the basketballers, but this time the debate stays friendly and even her 8:00 class wakes up. Lou knows that there is more to all this than the presence or absence of the new park, that hopelessness pervades the neighborhood, that kids are facing futures of narrowed possibility. She remembers vividly a conversation with a bright young African-American student a few years earlier: "My people wouldn't sell drugs if there were jobs for us," he said. Now, as Ada and Lou invite their classes to explore tensions on the northwest side, he sits in jail, accused in one of the recent shootings.

Perhaps to many, it seems simpler to keep the traditional divisions in place. Ada and Lou often say that upper-level kids tend to be cautious and conservative, resting complacent once they feel they have "cracked the meaning" of a poem or story. By comparison, they quickly add, the kids in their skills and integrated classes are much more willing to take risks. They may be occasionally sleepy or insensitive, but Ada and Lou see them as having less to lose and more to give. But theirs is a tale that seldom is told, at least not publicly, for the same spirit of cautious conservatism that drives Hamilton's upper-level classes also drives a school image built on measurable excellence and tangible acclaim. The other Hamilton remains enveloped in silence, physically removed, assigned a different track, a reduced set of options. As for the integrated class, notes Ada, "Nobody seems to be paying much attention." "No one visits, no one asks," Lou observes. But quietly, word is spreading among parents, and now and then Ada and Lou get calls from people wondering how to get their kids into one of next year's nonleveled classes. "I hope there'll be enough for at least two sections again," says Ada, "but you never know." "You never know," Lou repeats.

DEPARTMENTAL

Hamilton's district has mandated a shift to multicultural literature at the 10th-grade level, and Ada and Lou are meeting with colleagues this winter to select books to purchase with their $10,000 budget. The meetings take place in Lou's room; they are scheduled for the lunch period because so many faculty have other commitments before or after school, and by the time everyone gathers up snacks and walks to the industrial arts wing, little more than half an hour remains. But these meetings seem much longer, full of hidden depths and treacherous cross-currents. "Sometimes you have to scale back personal power," Lou remarks just before one of the meetings, "but with this group, I need everything I have."

Lou serves on the district's 10th-grade curriculum committee, and she is a source of order forms, deadlines, and copies of possible texts. At these noon meetings she passes around stacks of written materials—lists of books,

extended summaries, endorsements from students who've read particular texts. No one openly disagrees with what's on the handouts, but no one
studies them, either. Lou tends to lead the discussion while the others voice
complaints—this book has too much profanity, that one is inappropriate
for top-level kids, all of them seem somehow less appealing than a big
glossy anthology. "I'm curious to know *what* you didn't like," Lou often
asks, but the negativity remains vague. On a rare occasion when they seem
close to consensus, the vote is delayed at the last minute: "Scott hasn't read
it yet," the chair points out, gesturing toward a colleague. "I wouldn't *mind*
reading it," Scott remarks unenthusiastically. Unflaggingly upbeat in public, the department chair privately acknowledges her frustration: "I'm not
thrilled with the meetings," she says. "I've tried to organize it so everyone
has an assignment for our next meeting, so we have something to discuss.
And the assignments aren't being done."

One of the books Ada and Lou like is a novel about a Southeast-Asian
girl coming of age called *Rice Without Rain* (Ho, 1989). A colleague seconds
the department chair's concern that too many of Ada and Lou's selections
focus on women: "Again, it's a woman's point of view," she complains,
going on to note the "graphic birthing scene" toward the end of the book.
"Oh, I don't remember that," Ada replies mildly. Lou chuckles, remarking that the curriculum has long featured dead white guys and no one
seemed to mind *that*. The colleague backs off a bit, adding that she basically liked the book, but then "there's the part where she's having the ille-
gitimate baby." "I didn't notice that," Ada repeats.

These are colleagues who compete for top-level courses, and they function from a logic so different from Ada and Lou's that it is hard to imagine
them as members of the same department. Lou leaves her classroom door
unlocked as colleagues straggle in for a book-buying meeting, and she has
to tell kids that this is not a good time to visit. "I guess they just feel like
they belong here," she explains to the adults gathered in the room; "they
don't have much humility." Humility is hardly a prime virtue in Lou's eyes,
but one of her colleagues misses the glint of humor: "That's something they
could *all* use a little more of," he remarks drily. And Ada and Lou's colleagues sort literature into the same skills, middle, and upper categories
they use to define students. "Oh yeah," Lou says to Ada in a private moment, "I'm sure William Stafford sat down and said, 'I think I'll write an
average-level poem today.'" But neither speaks ill of particular people, and
both applaud their colleagues' good intentions, reminding me again and
again that some of the most traditional are also masters of their craft. Still,
Ada and Lou frankly acknowledge their difference, admitting their affection for this remote corner of the school, far from the central corridor where
the bulk of the department lives its parallel life.

ANOTHER WORLD

One dank February morning Ada takes me on a tour of the English department wing. "It's much quieter up here, isn't it?" she whispers. She has a theory that kids "loosen up" when they come out to "Russell and Finch," that theirs is a "hang-loose kind of place." This corridor feels prestigious, a way-station on the path to upper-crust universities. The English department office is halfway down the hall, a small, neatly kept room with green carpet, a new Macintosh computer, a printer, a fancy phone with lots of complicated buttons, a refrigerator, and a coffeemaker. Class sets of various texts rest on floor-to-ceiling faux walnut shelves: *A Separate Peace* (Knowles, 1960), *Lord of the Flies* (Golding, 1962), *Cry the Beloved Country* (Paton, 1948), a scattering of Shakespeare in paperback and a dusty replica of the Globe theater. A small round table is a congregating place for faculty, and the department chair keeps it stocked with a small basket of seasonal candy, currently valentine chocolates wrapped in pink foil. Here Ada and Lou's colleagues unwind and catch up on news, enjoying their own interval of adult company.

Jean Ford is a regular here, a stubbornly cheerful woman who keeps the candy basket full and greets visitors with bubbly warmth. She invites me to pull up a chair as she and the self-described "lunch bunch" continue their conversation. The circle opens to make room, but Jean's eyes are on the colleagues seated around the table, her focus on encouraging the conversational flow. A former student had a close call during a recent hospitalization, and those who know the story share it with the others. They recount memories of this student, what he was like, what his brother was like: "Their IQs were just on opposite ends of the chart," says one, and the others laugh knowingly. This is the same group that I see here again and again, five or six regulars who comprise the department's visible core.

Outside the principal's office is a framed newspaper article about Jean, the accompanying photos catching her classroom grimaces and gestures. Her work as chair demands a wide performative repertoire, but she most often seems to be playing the conciliatory hostess to a vexed dinner party. "I have an incredibly volatile staff," she admits privately; "at any given moment, it could blow." She praises and accommodates, writing teachers notes saying how good it is to have them as colleagues, making sure everyone is fully stocked with needed supplies, smoothing the rough surface of past debacles—meetings she describes as "horrendous," "explosive," "big blowups." "We still have some real problems, in the sense that a lot of them want to teach top-level students," she explains. The principal has assumed responsibility for assigning class schedules, but teachers sometimes lobby Jean to argue their cases. "It causes hard feelings," she admits.

Then Jean turns to the Ada and Lou situation. "I just really don't like it that they're over there," she admits, gesturing toward the industrial arts wing. Jean says she tried to talk Lou into moving when main-corridor space came available two summers ago. "We felt that would provide more of this collegiality," she says, still troubled by Lou's refusal. Lou wondered if her bad back could withstand the rigors of moving, and she worried, too, about exacerbating the lack of student integration out in the industrial arts wing. "It's really no one's fault," Jean adds; "I'm not blaming anyone." Of more immediate concern is Lou's role in setting off occasional fireworks, as when she remarks impishly about the dead white males that crowd the department's curriculum. Some of the white men on the staff have been "*very* offended, *very* hurt," Jean confides. "If she only knew the effects she has."

"There is not a lot of collaboration of the type that Ada and Lou enjoy," Hamilton's multicultural coordinator acknowledges, hastily pointing out that "there are not very many people on our staff who *teach* the way that Ada and Lou *teach*." For both, challenging the canon is of a piece with the conviction that education should be concerned with more than imparting information and preserving an academic aristocracy. Their beliefs and work present a touchy set of issues for their colleagues, and even Ada's tactful diplomacy does little to change that. One man speaks of curriculum as a swinging pendulum sensitive to the whims of passing fashion, and cautions that "we often are forsaking something good for something new . . . so often the new ideas are taken to such an extreme that we make them *bad* ideas, and the pendulum is either far to the right or far to the left, and rarely is it in its central location." Multicultural literature is fine, he says, but he worries that the works Ada and Lou are introducing are not only off-center, but also downbeat. "What I would like to see in that sophomore class," he explains,

> is to *celebrate* the diversity rather than focus on the oppression. I don't want to deny that it exists or existed, but I think education is doing kids a great disservice if they're not focusing on people who overcome rather than people who succumb. One of the more inspirational books we've just finished [in my class] is Zora Neale Hurston's (1978) *Their Eyes Were Watching God*, which is this celebration of what it is to be a woman who, yes, experienced oppression but did not allow herself to be suppressed in the process.

Meanwhile, another colleague worries that if students spend too much time reading multicultural literature, they will miss the mainstream tradition:

I think it is important to be global, multicultural, all of those things, taking into account the ethnicity of other people. It's very important in this building because of the diverse population we serve. The problem that I have with it is that we seem to exclude all forms of American literature . . . I think a truly global view takes in your own culture as well as other cultures, all our ethnicities. If you buy into the American dream, that we're all part of a large melting pot, then yes we have to be cognizant that we have our own American heritage and culture, too, and that needs to be preserved. I think there's a danger in ignoring that entirely.

She wishes Ada and Lou would take up multicultural literature in an "elective class," where it would not displace canonical texts and leave college-bound students at a "distinct disadvantage." A focus on global concerns is worthwhile, she emphasizes: "I'm certainly not one that would promote an isolationist view." Ada and Lou are the real isolationists, she argues: "We've got an isolationist backlash here. That would be the way I would characterize it, as a flip-side of the argument."

Many of Ada and Lou's colleagues see them as removed both physically and philosophically—as "autonomous," "in another world." "They're in their own little heaven up there," notes one, gesturing uncertainly; "wherever—up there on the second floor of that far-off wing." "I think that there is a sense that we have two departments here," says another, "and I think that sense comes primarily from them":

It just seems that they have adopted the idea that what they are doing is absolutely right. And I don't question that at all. I certainly feel that a lot of what I do is absolutely right. But there seems to be a divisiveness in terms of an alienation. We have a physical alienation in the fact that they're so far removed from the rest of the department, but it's almost by choice. . . . Because of that distance factor, there's a perception that we do language arts one way over here, and they do it the right way over there. And we keep hearing that.

Some of the department's traditionalists seem to regard Ada and Lou as vaguely threatening, as if trying something new amounts to an implicit criticism of the old ways. "There is so much that is gratuitous and self-righteous in their approach," says one; "they're just not open-minded enough to see that there's great stuff happening in *every* classroom." Two months later, there is frequent mention of the fact that Ada and Lou were no-shows at the yearly December party: "We had a really congenial Christmas party, so we can get along that way. Neither of *those* two came," complains one. And another: "You make time if you want to—and if you don't care, you know, some people are in their own little worlds." In this department variously described as "ferocious," "notorious for not getting along," and "a real maverick group," some see Ada and Lou as occupying a far territory.

The walk to the English corridor is long, and days here are full. Ada and Lou stick to themselves, savoring their too-brief times together. But their absence is read as separatism, and misunderstandings run freely. Sometimes colleagues preface remarks with "I don't know this directly but I've heard it from another person . . . ," the repetition of information lending an air of authority. Several are convinced that Ada and Lou are pushing to incorporate a required speech component into the integrated classes, and those certified in speech—one is certified *only* in speech—talk at impassioned length about the wrong-headedness of the supposed plan. But there is no such plan; Ada and Lou's integrated classes will dissolve at the end of February, moving into a final trimester of speech with another teacher.

"What's your perception of the integrated class?" I ask one of Ada and Lou's colleagues. "I don't see them enough to have much evidence that the integrated class is *hurting* kids," comes the uncertain reply. Those who begin with the assumption that the class may somehow cause harm need contact with Ada and Lou, and lots of it, before their minds will be changed. But Ada and Lou are far away, conserving time and energy, already stretched thin by the many challenges of their experiment. Several of Ada and Lou's colleagues dismiss the effort as mere packaging, insisting that the "integrated" kids are really "average and below-average students." "There are a number of parents who have kids in top-level classes who are listened to a great deal here at school," one teacher reminds me, "and to do away with top-level classes, I think, would produce anarchy here. I really do . . . that's something that our principal is very sensitive to."

I am often told that other members of the department are collaborating too—humanities teachers who exchange lesson plans, others involved in a district effort to enhance connections between language arts and social studies curricula. By most accounts, such efforts seldom delve very deeply. The woman who gave Lou the tractor pin served briefly as English department chair; she had just come to Hamilton from the city's alternative school, and she was determined to promote greater collegiality in this mainstream environment. "I thought we were getting to a point where we really were going to do more collaboration," she remembers sadly.

I thought there was going to be a bigger change than there really was—it sounds like the 60s all over again, doesn't it?—"I thought things would be different." And then it became clear to me that it was not going to be an actuality, it was just going to be talked about. Nothing big was going to change.

What would have to happen to promote collaboration among Hamilton's English faculty? Jack Graham holds no lofty hopes: "I would say that it would depend on me having the power to administratively transfer about a dozen people," he says. The department has only 15 members. Rarely is Jack so candidly discouraged:

> That's about what it would take. The department was pretty much that way when I came here 13 years ago, and if anything it's gotten worse. Although they're not for the most part hostile to each other. There's just a wide difference of opinion on how the English language should be taught, and a lot of very judgmental people. And it's, I would think in some ways the least collaborative department in the school as a total department. But on the other hand, there are pockets of the greatest level of collaboration, like probably Ada and Lou would represent.

Hamilton's English department is divided, its faculty holding rock-bottom beliefs that remain irreconcilable. The schism has origins both deep and wide, bringing to mind clashes between Deweyan progressives and Arnoldian classicists earlier in the century, and more recent debates concerning cultural literacy, multiculturalism, and the boundaries of the literary canon (Applebee, 1974; Gates, 1992; Hirsch, 1987; Levine, 1996). But there is little time or opportunity for Hamilton's English faculty to address any of this, only to notice the conflicting pedagogies these differences promote, and to regret the personal clashes that render their divide even more intractable. No wonder several of Ada and Lou's colleagues have made a conscious choice to work primarily alone; no wonder Ada and Lou avoid the upstairs office, seeking out one another and a small cadre of others. "I think it would be nice if people would talk about those differences," says Lou, "but I think we would still be very different." She laughingly recounts her colleagues' referring to the two of them as "'free spirits.' And that's not a good thing." "Oh yeah," Ada adds with a smile, "'loosy-goosey.'"

The reforms they envision are complex, requiring broadly based support, but as Ada and Lou look beyond their classrooms they encounter added challenges and formidable roadblocks. They remain an island of innovation, undertaking a big project without much help. But when I ask if they feel strongly about continuing the integrated classes, they utter a firm and united yes. "I don't think there are a lot of people in our department that really care," admits Lou; "but I think it's important that Ada and I can say that we tried it, and can say that it worked." They look to one another for emotional as well as pedagogic support, underscoring their successes even as they acknowledge frustrations. "I think Ada has made a whole lot of difference," says Lou with an affectionate smile. "It makes it more fun and free, and you can feel that you can be yourself," adds Ada; "it rubs off." "It's a joy," agrees Lou, "you know you're not crazy." "That's right!" says Ada. "You've *got* to know that you're not crazy. And you have to know that you *are* crazy, and that's part of knowing that you are not. It's been fun. You can't feel lonesome with Lou around."

IT HASN'T BEEN BAD

March arrives, a betwixt-and-between month of muddy slush, and Ada and Lou meet to survey the winter's work. For Lou, there's the lingering frustration of only half-knowing how to teach the new 10th-grade curriculum, of days when her students seemed tuned-out or at odds, when conflict hummed just below the surface, "subtle and underneath a lot of things." She says Ada picked her up on the "one or two" occasions when she felt discouraged, but she regrets that they hadn't more time together, that "most of our collaboration has been [while] running down the hall, grabbing a sandwich." Ada looks on the brighter side: "But it hasn't been bad," she says cheerfully; "in fact, what we've said has been really important. . . . There is a difference in that you look at things as the possibilities, and as a sort of critical 'this is our lot and we have to deal with it.'"

They talk of ways that the integrated classes made their jobs both more difficult and more interesting. "I mean the classroom can't look quite as neat or managed," admits Ada; "it's harder, but I think it is worth the risk." Both recall moments that felt touchy or charged, times when "dangerous" topics came up, where racism or classism found a voice and demanded a response. Lou observes that their classrooms are places where all kids can share something of "what their lives are, what their neighborhoods are like," and sometimes that makes for real-world tensions. Perhaps, adds Ada, the kids who stand to learn the most from the conversation are those traditionally marked for the upper ranks:

> An upper-level kid, who thinks he's *such* an upper-level kid,
> realizes that the experience and the knowledge that other kid is

bringing into the classroom is valuable to teach him a whole lot of things that he doesn't know. Once you get that done, you realize that it really doesn't matter that that kid has been to Europe and read all these books, but that *this* kid just came from Chicago, and he knows stuff that that kid doesn't know. Everyone is just as valuable as everyone else in the room.

Ada and Lou recall students they have shared over a year or more, kids who have moved toward mutual openness and trust. If only they could have this extended time with all their kids; if only more parents would come up at church or parties to express an interest in the nonleveled approach. "There aren't too many," Lou allows, "but I'm hearing more of it—though I think there are a few people who are looking at it and saying, 'this is kind of aberrant.'" Pro-tracking parents worry about keeping their sons and daughters away from "dangerous kids," Lou adds. "You have to understand that this is a public school," she answers them, "and *everybody* comes here." "Parents always like to go back to what they knew in school," Ada observes, "and things are not the same. Lou and I share the same feeling when we say, 'It's your loss if you choose to put your son or daughter someplace else, because we will make sure something great happens to your kids.'"

Ada's and Lou's students are meanwhile glad for the integrated option. "It was like a bunch of different people learning in the classroom," one observes, "not just a whole bunch of *smart* people." "I'm not stupid, but I'm not smart enough to be in an advanced class," says a boy formerly tracked as "average"; "right here, you can learn a lot better." A number of students feel that the presence of more-abled peers motivated them to do their best work: "You probably learn more," says one girl, "because you have everybody in there, not just all the same old people, but people of all different levels." According to a classmate, the effect is particularly noticeable when they work in small groups: "If there are people that aren't doing well, and then there are people that are, if they had them in their group it might encourage them to do better. All in the same level, I don't think it encourages anyone to do any better."

But the kids know that what was good about the classes had a lot to do with their teachers. "Mrs. Russell is a really good teacher," says a boy who has had both Ada and Lou. "She's there for the students, the same way as Mrs. Finch. They want you to do good in the class. There are some teachers here that don't care." Several describe them as "a lot nicer and more understanding" than other teachers they know, as people who "really listen to you and will help you," who "would both be there to help" as problems arise, who'll "tell you you're doing a good job." Ada's class describes her willingness to "get close to her students," to help them "relate stuff we were reading to our own lives," to be "real patient" and "easy to talk to." Ada's and Lou's students watch them go to lunch together, but only a few are aware of their professional collaboration: "I think that it helps all their students," says one of these. "If they both have input in their classes and the ideas, it'll help make both classes better."

FRONT STAGE/BACKSTAGE

If we know so much about how bad tracking is, why do we keep doing it? Why do so many teachers and administrators continue to argue its merits? Why do a vocal majority of Hamilton's English teachers ignore their own professional organization's opposition to tracking (National Council of Teachers of English [NCTE], 1991; see also Lloyd-Jones & Lunsford, 1989)? Oakes (1985) argues that successful untracking requires that we confront a host of wider issues, including Bowles and Gintis's (1976) assertion that schools are organized to reproduce the inequities of the wider society. Beyond this, we have relatively few models of successful experiments in untracking, few voices charting the tangled connection between such reform efforts and the institutional and political situations in which they are enacted (Oakes, 1992; see also Freedman, 1994b, and Cone, 1992). Doing away with tracking requires leadership (Oakes & Lipton, 1992), support across diverse constituencies, and rethinking other features of schooling as well—things like fragmented curricula, norm-referenced assessments, and competitive ways of being for students and teachers alike (Oakes, 1992). It is a tall order, and Hamilton might well wonder if the effort could ever be worth it, especially given a present system that seems by most public measures to be working so well.

Ada and Lou's experience might be read as thoroughly positive, an instance where teachers were given the necessary freedom to try something new. Put teachers in charge, we often hear, give them control over their own collaborative ventures and all will be well—but to sum up Ada and Lou's story in these terms is to ignore the departmental factionalism that presented powerful resistance to change (Datnow, 1997). Mutual support can empower teachers to attempt needed reforms, but collective energies can also be directed toward preserving ill-advised habits such as tracking (Finley, 1984; Oakes, 1985; Oakes, Gamoran, & Page, 1992). Ada and Lou's collaboration served to open up new possibilities, to question traditional ways of doing business, to confront snags and failures. It was a model of what they wanted for kids, informed by a belief that schools should reflect the challenges of an increasingly diverse world, their interest in joint work part and parcel of their taste for diversity. Meanwhile, Ada and Lou's more traditional colleagues remind us that togetherness can also be a way to quiet questions and preserve familiar hierarchies.

Pressed for time, fighting off a succession of viruses, struggling to figure out a new curriculum and a new sort of classroom, Ada and Lou have nonetheless managed to give Hamilton's tracking tradition a bold nudge. In the months and years ahead they will once again lobby for the integrated option, informing, reminding, and teaching a couple sections every trimester. They are kindly people, not the sort to set off needless waves, but they continue to believe that students are better served this way. Others might hold them in disdain, but they go about their business with steadiness of purpose and generosity of spirit, careful with what they say, careful always with people. "Professionalism" is a word one might associate with their way of doing business, but it's also more than this. Ada and Lou have a stubbornly inclusive turn of spirit, and their affection for their crankiest colleagues remains quite genuine. These are ordinary people whose lives and work approach the extraordinary, people with big psyches as well as big ideas. What they are trying to do is hard on multiple levels, but they keep trying, and they somehow keep doing it.

Sometimes Ada and Lou's notions make others uneasy. These days lots of people are longing to know where the center might be, the place where the cultural pendulum can rest awhile. Some of Ada and Lou's colleagues claim to know, arguing the need for a centrist literary canon that honors our country's melting-pot past. Such arguments hold considerable appeal, perhaps especially for those who treasure the tradition of old wealth and established pride that is the public Hamilton. An antitracking coalition is not out of the question, but it would be a risky venture for teachers and parents alike, inviting hostilities and jeopardizing the progress already quietly made. There are no organized protests over in the other Hamilton, and so the tradition continues.

A member of a team that evaluated the school several years ago describes the school as "a machine-like corporate structure just running on its own rhythms," the "stage always set, the lights down," the school a gigantic front stage built by a powerful director. It is a first impression many might have of this place, but Ada and Lou are unconvinced. They know Hamilton's backstage well, and they know what lurks up front, too—well enough to know that this place was built by people and influences that reach beyond Jack Graham, even beyond these walls and times. Sole credit or blame is often assigned to school leaders, and it is tempting to regard Jack, the focus of so much public acclaim, as a private villain here. But Hamilton's principal readily acknowledges the limits of his power, the collective strength of tradition-minded teachers and community members.

The structure resists, stolid and impermeable through the seasons and years. Rather than proud owner, Jack is perhaps just another player who understands the construction's sturdiness, another observer who wonders when the time will be ripe for a few renovations.

Ada and Lou know the odds and still dare to scheme, spurred on by each other and their abiding affection for students. I leave them as they continue their behind-the-scenes hammering, still doggedly determined, still playing to small audiences, still hoping that more will heed their distant racket with time. They need helping hands, and maybe one day they can find them—people who find excellence in equity, who stand ready to turn up the lights on a new Hamilton, a place that, like Ada and Lou's classrooms atop the auto shop, is well worth the risk and mess.

Chapter 4

Together on the *Titanic*:
The Dynamos

Moving up through this mighty ship on newly carpeted stairs, I'd become aware of the special smell of the Titanic, different from the Mauritania, both saying that we were at sea, but pervading the air of the Titanic the unique smell of—I recognized it now—newness.

(Finney, 1995, p. 287)

March continues its halting ascent into spring, cycling between snow flurries and warming sunlight. I drive past neatly plowed farmlands, silos bearing the remnants of last year's corn, the occasional resident tending livestock. Up ahead an urban center sprawls around one of the nation's great rivers, and suddenly the landscape is cluttered with car dealers, midpriced motels, fastfood colonies, arrows pointing the way to the several towns clustered here. Just off the interstate are the new developments encircling Anspach, an affluent European-American city nestled beside an older, more diverse, more ostensibly troubled neighbor. The freshly constructed houses are mammoth, pastel clapboard and brick facades rising abruptly from the flat brown earth. Further into town the construction looks only slightly more rooted, the older trees perhaps two decades old, vaguely colonial or faux Tudor architecture suggesting a taste for tradition. Most residents earn their daily bread in neighboring cities, places of grandfatherly oaks, nineteenth-century homes, and less enviable crime rates. Anspach is a bedroom community, a centerless upstart with an aura of safe prosperity.

People all over the state are talking about Anspach's middle school—a place, I hear again and again, to see teacher collaboration "really working." Two years ago a new principal was brought on board to reorganize the school into interdisciplinary "houses," assigning teams of teachers to subsets of the school's burgeoning student population. The idea is gaining currency across the country, as research continues to report the negative consequences of the seventh-grade shift from self-contained classrooms (Eccles et al., 1993), and the need to provide developmentally appropriate support to students negotiating the rocky years of early adolescence (Eccles et al., 1991; Eccles & Midgley, 1988; Egan, 1992; Eichorn, 1966; George & Oldaker, 1986; Lipsitz, 1984). In the words of one influential task force, middle schools "are potentially society's most powerful force to recapture millions of youth adrift, and help every young person thrive during early adolescence," yet schools too often "exacerbate the problems," presenting a "volatile mismatch" between "organization and curriculum" and "the intellectual and emotional needs of young adolescents" (Carnegie Council on Adolescent Development, 1989, pp. 8–9). Reformers increasingly see schools for early adolescents as too big and impersonal, too preoccupied with maintaining control, as failing to provide the sorts of intellectually substantive and individually appropriate support these young people need.

Hence the growing popularity of schools within schools like the kind recently instituted at Anspach. Over the past year and a half, teachers have been meeting in house teams one instructional period every other day, talking about the students they share, developing curricula, and planning activities. Eager to maintain a reputation for cutting-edge excellence, district leaders hired a new principal 3 years ago, charging her with managing the shift to houses. While the reorganization is still new, it has already garnered a prestigious state commendation. In a few weeks the governor will stop by to present the award, and district officials plan a lavish public ceremony, proudly displaying this further evidence that Anspach's district is among the best in the state, a further reason for well-heeled families to flock here.

WHERE PRIORITIES COMPETE

Anspach Middle School is a single-story building faced with pale brick, a small stone monument to the "men and women of Operation Desert Storm" set beside its flag pole. Just inside the school's front door is a small lobby, a teachers' lounge to the left, a tiny school office to the right, and glossy color everywhere—yellow and orange cinderblock walls, long banks of pale blue lockers. An engraved plaque lists top scorers on the Iowa Test of Basic Skills, displays proudly detail the school's business partnerships, and a huge banner commemorates the recent state award. Under the motto "Where Children Are the Priority," a framed poster proclaims the district's mission statement: "To provide a quality learning environment which promotes teacher/student/parent relationships that offer each student the opportunity to acquire the skills, attitudes, and knowledge to be a responsible citizen and life-long learner." The school is a well-kept but unglamorous place, its distinctive smell vaguely nostalgic, described by one teacher as an unmistakable mixture of "floor wax and bubblegum." Beside the front doors someone has taped a hand-lettered sign, a low-cost effort at official cheer: "Have a Nice Day."

Despite its glowing reputation, Anspach Middle School is increasingly overcrowded and underfunded, and if children are a priority here, so too is reaching them with economical efficiency. Anspach is an expensive place to live, and voters are reluctant to offer still more money to schools, recently voting down a series of bond measures that would have provided funds to improve and enlarge cramped facilities. Teachers on the team I will follow here—the "Dynamos"—see 182 kids every day, a number that climbs perilously close to 200 if they count their early-morning homerooms as extra. There is no time for sustained conversation with students, nor have they sufficient chairs, room, or fresh air. Big loops of plastic hang from the ceilings like oversized hammocks, intended to remind visitors that the roof leaks, that an upcoming bond measure deserves their support. Teachers worry about the safety of passing periods, when a human tidal wave rushes down the corridors. I join the moving crowd and staff cry out that I'm taking my life in my hands—but later they confess that their concern is real, that they wonder at the danger of all those lively bodies, don't know if they could get everyone out in a real emergency.

The Dynamos are at the far edge of the school in a structure known as the "pod"—all except for the team's leader, a science teacher who spends his days in the aging lab facilities on the other side. The building is all odd angles and strange add-ons, but finally I reach a juncture where the main corridor connects to the hexagon-shaped pod, a paper banner proclaiming this the home of the Dynamos. The language arts department was previously located out here, and relics of former times rest in a display case, including a National Council of Teachers of English Center of Excellence award. One of the recipients was Steve Rush, a veteran teacher in his mid-forties now assigned to the Dynamo team. A few years ago Steve and two colleagues reinvented their language arts classrooms, setting up work stations in a large multipurpose room, its grooved ceiling accommodating vinyl dividers that teachers could close or open at will. The space was dismantled along with academic departments, plastic panels assembled over the old ceiling and permanent walls inserted—the new principal wanted the area configured this way, a teacher tells me, and this was the least expensive way to do it.

The Dynamos' windowless classrooms have likewise been reimagined several times over. The pod was built two decades ago as an open-architecture environment, an expansive space where teachers' workdays were visibly and noisily shared. Colorful prefab walls were added a few years later, creating separate language arts, social studies, reading, and math classrooms, seriously taxing the ventilation system even before overcrowding reached crisis proportions. Access is an even bigger concern: The social studies and language arts classrooms have doors that open onto a hallway, but to reach reading and math students press into the far reaches of the revised structure, passing through one or more crowded classrooms on the way. Other courses require special facilities, and kids hustle to remote segments of the school for science, music, art, and physical education. Nor is there a bank of lockers adjacent to the pod, where the Dynamo team keeps a watchful eye on students' comings and goings. "This school just wasn't built for houses," the teachers often say. Anspach's architecture stands as a monument to cycles of change, its new walls like tree rings grown up around an earlier center—but there is no organic cohesion to this layering, just the haste of reformers in a hurry and on a budget.

THE DYNAMOS

The glass panel next to Steve's classroom door still bears last December's stenciled snowflakes and holiday greetings. As his last class scrambles out, I find him busy preparing materials for today's team meeting, level and deliberate despite a scant 4 hours sleep last night. His sandy brown hair is thinning and he jokes about middle-age spread, but he functions with perpetual efficiency, juggling professional demands with steady care. Once a long-distance runner, Steve began his career as a track coach, and he still carries an air of disciplined energy, his language arts classroom meticulously organized, his monthly calender crammed with far-flung responsibilities—serving on national task forces, organizing the state language arts conference, working as a union representative, and stepping into a host of leadership roles at the school. He will be the Dynamo's official leader next year, but Steve is already a key presence in these meetings, often ready, as today, with handouts and agenda items.

I am greeted as well by Emily, a student teacher who joined Steve just over 2 weeks ago. She was originally placed in an inner-city school in a neighboring district, but eventually made a hard decision to transfer out. The main trouble was a philosophic clash with her tradition-minded co-operating teacher, but the preponderance of gangs and violence made the challenge seem insurmountable. A university supervisor who knew Steve thought that he might be the kind of mentor who could resurrect Emily's wounded self-confidence; his principal was miffed, Steve tells me on the sly, but Emily has settled in nicely just the same. She seems happy and relieved, saying that she loves it here, that she feels fortunate to be working with Steve. She admits to knowing only around half the kids' names, but she says that like everyone else, she manages.

Their Dynamo colleagues drift in, gathering around one of the big tables where Steve's kids talk about writing and young-adolescent books through much of the day. Patti wanders in first, a veteran reading teacher with a southern drawl and frizzy blond hair. When she came to Anspach 25 years ago, reading teachers dealt in books while "language arts" meant grammar and writing. These days Patti's work overlaps with Steve's, but there is little mention of this, no talk of combining their classes or meshing assignments. Patti amicably pursues her parallel path, her sense of humor marked by long association with young adolescents. Later in the day I hear her joke that one kid's an arsonist, another a monster, and watch both look back with smiles, basking in the glamour of notoriety. Hers is a voice of compassion in team meetings, of someone genuinely intrigued and charmed by eighth-graders. Her metaphors are vivid—a bashful kid is "squishy," a teacher-pleasing one "velcro-like"—and she often warns that if I quote half the things she says, she might come off "sounding like a fiend." The team has long since agreed otherwise, knowing Patti's good will and warmth, looking to her often ribald humor as a buoy.

After a few minutes Laura comes in from the math room, carrying a ceramic mug with the logo "I [heart] giving pop quizzes." She drops her stern classroom persona for the meeting, her round face brightening as she greets Steve and Emily. It is an expression her students seldom see, and even here she plays the bad-cop role, advocating the tougher course with wayward students. Laura started teaching in 1963, and she remains passionate about her subject, her first goal "to make kids have an experience that makes them feel positive about their ability to do math." She will give a talk this spring at the National Council of Teachers of Mathematics conference, and over the summer embark on a master's program in math education. "It's a lot of fun," she says of her work. "When you see that light click on and all of a sudden they get something—that's what keeps you in the business."

Judy joins the group a few minutes late, a tall, lean woman in her 30s with an athlete's smooth stride. She teaches social studies, but just now her heart is in coaching. Her girl's basketball team will win the state championship in a few weeks, and she moves through these late-winter days distracted and sleep-deprived, her mind on games, practices, and her group of closely bonded young players. She enters each day vigorously chewing a good-sized wad of gum, placing it aside as the team passes around boxes of candy or ice cream bars. Judy's been teaching for 10 years, but they affectionately refer to her as the team's "baby." While she seems young and boisterous beside the others, her busy schedule is pressing her into heavy reliance on prepackaged worksheets and machine-scorable tests. Judy is often distracted in team meetings, but the others regard her with eager interest, asking about her games like proud boosters.

Finally Don, the team's elected leader, saunters in from the school's science wing. He seems confident and vaguely bemused, a gray-haired veteran teacher with little left to lose. He dresses more casually than the others, often in faded jeans and cotton shirts, and his leadership is so laid back that I realize his role only after the others explain it. One of the few Dynamos with a classroom computer, Don often comes to meetings with a bundle of spreadsheets in hand. Like the others, he greets me cordially, listening politely as I explain my project. Accustomed to visitors by now, Don is eager to move past all this, to get introductions and permissions over with, to set the meeting in motion.

We are joined by a counselor who visits the team now and then, and by Mary Jane, a special-education teacher who provides assistance to Dynamo kids with low standardized test scores. Eight adults crowd around the table, lots of perspectives to gather and integrate in a 40-minute meeting, but aside from the stone-faced counselor, they laugh and nod readily, their warm bond immediately apparent. Steve takes the lead, asking what kinds of supplies they need for the following year, compiling a list to give to the principal. There is talk of paper, erasable ballpoint pens, protractors, rulers. One teacher jokes that the district will probably give them each one box of Kleenex for the year. The school's lab is badly outdated and only a few teachers have computers, but someone asks for diskettes. There are lighter moments too: When Steve adds tape to the supply list, Patti turns to him in mock disbelief. "Tape?" she asks. "You're going to trust our kids with tape?"

But then one of the teachers asks Steve about a recent meeting with the principal, and the meeting takes a somber turn. "You won't like hearing this," he says, "but we're broke." Steve says he has been enlisted to advise the team to feel sorry about the budget crunch, not to ask for things they need, not to demand that the principal go to the central office and beg for funds. He adds that to avoid controversy, the administration wants to split any available money across the three eighth-grade teams, clean and simple, ignoring the fact that the Dynamos have more kids. "That's ridiculous," someone snaps, and there is talk of a face-to-face "showdown," Laura suggesting that perhaps the principal needs help "figuring the math." There's more talk about how urgently the team needs computers, Don shaking his head, describing some of the new science software now available. Maybe if they could get even one new machine, Laura says, perhaps with a rolling cart, so the team could share it. Patti taps the surface of Steve's notepad. "Wouldn't hurt to put it down," she murmurs.

A tense meeting ends on a milder note, the teachers agreeing to talk about particular kids next time, to continue a series of "little motivational chats" with those in trouble. They laugh at this, the edginess suddenly gone. Don tells Patti about overhearing students rehearsing book reports for her class, and she recounts a conversation between two kids about "homo sapiens"—they thought "that's when gay people get married," she says, inviting a wave of laughter. Steve grabs a few minutes to finalize the supply list while the others gather around Judy to review last night's game. Kids are already flooding back in, but Patti offers to take me on a quick tour of the pod, through her classroom, crammed with paperback books and wall-to-wall desks, back to Laura's math classroom, with its tighter order but similar space problem. Students rush by, passing through Patti's classroom en route to Laura's, but there is no time for real introductions, just more rough joshing. "Oh, they're not anybody you'd really want to know," Patti says to me, but the joke is really intended for these kids. They grin as they rush past Patti, long accustomed to unnamed strangers come to see their exemplary school.

The pod has a small workroom that used to belong to the social studies department, still stocked with history worksheets and quizzes filed in neatly labeled cubicles ("Index Skills-Plan C," "7th Geo Skills-Ans. Key"). Here, too, is the refrigerator where the Dynamos store the lunches they consume during their half-hour midday break and treats for their afternoon team meetings. The team brings in something special when Judy's team wins a game or someone has a birthday, and today I am invited to sample the crumbling remains of a rich chocolate cake. Then the bells sound and it's time for the last two classes of the day. The teachers remain cheerful but hurried; their talk to me, as to one another, is in half-sentences, snippets I can piece together only some of the time. I wonder what they think of my being here, yet another visitor drawn by Anspach's reputation for innovation and excellence. I wonder if they have time to think, to formulate questions, to probe one another's philosophies and ideals. There is indeed so little time here, so little opportunity to ponder any one element in the surging tide of people and concerns. I try to recall names and faces a few hours later, but all that comes to mind is a jumble of movement, of sentences that begin and begin again, inexorably replaced by a half-finished something else.

WHERE HAVE YOU BEEN?

I am scheduled to meet Shelly Hays, Anspach's principal, and Steve walks for a few moments beside me, back to where the pod meets the school's main corridor. We pause near the display case filled with artifacts from the heyday of Steve's language arts department, and he points to the various awards their efforts received, his voice registering equal parts pride and loss. He speaks briefly of the old writer's workshop, of how he and his colleagues watched kids prosper, of the good times they had together. The new principal wants only recent awards displayed in the school's lobby, Steve says, only those given during her brief tenure at the school. By now the last kids are straggling into the next hour's class, leaving Steve less than a minute to make one last point. "See over there?" he asks, pointing down the long corridor to where glass doors open onto the lobby. "She hardly ever comes through those doors, which means kids don't see her much. We'd like to keep it that way. If you write anything to change that, we'll be very unhappy." Steve smiles, but there is an instruction in his eyes, a caution. The message is spare and penetrating, as clear as a warning glance to one of his eighth-graders.

Shelly Hays sits before me a few moments later in her cramped office, a slight, middle-aged woman in a crisply tailored black suit, silk blouse, and high heels. She is cordial and talkative, but her manner is stiff, her words carefully chosen, a hand sweeping up now and then to touch her heavily sprayed hair. I wonder how many times she has recited this litany— the long list of the businesses engaged in partnerships with the school, what these mean in terms of resources and advantages, how excited everyone is to participate. She pauses when I explain for the second time that I'm studying *teacher* collaboration, and she lets her disappointment show when I mention the Dynamos. "That team has some growing to do," she notes, adding that the Dynamos have not produced interdisciplinary units, that they are still more "secondary" than "transescence" in orientation, still privileging their traditional fields of study over the developmental needs of early adolescents. Perhaps the school's transformation is incomplete, she allows, but they have come a long way and paid a heavy cost. When she first arrived 3 years ago, the whole place was "more like a secondary school." The recent restructuring has meant "lots of stress, lots of growth," Shelly admits. "Breaking up departments was in some cases like breaking up families."

I soon recognize it as the kind of remark that invites private jeers from teachers. Opposition to Shelly has an underlife quality, leaving her wondering but never quite sure. The teachers have a hand gesture they use in staff meetings signifying "tedious, uninteresting, and boring," with a slight variation indicating "very, *very*, tedious, uninteresting, and boring." Their new habit of wearing jeans on Friday came in response to Shelly's habit of complimenting those who dress up. By now the teachers have a large repertoire of stories underscoring their principal's top-down management style and lack of connection with kids. A favorite of the Dynamos hearkens back to her earliest days at the school, back when she first introduced the new house plan. Shelly paid a May visit to a seventh-grade assembly, explaining to the students that they would be moving into interdisciplinary houses come September. "She really built it up," one teacher told me; "'you're eighth graders, so you'll get the big lockers, and the air-conditioned classrooms.'" Shelly called on a student with an upraised hand: "Would this mean that we wouldn't get to go home early on hot days?" he asked. Shelly said something about how she was certain they would prefer to be in school, being grown up eighth-graders and all. The kid had a reputation to uphold, and these were the daring days of late spring: "Lady," he shot back, "where have you *been*?" Steve was sitting beside Laura, one of the school's renowned disciplinarians, a woman accustomed to stomping decisively on snide remarks. They dared a quick glance at one another, swallowing laughter.

To the majority of Anspach's faculty, their principal is out of touch, an intrusive leader who undercuts the staff's authority and fails to acknowledge the day-to-day needs of teachers and students. In an effort to promote "shared decision making," Shelly called a series of meetings early on to invite faculty involvement in school goal-setting. She instructed the teachers to formulate three goals for the year, two cognitive and one affective, then displayed sample goals on an overhead. As teachers offered suggestions, Shelly pointed to similar items on the preformulated list. "Teachers don't like that," Steve tells me; "they don't like being asked to set a particular number of a particular kind of goal, and they don't like being given a list to choose from." Afterward he conferred with angry colleagues, put up a large sheet of brown paper in the teachers' lounge, and invited teachers to write in their own goals. In meetings they called themselves, teachers synthesized their ideas and prepared a list to submit to the principal. "It was unusual in that it was participatory," Steve remarks; "usually 'shared decision making' means 'I'll make a decision and share it with you later.'" But the teachers have seen little movement on the goals they advocated: more time for planning interdisciplinary curricula, better technology, a campaign of support for the upcoming bond measure.

Distrust of Shelly runs so high that teachers suspect her of controlling almost everything—the election of house leaders, budgeting, the timing of tornado drills, furniture and space allocations. When a box of tampons disappears from a faculty restroom, a new joke is passed around. "I know what happened," one woman tells another, "*She* took them." There is no pause before the rush of laughter, no need to identify the pronoun reference. Increasingly distanced from Anspach's teachers, Shelly has become an icon, an abstraction. It has become funny to think of her bodily functions, her vulnerabilities.

Shelly's hallway persona is wooden and remote, but in our private conversations she reveals another side, describing her uncertainties as a young teacher, times she sat alone in her classroom weeping, how frightened she was of each new challenge—teaching courses in her minor field of study, working in an open-architecture environment, setting up a learning lab. "I tried to tell my staff this, that 'I have been where you are,'" she explains, a slight quaver in her voice. "It's very hard for people to believe you. I wish I had a videotape of me years ago." When her teaching position was cut she thought about leaving education for a career in law, but her department chair encouraged her to go on for graduate work in education. Then came a stint as an associate principal at a big-city high school, and a few years later, the invitation from Anspach's superintendent. "I was brought in as a change agent," she explains,

> which didn't make me too popular. There are still some remnants of that. That's a difficult spot to be in. It's very threatening to people, and it has placed me in a position where people look back, they were forced to change, and people don't forget. Some people aren't too excited about seeing me come in still, and probably won't be. But I feel very strongly this is the right thing for children, and we are offering more to our children than we were before.

The attacks have grown personal, but they have moved to the back corridors, to the team meetings, to the teachers' lounge. No one here seems to have time or energy for an open confrontation. Shelly is frequently off campus these days, and when she is present the teachers quietly avoid her. September is a distant memory, but summer is still a long way off, the upcoming spring break a too-brief reprieve. Like the others, the Dynamos protect their solidarity, getting by on dry humor and mutual support. With one another they vent and laugh, but their public cynicism is more abstract and general, their sarcasm pointing to no one in particular. "I hope I die during an in-service," reads a hand-lettered sign in the teachers' lounge, "because the transition between life and death would be so subtle."

COMMITTED (OR OUGHT TO BE)

The Dynamo teachers are planning a May trip to Chicago, a reward for kids who do their homework and obey school rules. They will go to museums and then a shopping mall, stopping along the way to buy burgers at McDonald's. The teachers joke about how stunned the fastfood crew will be at the sight of nearly 200 eighth-graders, but as the day grows nearer they find themselves feeling a little stunned as well. They have planned other reward trips over the year—several bowling outings, and a skiing junket in January—but the Chicago trip is the end-of-year cap-off, an important goal for the kids and a major logistical challenge for teachers. They did it last year, too, stumbling out of bed well before dawn, asking one another if they're crazy or what, in overdrive through the long day, ever vigilant lest one of their charges discover a hiding place in the entrails of the museum. "The worst thing that could happen," Laura predicts, "is that it'll go really well and we'll want to do it *again*."

The trip itself occupies only one day, but it is on the teachers' minds all spring, setting the central task for the season's team meetings. A number of kids are in danger of ineligibility, and a form letter has been sent home to parents, detailing expectations and flagging those at risk. These borderline cases receive a summons to appear at a team meeting, each teacher reading off a list of deficiencies, Laura and Don leaning hard, the others backing them up: "In my room," begins many a comment, "it's the same thing." Steve is part teacher, part coach, part dad on these occasions, delivering a vigorous scolding, then asking what's up, if there's anything he should know about. One student has been blowing up now and then, another faking excuses to stay home, yet another refusing to wear prescribed reading glasses. "We want you to succeed," the teachers say again and again, "but some of it has to come from you." Kid after kid looks down, shrugging noncommittally when the teachers ask about possible reasons for the misbehavior. "It can be a whole new ballgame for you," Steve often says, always ready with a sports metaphor, "a new start." The others talk about being adolescents once themselves, about being more empathetic than students might realize. Come talk to us, they say, we're here to help. The kids leave the room with lowered gazes, smiling shyly when the teachers josh them about the ordeal of coming in, of being so firmly pinned to the hot seat.

The teachers are caring but overloaded, catching up on paperwork while a colleague takes the floor, seizing the brief interludes between students to raise fresh concerns or catch up on news. One day a group of boys are roaming around school showing off mercury stolen from a broken blood pressure machine; there is wry talk of the assistant principal's response, and Don explains the dangers of heavy metals. A number of students fall in and out of love; the teachers imitate the antics of the smitten, staring worshipfully into one another's faces. "He's good looking," Patti says of one object of affection, "but he's about 5 years old! I don't know what she *sees* in him." There is uproarious laughter when Don recalls a snide remark from a classmate of the new couple: "Take it to a hotel and get it out of here!" The team delights in their students' giddy sexuality, their own humor tumbling down similar paths. A tired teacher remarks that she'd rather be home in bed, and the others speculate about who the lucky company might be. When a colleague appears on local television, someone observes that he would feel naked before a video camera, and there are lots of giggly asides about the fate of my research if they were to show up unclothed at a team meeting. I assure them that I am only audiotaping, and the group feigns relief, by now breathless with laughter. The men and women share equally in these asides, comfortable with one another, trusting in their mutual commitment but knowing as well its wackier side. "We fit my old standard for middle-school teachers," Laura remarks: "You're either committed or you *ought* to be."

Parents come to see them with increasing frequency as the weeks go by, a lengthening procession of concerned men and women who seem as varied as the kids who pass through the pod each day. A strapping man in a satiny baseball jacket comes by, wanting to know if his son "mouths off": "Oh, no," says Patti, "he's a nice kid!" But the boy tends to be the butt of mean teasing, and the dad is clearly worried, wants to know more about how he seems at school. Mary Jane speaks at length about the boy's learning difficulties, explaining that he's sometimes tempted to ask a classmate to repeat a teacher's spoken directions. The counselor asks the teachers if the boy has any friends, but none can name even one. "I have three kids at home," the father says heavily, "and it's not easy." The teachers emphasize that his son will be okay, but that it will take lots of hard work, that there can be no more absences. They want to get him ready for high school next year, they say—"so his attitude is in gear, so he knows what it takes to get by."

A woman sits before them who looks hard and worn. "We're sorry," Steve tells her, "but we can't talk about this stuff without eating something really decadent." The teachers gather peanut M & Ms by the handful, arranging them in color-sorted rows as they talk about one of their more troubled students, choosing words carefully. The mom brushes aside the offered treat, focusing only on her daughter, describing what she was like before things fell apart for the family and then adolescence hit. She passes around pictures of a well-groomed, smiling girl of 2 years ago, and the teachers study them thoughtfully. Just moments ago the team was going through its usual litany—abominable test scores, Ds for effort, they're forever needing to remind the girl to "stay focused, stay focused," anyone who doesn't try harder in math will only land a dead-end job. But now the talk turns to the happy girl in the picture; the mom says she wishes the teachers could meet that girl, and they smile, agreeing, wondering what it would take to turn things around. The team gives this mom the entire period, and she lingers afterward, too, still talking with Patti and Laura. Steve catches

Don's eye, reminding him how far behind they are, about urgent business to take up next time.

The teachers make time for parents with less pressing concerns, too. They meet with a mom whose daughter is hanging out with the wrong crowd, who has warned her daughter that if her study habits don't improve she'll personally accompany her to school, sitting in her classes wearing a scruffy sweatsuit. Judy smiles knowingly, remembering a time when her own mom did just that: "And I straightened up real fast," she says. The others laugh heartily as the mom warms to the occasion. Don usually takes the lead in urging parents to monitor their kids more carefully, but today he finds the tables turned. This mother has instructed her daughter to bring home a signed report from her science teacher every Friday: "And I don't want to ground her for the weekend just because *you* didn't write the *note*," she tells Don. Steve beams, commenting that he wishes they could clone her, put some of her good sense into other parents' heads. "I'm not the perfect parent," she shoots back. "Well, you sure are throwing some strikes here," says Steve. They work out a plan: The girl will write a weekly report on each class, using this to satisfy her mom as well as Steve's journal requirement. Don will sign off on the science portion, and the mom will offer further response if she likes, "to reinforce the writing," Steve explains. The mom has more to say: She's revoking all library passes for the year, and she wants the teachers to make sure her daughter isn't sitting near kids who might lead her astray. "She'll get over, excuse the language, getting pissed," says the mom, "but she won't get over not learning." Many parents seem cowed by this assemblage of teachers, but this woman has taken the team in hand. By the end of the hour they are friendly peers, laughing at memories of their own adolescence and the rigors of parenthood.

The talk moves up and down the teachers' ladder of priorities as they respond to requests and try to get moving on their own initiatives. The team talks of kids they hesitate to bring on the field trip, kids who might try to run away, kids who don't know, as Mary Jane puts it, "what a city like Chicago holds." Then a pillar-of-society mom and dad come in, both dressed for white-collar jobs, stealing a long lunch hour to talk about their son's spotty study habits. Again the conversation relaxes into friendly banter, with personal stories from the teachers, laughter from the parents, lots of reminders that supportive adults can only do so much, that the student has to "want it." "You have a good kid," one of the teacher says. "We know what we've got," the mom replies. Afterward the team has a brief moment alone together, sharing Dove Bars in celebration of Judy's birthday. Her boyfriend has sent a dozen red roses, and one of the teachers brings them down from the main office. Talk of students ends as suddenly as it began 40 minutes ago, and they steal a few moments for jokes and laughter.

The recent school award was for team-generated curricula, but I never hear the Dynamos talk beyond interdisciplinary spelling tests. I was once told that they'd be doing a Civil War unit this spring, but those plans are lost somewhere in the press and shuffle. In these meetings with kids and parents the team is at its best, opening its borders, inviting others into the joint effort, backing each other up, standing tough. This sort of attention takes lots of time, more time than they have, but they make do, suspending planned business when a parent or counselor drops by, remarking only now and then that they wish they could talk about *all* their kids. Interdisciplinary curricula would be nice, they explain when I ask, but they have to set priorities, managing with limited support, limited opportunity. The attention they give to students in trouble is not magical or complete, but the team sees it as worthwhile, every teacher in the room together, no pitting one against the other, no playing games. Just down the road is high school, and the team describes it as a whole new world. This year, the notes they send home to parents are on Dynamo letterhead bearing all the teachers' names; at the top is their logo, overlapping circles bearing the words "students," "teachers," and "parents," below it the team slogan, "cooperation not competition." Next year no one will be watching these kids the way they are now, they often say; next year it'll be sink or swim.

PRESS ON

The margins between Steve's tables seem even narrower as team meetings come to a close and students flood back in. But the room soon settles to its predictable rhythms, Steve moving about, recommending books or glancing at student writing, gradually increasing Emily's responsibilities as the weeks pass. The edges of the crowded space are arranged with meticulous care: a metal literature organizer filled with an extensive collection of handouts, racks of resources, shelves of books. Colorful bulletin boards are packed with student work—posters describing research projects, book reviews Steve helped them publish in the local paper, letters exchanged with novelists, and cartoons, including one of Steve wearing a "Disco City" T-shirt, standing in front of a building labeled "Books." Steve has posted an assemblage of quotes and slogans: "I refuse to have a battle of wits with an unarmed person"; "I used to have a handle on life, but then it fell off." There are also posters from Steve's professional organizations— the National Council of Teachers of English, in which he is increasingly active, and the state affiliate, in which he has long been a leading voice. "I write to discover my soul," notes one; "I read to discover yours."

Back in the early 1980s Steve attended a local Writing Project work-shop, an experience that transformed his teaching and created a lasting hunger for professional growth. Steve remembers it as school for grown-ups, with lots of freedom to set his own terms, lots of opportunities to write about his own learning:

> I got to write about my grandfather again—my dad's father, who never taught anything the way I thought it had ever been taught before, but taught by example. It used to drive my mother crazy, because when I was seven or eight I would use power tools with him. She'd go nuts, because I was too young to be using them. But he was very good at doing a task, and when you came over, he'd give you a look and let you step in. As you stepped in, he'd be there a while, but once he felt you were okay, he'd walk away. He very rarely said anything—you learned it all by seeing it and doing it. Writing about that, I got to thinking about my teaching.

Steve has since written about his teaching in published articles, de-scribing how he learned to put more responsibility in the hands of students. "They don't learn how to use it if they're not given it," he said in an interview that ran recently in the local paper. He gives Emily the same advice he offers all student teachers: "Make sure the kids are putting in most of the effort, make sure you aren't doing it for them." Steve's classroom is a place where students come to work, and he insists on a steady flow of purposeful activity, leaning hard on those who test him, setting stiff stan-dards from day one. He maintains careful balance and structure, each class session split between lecture, student interaction, and individual work; each activity involving direct instruction, ongoing guidance, and hands-on ex-perience. There is lots of activity in Steve's room, sometimes lots of talk, but he maintains firm control, his letting go always tempered by a careful system of accountability. Steve has been influenced by leading figures in middle-school language arts—Linda Rief (1992), Nancie Atwell (1987), and Donald Graves (1983)—but the strategies they describe have been filtered through Steve's prism, recast to fit his individual style and the demands of Anspach's overcrowding. His classroom is like a well-oiled machine, every detail deliberately designed to complement the whole.

Despite its reputation for innovative excellence, the district is in many ways as conservative pedagogically as it is politically, and some of Steve's colleagues wonder aloud if his classroom lacks structure, if any "real learn-ing" goes on here. In his earliest days at the school, Steve confesses, he was something of a "bull in a china closet." Even before his Writing Project experience, he found courage to toss out the grammar curriculum he was handed and search for something more engaging—in the words of his present course objective, inviting kids "to use language (read, write, speak, listen, view, and think) in a variety of ways for a variety of purposes and audiences." English teachers at the local high school place great stock in a placement exam emphasizing grammar, and a recent drop in scores brought renewed grumbling about Steve's pedagogy. Such concerns are shared by several of his language arts colleagues—the kind of people, Steve says with a sly grin, "who have kids memorize 48 prepositions in alpha order, that kind of thing." One particularly traditional teacher "started hitting grammar" even more after a recent drop in Iowa Test of Basic Skills scores, stepping up her efforts to garner parental support. I often find her in the faculty lounge, red pen poised over a stack of quizzes: "See?" she says of the low scores on the high school's grammar test, "it catches up with them sooner or later! I just think that we're really shortchanging these children if we don't do it."

Steve acknowledges that similar worries prevail among a small but rather vocal group of Anspach parents: "'Are we teaching enough grammar?' 'Are my kids learning phonics?'—same old stuff." Such resistance has only strengthened Steve's determination, making him even more adamant about addressing grammar only in the context of student writing (Weaver, 1979, 1996). Something similar happened back in the heyday of his award-winning writers' workshop: "We also were doing things the rest of the department hated," Steve recalls, "so that *encouraged* us. I think if they had backed off, it would have been different. Keeping the pressure on us to conform was enough to keep us as far left as possible." Steve and his two like-minded colleagues worked closely, sharing ideas and plans, writing units for each other, bringing their groups together so that they could team-teach. "I was blessed," he says. One of Steve's old colleagues is still nearby, an embittered man who calls Shelly "the princess" and often neglects to go to meetings with his new house. The other is off in an aging wing of the school, embracing new opportunities but still missing the old: "You teach with these guys for 18 years," he tells me, "and then maybe you see them once a month."

Steve detects a false dichotomy in Shelly's talk of privileging developmental needs over disciplinary content: "Because the kids are in their early adolescence doesn't mean they can quit learning stuff," he argues; "it just means you have to deal with them differently—it doesn't mean you just shut down the content." Early on, he and his colleagues worried that the switch to houses would mean less attention to curriculum, that events like the Chicago trip would become "just another thing for the school resumé," events as meaningless, Steve feared, as the school's much-touted business partnerships. He recalls a standard joke from those initial meetings: "It doesn't matter what you're teaching, just when your next field trip is." Then came the numbers crunch, and along with the advent of the new school structure, Steve watched his student load swell from 140 to over 180, both figures far in excess of the contact hours recommended by the National Council of Teachers of English (Lloyd-Jones & Lunsford, 1989; NCTE, 1962). With these kinds of numbers, Steve estimates that he can talk with the typical student a grand total of "1 minute and 15 seconds per day." He wonders how serious Shelly can be about the school's becoming more child-centered over the past 2 years—or, for that matter, how serious the district is about its proclaimed commitment to supporting teacher collaboration:

> High school teachers are teaching 150, middle school 180, and elementary 28. Then you have district committees to create documents to report to the state, and you have people going to one, two, or three meetings a week. How much do you really want them to talk? There's this subversive kind of underground tenet that says they're trying to keep us busy enough so that we *can't* talk.

But what about the Dynamos, I ask Steve—what would he say to the people who told me that Anspach is a place to see teacher collaboration "really working?" "I *think* it's working," he replies, hesitant at first. Then, after a pause: "It's almost like we're on the *Titanic.* We may have been strangers 5 minutes ago, but we're saving each other's asses right now. There is that sense of desperation almost, that says 'we have to work together, we *couldn't* do it alone.'" Their coming together may have been "pure luck," but to Steve the Dynamos remain "a match made in heaven," "a great bunch of people" who have made "losing the contacts with other colleagues a lot easier." They share a "bizarre sense of humor," an ability to laugh at themselves, and a dead-serious solidarity. "We almost immediately came together and started to defend each other," Steve recalls:

> There's a real openness, you can say what you want to say and be real honest. It opens up the possibility for making a better education for kids. There's nothing that can compare with working with somebody you have a lot of respect for and care about. If suddenly they were gone, you would feel a deep sense of loss. That's the way I feel about people on the team. I think that leads to a sense of support, people to bounce ideas off of, to have fun with—it's not all work.

While the team holds many joys and benefits for Steve, he also sees its efforts as rather sharply constrained by external circumstance. He emphasizes that his Dynamo colleagues "are very caring and genuine, and care deeply about kids." But meanwhile they face the constant reality of over-crowding: "The hardest thing for all of us to stomach," he explains, "is what doesn't happen for the kids, because of the numbers." When they met for the first time, Steve convinced the others of the need to write notes home to all kids' parents, to resist the temptation to attend only to those in crisis. Knowing they would have "a dozen or so problems" in a house so large, they made a pact "to at least send a note home. But that doesn't work," Steve admits:

> There's enough business, enough problems that arise, by the time you have a few parent conferences it's semester time and not every kid has a note yet. So you get the kids who do really well and are self-directed and don't get notes for a long time, maybe ever.

Steve surmises that they "are doing a much better job with kids who have problems," especially since the team is able to approach them as a united and closely coordinated front. But such attention is typically to study skills, attendance habits, classroom deportment. Seldom does the team have time to talk about how kids learn, how instruction in their various classes may or may not be fitting individual needs. "I'm real worried about con-tent," Steve admits, "and any kind of content transformation that might go on. I think there's a general concern around the school that we are going to continue to grow without the emphasis on content, because I don't know if we serve everybody better." For Steve, a deeper sort of collaboration would involve opportunities to design curriculum and evaluate student progress together. "I think the reason most schools don't have that is they don't have that singular sense of mission," he explains, "they don't believe in the same things. And you've got management that wants to be top cow."

Hungry for opportunities to rethink his practice, Steve has enrolled in a doctoral program in English education, commuting to a distant cam-pus a couple evenings a week and spending weekends writing papers. It adds yet another wrinkle to his busy life, but the coursework satisfies his need to examine what he is doing and why, to think more deeply about his students, to extend his ability to articulate his intuitions and insights. In his wildest dreams, this would take root at Anspach:

> I'd like to see us talk more about what it is we need to do—to think about reading and writing across the curriculum, look away from grading, and really look at what we're doing. The kind of profes-sional dialogue that goes on in graduate classes or at conferences, to have that here. Just do the kinds of questioning that professionals

do, but because of the numbers, we really don't. It's one of the reasons that I want to come back to graduate school. I needed an environment to go where we would talk about how kids learn, about how they write, about learning things.

Steve also acknowledges all that impedes this kind of talk, especially among colleagues as overburdened and beleaguered as his. Talk about basic beliefs can highlight fundamental conflicts, creating dividing lines that threaten much-needed solidarity. Steve knows that his colleagues' classrooms look rather different from his own, that language arts has become a special place, a reprieve from quizzes and worksheets, a time to explore emerging ideas and possibilities. He estimates that it takes around 5 years of trust-building before teachers can disagree openly about things that matter; next year is only the Dynamo's 3rd year together, but he thinks they may be ready then for some touchy subjects, the bonding process sped along by their shared disdain for Shelly. Meanwhile, given the realities of overcrowding, Steve understands that a teacher-centered approach has its appeal:

It's probably cruel and heartless and self-centered to say this, but I don't think there's a commitment to interactions between teachers and students when you put that many students in front of a teacher in one day. I also have to believe that there's not a commitment to encourage that kind of classroom talk and interactions, and even cooperative learning, hands-on, scientific-method kinds of teaching. If you're going to give that many students to so few teachers, it just lends itself to straight rows, shut-up-sit-down-and-work kind of pedagogies.

Steve's work stands in defiance of opponents and constraints. He manages his classroom with artful ease, a steady and determined member of the Dynamo team, and an active participant in a larger network of literacy educators. One Monday he moves a little more slowly than usual, and I ask if he ever gets tired. "Seldom," he says, "but I'm tired today." Steve is involved in several reform efforts sponsored by the National Council of Teachers of English, and he has spent the weekend away, working with colleagues from around the nation, talking shop far into the night. He admits that coming back is always a little hard, no reprieve here at school, no opportunity to slow the pace, no one who asks about his activities outside the walls of Anspach. During lunch, someone wants a word with him about contract negotiations, and then there is paperwork to do for the team, a stack of student research papers on his desk, kids to corral back to work.

But he doesn't mind being stretched, he says. All his life, he's always wanted to see what more he was capable of. Back in school he ran the half-mile as fast as he could, then his coach said he could be a really strong miler. He ran his first marathon at 26, and in some ways he hasn't slowed down yet. Steve pauses, observing with a laugh that when he's really worn out like this he starts to sound like the coach he used to be. He offers an alternative comparison: When he thinks of his job here at Anspach, he's often reminded of Chuck Yeager's autobiography, *Press On* (Yeager & Leerhsen, 1990). "If you're in a burning jet, you're going down anyway," Steve explains, "so you may as well make the most of it—you press on." I remind him of his metaphors—the *Titanic*, a burning jet—and ask if things at Anspach are really that bad. He thinks it over for a moment or two, but answers only with a smile.

WE'RE HAVING A QUIZ SOON

Dynamo students sit quietly in rows through much of the day, and when they speak, it is usually to reach for answers the teacher already has in mind. I visit Judy's social studies class the day before a test on the Oregon Trail. "Gonna be tough as nails," she promises. She moves all period through a series of review questions, pumping students for answers, finally supplying most herself. "Why did people want to go to Oregon?" she asks. "To start a new state," replies a student. "Eventually," Judy replies, "but originally?" Another: "To start a new life." "You're close. The driving part was that people heard there was good land, it got 'em to go. Why did people want to go on the Oregon Trail?" Judy's manner is both warm and tough: "Not even close to cute, man," she tells a misbehaving student. Most of the kids seem to like and respect her, raising their hands, playing their part in the script, the rules and rituals familiar and expected. Judy's walls are papered with social studies posters, but here and there are motivational slogans: "Never settle for less than your best"; "SUCCESS" spelled in crossword-puzzle fashion over the U in "ATTITUDE."

Over in science the drill is much the same: Don tells them that the one thing they should remember from last night's reading (section "20-1") "is how this thing called our solar system got here in the first place." Then, perhaps remembering the power of Anspach's religious right, he adds that "nobody knows for sure. But what hypothesis did your book come up with? It's the most widely accepted explanation in the scientific literature." "There was a cloud," a student offers vaguely. "What was the cloud made of?" Don asks. "Gas," volunteers another. "What kind of gas?" Don responds. "Nitrogen." Don: "No. What's the most common gas in our solar system?"

He fishes for answers, leading them through the material, drawing swirling clouds in different-colored chalk to suggest how "leftover star material" became "protoplanets." They become fully formed planets with a few more sweeps of chalk, and a student accurately observes that the inner four are called "terrestrial." Don brightens. "Why are they called terrestrial?" he asks. "Because they're like earths," someone offers. "Yes. And what makes them earth-like?" "They all have a rocky surface?" someone ventures. "What about other characteristics they have in common?" Don asks. Silence, then he answers his own query: "They're all very small. These are very small planets. Remember, the Earth is the biggest terrestrial planet." Don adds a few lines to the chapter outline he is building on an adjacent chalkboard. Then finally: "Any questions? We're having a quiz on this soon." He finishes class one minute early, and light chatter breaks out as his kids wait for the bell: "If you want to be dismissed on time," he warns, "you should probably be quiet. Let's see how quiet you can be."

These classes are a typical size by Anspach standards, over 30 students to a room, and a high premium is placed on maintaining order. In less practiced hands things could spiral out of control, but here the mechanism runs smoothly, fueled by quizzes, points, and the promise of a trip to Chicago. In speaking to parents, the teachers sometimes reference more far-off threats and rewards, too—the need to prepare for high school, to think about college or the job market beyond that. Patti admits that her students think her an easy grader, that she is at peace with this, just wants them to enjoy reading; and then there is Steve, the radical of the bunch, urging his students to think things through, to weigh this perspective against that, to argue and discuss, to find a place to stand. But in their other classes, kids are required to learn content, to memorize, to get the answers right. There's lots to get through, so much to manage, so little time for controversy. In social studies, our nation's westward expansion becomes a benign set of facts, unchallenged by charges of imperialism or genocide. In science, there is no discussion of how "the hypothesis your book came up with" compares with other explanations, why the next quiz focuses on it alone, no talk of church and state or competing modes of knowing.

Why learn all this? What's it for? These are the questions Steve longs to see the team address, but there is so much to cover, so many students. I spend a half day in the pod and feel as though I've flown halfway across the continent, my head foggy from lack of oxygen and the strain of cramped quarters. But these teachers manage, coverage and control the first goals, everything else waiting until that distant day when they have time to think, time to talk. The school year is no longer young, and teachers joke about the squirrel index, the sap rising, and, more seriously, how to up the ante on penalties and punishments. When the Dynamos speak of a rebellious

student in team meeting one day, Judy tells them, incredulous and outraged, that the girl recently went so far as to pull her chair out of an assigned row. Over in Laura's math class the restrictions are sternest of all.
"I *want* you to *get to work*," she tells them firmly, then turns to a student
retrieving a paper he left on her desk. "Why do you think you have the
right to pick things up off my desk?" she asks, leaning over him now, glaring, the room still and tense. "*I* am the adult in this classroom. *You* are the
student."

The teachers acknowledge that they talk mainly about the same kids,
a small percentage in serious, recurrent trouble, the ones untouched by
offers of rewards or threats of punishment. Like Steve, Don is frustrated
that they haven't made good on their promise to send letters home with
all the kids or work on interdisciplinary units. Instead, he confesses, they
focus on a problematic few:

> For the second year in a row, we have seen that small percent is
> dictating our time. You find you get so involved with these students
> that are turned off, students probably turned off from most any-
> thing. They take up too much time. But do we ignore them? When
> you see them not working, you hope you can solve their problems.
> But I don't think we spend enough time on the good kids. We don't
> get to do work on interdisciplinary ideas. We don't have contact
> time to do what we want in areas, because students are taking up
> too much of the time. We feel that we owe some of our off-time to
> classroom preparation, etc. So there's only so much time you can
> give to house activities, and all of us would agree that our small
> groups of students are taking up too much time.

The teachers come together for 45 minutes every other day, time enough
to boost blood sugar and spirits, to put out a fire now and then. But there is
no time to survey the reach of their jobs, to talk about the full diversity of
their students, the few who are soaring, the vast crowd in the middle. Steve
tells me of one of the latter, a nice kid recently grown quieter than usual.
Anyone would be pleased to have her as a daughter, he says; she's bright
and conscientious, good at sports, affable and kind. Worried about the change
in her behavior, the other day Steve left his class unattended for a few risky
minutes, making time for a private hallway chat. He asked if anything were
wrong, and the girl burst into tears that wouldn't stop. Here at Anspach, Steve
says, she's scarcely known, her troubles easily hidden. There is no time to
connect with each kid, no time to notice the quieter crises.

Nor is there time to know one's colleagues in any kind of depth—to
explore the beliefs that lie behind their practices, to confront differences,

to chart more finely networked paths. While emphasizing their great affection for one another, the Dynamos acknowledge their curricular autonomy. Laura notes that "there were a lot of pressures" to integrate instruction back in the early days of new system. "But," she adds,

> we have managed to say "we're doing really well by ourselves, thank you." I guess we all have different types of classrooms. I've never felt that any of us have had to give up any part of our identity to be part of the team. All of us are so curriculum motivated that we've felt that our curriculum has to stay intact. Anything that we do interdisciplinary still has to have a purpose and meet some goal in our curriculum practice.

In meetings with kids they balance one another, moving easily into what Don calls their "good cop/bad cop routine," he and Laura "hammering down," Judy the mediator, Steve and Patti the "soft-pedalers." These sorts of differences are both allowed and embraced: "Nobody on the team is so pig-headed that they can't see another person's point of view," he explains. But unlike Steve, the others privately acknowledge a desire to keep their classrooms distinct, to close the door and go about their separate business.

Emily is interviewing for middle-school jobs, and is often asked about her experience on the Dynamo team. She is thinking hard about what interdisciplinary collaboration might mean to her work as a language arts teacher, about ways to connect with colleagues. Laura and Patti have been particularly welcoming, but as Emily explains, "there's not much casual conversation between classes. There doesn't seem to be much time for that. People are too busy." She's exhausted when she arrives home every day, and understands how teachers "could get run down," how important collaboration must be to "creating energy." Emily sees the potential but lives the daily reality, not yet at peace with its compromises. One afternoon she puts words to what any new teacher might feel here: "I'm overwhelmed by this."

THE ONLY THING MIDDLE

Anspach Middle School is on Middleridge Road, and Shelly is fond of saying that when she first arrived, the only thing "middle" about the place was its address. She repeats the line at an awards banquet, and it is the subject of much derision at the next team meeting. Shelly is referring to the shift to interdisciplinary houses, but the Dynamos find the remark unfathomable. They insist that they have always embraced the core tenets of middle-school philosophy—close attention to the developmental needs of early adolescents, collaborative problem solving, a commitment to building an inclusive community. "This has been a middle school with a middle-school philosophy since I came here," Patti snaps. "We've always worked on teams, and we team planned and we had meetings, and we did bond with people who knew how to do it. They weren't simply *interdisciplinary* kinds of teams."

Some say that they can see how recent changes could dovetail nicely with what was already in place, that they were more opposed to the method of reorganization than the idea of houses. "When it all started 4 years ago," Don tells me,

> a meeting was called in the spring of the year. The principal walked in and said, "You will be in interdisciplinary houses next year." I asked, "Does that mean we're going to study the interdisciplinary approach and decide if that's what we want to take?" And I was told, "No, you will have it."

Steve, too, bristled at Shelly's top-down approach:

> We just wanted questions answered, we wanted to know more about what we were going into before we got into it. The concept itself wasn't anything that didn't appeal to everybody, but some of the nitty-gritty logistics. Then we heard these wild promises about how the class size would go down, it would be less expensive to do the interdisciplinary approach. That's all bogus—it would cost *more*. The class size didn't go down, we didn't get more time to plan, we just got more kids. I think most people in the school agree with the concept, but it's the way it was enacted.

Even those who most supported the change acknowledge certain issues in its implementation. An assistant principal insists that by now the vast majority of Anspach's teachers "believe in the middle-school concept and the house concept, because they see the good it's doing for children." Still, she admits, "there was a time when that wouldn't have happened":

> I think they felt like it was crammed down their throats. Anytime you're going to do change, you need to do as much as you can possibly do to let teachers, parents, community, all the constituents you are working with, have input. And I know that's difficult. But I really think an administrator really needs to listen. And ultimately,

someone has to make decisions. But you really have to hear people out, their concerns, their wants, their desires, and what they think is good.

"What if you had limitless options and resources," I ask the teachers, "what would you do to make your work with kids even more powerful?" Their own professional needs always figure somewhere in the answers, often beginning with workplace conditions and issues of governance. "I would like to be respected as a professional," Patti explains, "to have an administrator that looked beyond superficial kinds of things to do what is good for kids—not just what makes nice little headlines, to really believe that teachers have a knowledge of what's good for kids." Regardless of how the school is organized, the Dynamo teachers know that the press of numbers makes quality teaching and learning impossible. They shake their heads at school awards and Anspach's frequent appearances in the press, wondering aloud how the school keeps attracting such recognition. "There's a gap," one of Steve's old language arts colleagues tells me, "between how we promote this school in public and my perception of what it really is":

> I sometimes hear about all the wonderful things that are going on, and how we're doing this and doing that, and I think, whoa—not in the building *I'm* in. In the building I'm in, the roof leaks, and we don't have any budget. I'm told that next year "I don't really know yet if we can get you furniture." I've had kids stand up before, and I've said, "go home and tell your parents there are no desks for you." We suddenly have desks. I'll probably get a reprimand for it, but we do it that way. And it's just sort of this, we just go on, business as usual. But I read about how wonderful we are.

No one seems to care about overcrowding, and the teachers have grown sadly resigned. "Yes, it would be nice to teach five classes of 25 kids a day," Patti observes, "But I don't think that's going to happen in my lifetime or anyone else's." The team agrees that a student load closer to 120 would make their work manageable, but they acknowledge other constraints as well, including a lack of options built into the school's very architecture. "The building is not big enough for flexibility," Don explains:

> The *staff* is not big enough for flexibility. Ideally you could split the school and have two 600-student middle schools, which would be better—if you then gave the staff the room to go with it. With the limitations that we have, making changes is extremely difficult.

But they're getting by, he adds. They all knew from the start that they'd somehow manage: "There's too much pride in the staff," he explains, "to *not* make it work. But in 7 or 8 years, when people are getting burned out over the hours it takes to make it successful, who knows?"

My own home town hopes to replace its junior highs with middle schools, and someone tells a reporter that Anspach is the model to emulate. Soon a front-page article profiles an Anspach eighth-grader named Jenny, who "studies in a close-knit circle," an "academic world much smaller and more intimate" than a traditional junior high. Her teachers "talk about the eighth-grader and her progress in school regularly, and use their common planning time to coordinate homework and lesson plans." It is the image of Anspach the school's administrators paint again and again, their talk sprinkled with references to "what all the research shows"—that kids thrive in a situation that is "more student-centered," as an assistant principal puts it, "and not subject-centered." The idea, she explains, is to get away from housing kids this age in a "mini-high school," to "get to know those students a little bit better, to get to know what works and what doesn't work with them."

While administrators praise Anspach's new emphasis on the developmental needs of early adolescents, teachers maintain that their old departments attended to kids and curriculum alike, providing opportunities to address individual needs as well as the demands of one's subject matter. Even those who embrace the new system admit to a certain nostalgia for the old. Patti, for instance, misses teaching across the grade levels, and, especially, time with her longtime reading colleagues:

> I liked the fact that we had some time to plan some curriculum, that we could plan with other teachers of the same discipline, so you got a lot of good ideas from other reading teachers. I never see any other reading teachers now. So there isn't really that relaxed casual time to exchange ideas. For things like that I feel nostalgia. If you asked me which system I prefer, I prefer this one. [But] I wish there were some way we could incorporate some time where we could meet with colleagues of the same discipline.

"What's the heart and soul of your work as an educator?" I ask the Dynamos—"how would you describe your mission, your basic reason for being here?" In separate interviews, each frames an answer that references a discipline: to help kids enjoy reading, to enable them to tackle math concepts, to foster an appreciation of science. And if their students' learning is cast as experiencing the life of discipline, so, too, is their own professional growth. The challenge is eased a bit for Don: His lab equipment may be tired and outdated, but the school cannot afford to remodel classrooms closer to the various houses, and long-time science colleagues remain neighbors. "This is only our 2nd year in eighth grade and 3rd year in the building to have houses," he reminds me. "The previous 20-some years, we had a science department." Don swivels in his avocado vinyl chair, its arms falling off, stuffing protruding through good-sized gashes. He smiles like a man who has gotten away with something, explaining with a sly glint that "we have kept in touch well, and we know what we would like to be able to do." An interdisciplinary curriculum can seem "watered down," he says; "we try not to do that, because everyone has too much invested in science as far as their career goes."

The others see themselves as less fortunate, privately admitting that their professional development has been sorely disrupted by the split from discipline-based departments. Judy, the Dynamo's youngest teacher, fondly remembers a time when "we were part of a social studies team":

> There were six of us. We did a lot of special things, and curriculum-wise that's the ultimate: when you're working in your area of expertise with other people who are just as excited. I'm not saying that what we're doing here [on the Dynamo team] is wrong, but I grew more on that team than this team from an academic standpoint in my curriculum area. This allows me to grow professionally and understand other areas, but it will not feed me like my social studies team did. Have I grown? Yes, but I've also regressed.

The change was fraught with loss for the team's more veteran teachers as well. Laura likens the breakup of her old math department to a "divorce":

> There are materials that we had always shared because we had a common office area, we shared classrooms. All that material had to be split up and divided among people, all of the things that you'd always done. You had to start working with a whole new team.

The Dynamos are keenly aware that the new change takes little account of all that came before, that there has been scant effort to build on the successes of the past or acknowledge the constraints of the present. Something important has been taken away from each of these teachers, and they have tried to preserve what they could, protecting their individual classrooms from the turbulence of reorganization. When asked if his teaching has changed as a result of the shift to houses, Don answers, "Probably not a whole lot. My classroom situation is not a whole lot different, my schedule hasn't changed." For Laura, one of the benefits of the new team rests in the preservation of her curricular autonomy: "When I come into my classroom," she explains, "I shut the door and I'm not under any pressure to do other than what I feel is best for the kids."

Houses with smaller numbers of students have experimented a bit more with interdisciplinary projects, but these are modest attempts to link activities rather than a more radical meshing. Students learn about environmentalism in science class and write a related persuasive paper; students study the middle ages in social studies, then read King Arthur legends and make construction-paper stained-glass windows. The house next door to the Dynamos sponsors a much-touted "Heritage Days" event: The kids have been studying the old West, and for several days there's a festival of sorts, the teachers dressed up like pioneers, the kids preparing chili and corn bread, their classroom walls papered with tempera-painted images of mining towns. The teachers are in high form, telling wild-west jokes and snapping photos of one another, performing on a makeshift stage with papier-mâché curtains. They talk of how exhausted they are, 3 days in the same clothes, all the extra work, long hours on their feet. "The principal came by on Wednesday and had her picture taken," one tells me. His voice is sharp with sarcasm, and there is a moment's strained silence.

Shelly is proud of these kinds of efforts, talking them up before awards committees and visitors. It is a promising start, perhaps, a way to connect the work of seemingly disparate classes, to blur the artificial boundaries of content and learning. But I can't help thinking that these forays still seem a bit tentative and contrived, starting from questions of how ("how to design a science unit on ancient Greece") rather than why ("is this something kids want or need to know?"). Meanwhile, Shelly regards the Dynamos as a team with growing to do, even as the question of how to support that growth remains unanswered and even unacknowledged. The teachers know that the familiar dichotomy is phony at heart, that they need to serve kids' larger needs *and* teach about something they know. The trouble, given the present situation and the way it came to be, is finding ways and means.

PRETTY GOOD

The shift to houses has been too much too soon, and few insiders regard it as a transformation of the school's deep structure. Teachers can coordinate talk with students and parents a bit more readily; here and there, perhaps, they can even begin to coordinate curricula. Their workplace routines look a bit different—they have been pulled out of physical proximity with old colleagues, placed in new classrooms, given a shared planning period every other day. While teachers wonder if they are really serving students better in any overall sense, administrators insist that the rewards are already worth the upheaval. Typically absent from these discussions are the voices of Anspach's prime constituency, its students.

"What is a 'house,' anyway?" I ask some Dynamo kids. They represent the range, from superstar achievers to the troubled 2% teachers talk about in team meetings. All explain the house system in terms of grouping kids and teachers into more easily managed subunits: "They make it so you know all the teachers," as one explains it, "you don't have to keep going back and forth to different teachers, they're all right in the same hall." A few are unsure of the benefits in this, but most think it a modestly good idea. "I think it's just so the teachers will get to know you better," another says, "so when you're in sixth grade, you're not so scared." All the kids have the same teachers, which means the same academic rhythms: "You can talk with them," a student tells me, "and get information or help on your homework and everything." Like their teachers, the kids see certain obstacles in the school's architecture—the science room off in another wing, the wedged-behind placement of their reading and math classes. But overall, most say, the school-within-a-school notion seems to make a kind of sense.

Despite the Dynamos' best attempts to keep the content of their meetings confidential, the kids have a strikingly accurate impression of what their teachers talk about. "I've walked in on a meeting before," one student reports, "and they're talking about how students are and stuff. I walked in and I got yelled at because I was taking too long, and I could tell that they didn't like students looking at their meetings, because they really take it seriously." "I really haven't noticed much about how they work together education-wise," says another, "but they organize everything together, set up everything, and I see them talking a lot, so they get along well." The kids know that the team talks about upcoming field trips and kids in trouble, and they suspect efforts to stagger test dates and deadlines. A few mention the interdisciplinary spelling tests or the team's role in nominating students for school awards, but mostly the kids focus on the trips and parties. What sorts of things do your teachers do together? The reply becomes predictable: "Well, they took us to Chicago . . ."

From the students' point of view, the pluses of the house system rest in social and recreational concerns. They may get to know their teachers better when they share a day's bus trip or play together on a bowling team, and a few say that this makes teachers "easier to talk to." But the crucial concern for the kids rests in their relationships with peers: "If you make a lot of friends in your house," says one, "then I think you are in a good spot." Conversely, a number of kids raise the possibility that one's friends may be placed in another house, regarding this as the system's main danger.

"In one way," a first-year Anspach student reports, "I would like to be in a school without houses, because I came from a school that didn't have houses. You see more of your friends. But then the house is pretty good."

"Pretty good" more or less summarizes what the Dynamo kids have to say about the house system. It helps them get to know their teachers a little better, makes for fun field trips and parties, and, in a best-case scenario, aids in the important business of maintaining key friendships. They report minor academic advantages, but the kids note none of the connections across disciplines cited in the recent school award. Their classes remain separate worlds, language arts a unique island where they can "express viewpoints," "speak your mind." Several students note that in math or social studies, there is one right answer to every question—"it's just out of the book," as one student puts it. In language arts, on the other hand, "you have to think more, you write down your own ideas, what you're thinking." Mr. Rush's class is "more free," the kids say, "funner," while in other classes they sit at separate desks, quietly completing worksheets and quizzes, raising their hands to enter the question-and-answer recitation script (Cazden, 1988).

"Well, I don't think it's a big decision that's going to affect your life or anything," one student says of the shift to houses; "I think it's just the way they want to organize things. So, I don't know." What does he think the school's intention was in making the switch, I ask; does he want to hazard a guess? "Not really," comes the reply. "Except for small things, like to get to know more people." The students' perceptions become a familiar refrain, their teachers' work useful but not exactly earthshaking, "pretty good" the recurrent report: "They helped organize our trip to Chicago. They organize special things at the end of quarters, like a couple weeks ago we went bowling, now for second quarter we went skiing, which was a lot of fun. If there's a problem with some students or in a class, they figure it out together, which is pretty good."

TACIT ISSUES, QUIET TROUBLE

By late May the teachers are in survival mode. There is a rash of girls' yanking boys' pants down, and lots of half-serious speculation among the staff about appropriate punishments. They settle heavily into the tattered furniture in the staff lounge, reminding one another of the number of days left before break, their humor worn but still intact. The warm days take their toll over in the Dynamo house, where the kids are rambunctious and the air stiflingly close. When it gets really unbearable Steve guides his class down to the library ("at least you have a door that opens to the *corridor*,"

Patti scolds). The others stay put, and when I visit classes for even half a day I grow sluggish and muddled. Judy copes by showing movie after movie, the sound track vibrating through the thin walls that divide her classroom from Steve's and Patti's.

Steve shows a movie, too, an old one based on the H. G. Wells novel *The Time Machine* (1898/1949; Pal, 1982). Humankind survives nuclear war, evolving into the cannibalistic Morlocks and the passive, pleasure-loving Eloi. The Eloi behave like mindless robots, living the good life until they are mysteriously escorted to the Morlocks's subterranean dining room. They need to band together for the common good, but the Eloi bask in the sun, pluck exotic food from nearby trees, and fall into petty squabbles. Only with able leadership from the time-traveling Rod Taylor do they wise up, fighting for the common good, at last a fiercely bonded community standing up to the evil powers. Steve talks to the kids about how peer pressure can obscure one's better judgment, how collective action based on clear-headed principles can save the day.

The atmosphere around the school has grown wackier by the week, and the time seems right for probing certain parallels between the plight of the Eloi and Anspach's beleaguered staff. I mention to Patti and Steve that I was hoping to do some sort of final interview with the team, that it would be great to get it on tape. Steve just laughs, wondering aloud if I've noticed that there's no time for conversation here. Patti takes me aside and whispers her refusal to talk yet again about the team's collaboration: "It's sort of like sex," she says, "you don't sit around afterward talking about whether it was good or not." The fact that they aren't talking much about their work together is a sign that it's working just fine, she explains. "Couples do most of their talking the year before a divorce," she adds. She is reminded of a team of teachers who visited the school awhile back to talk about their "roles." Patti thought they looked foolish, as if they were trying to figure out who they are and how to act, as if they were thinking about it all too much.

The Dynamos are too busy to step back and survey their work, too absorbed in the now to observe their multiple lenses, their tacit conflicts. But their hectic pace serves as a sort of ballast, too, stabilizing their amicable solidarity, giving them an excuse to steer clear of rock-bottom differences. These people hold radically different notions about what it means to teach or learn, ideas conceived and nurtured within their diverse disciplines. They have been trained as teachers of particular subjects, their early growth shaped by contact with same-discipline colleagues, by reading a disciplinary literature, by attending discipline-based workshops and conferences. The disciplines have long shaped the way schools and professional lives have been organized (Grossman & Stodolsky, 1994, 1995; Little, 1993b;

Siskin, 1994; Siskin & Little, 1995), and there is scant opportunity to interrogate such traditions here. Steve has moved farthest from a focus on transmission of content, adopting a workshop approach that blurs the boundaries of student need and subject exigency, that renders him the most ready of the bunch for the challenge of interdisciplinary curricula. But unlike those who brag to the media about Anspach's supposed transformation, Steve knows that this is a complex challenge, requiring lots more time together than the team has enjoyed to date.

So too has educational theorizing moved beyond a vision of teaching as transmission or "banking" (Freire, 1970/1988), beyond a conception of learning as something that takes place within the well-bounded confines of one's own skull. These days we talk of cognition as "distributed" (Bruner, 1986, 1990; Salomon, 1993), of teaching and learning as intertwining social processes, as mutually orchestrated meaning-making. Charged with issues of power and culture, nestled within the histories of institutions and individual lives, engaged learning involves emotions as well as intellects, people struggling to challenge and connect. Whether the learner be an eighth-grader or a veteran teacher, the process involves both cooperation and dissonance, negotiations that challenge the boundaries of self and other.

But here certain dividing lines stay quietly put. For the Dynamos, still newly wrenched from departmental "families," disciplinary identities remain a major concern. In a relatively short time, they've moved toward mutual trust, established useful patterns of interaction with students and parents, and become friends. But moving to this next level of collaboration is hard, threatening all they have accomplished to date. The Dynamos grow defensive in the face of Shelly's assertion that their disciplines are perhaps too important to them, but their former affiliations remain significant, lenses through which these teachers evaluate student learning and define their own development. How much to let go of this part of their pasts? When—and why? Such questions require time and trust; as it is, the Dynamos seldom finish sentences, much less explore an unresolved issue in depth.

A move toward interdisciplinary curriculum would be demanding, requiring something far more fundamental and humanly nuanced than the reorganization Shelly has brought to Anspach. It would mean letting go of familiar ground, leaving behind the notion that one teaches to impart knowledge based in well-defined fields of study. This would mean abandoning accustomed certainties, moving toward a stance that privileges questions over content, that would truly require the shared pursuit of new meaning, the opening of what Maxine Greene (1988) calls "intersubjective spaces." The disciplines can play a part in this process, Greene argues, but only if we think of them as offering realms of possibility rather than fixed answers:

> The languages required include many of the traditional modes of sense-making: the academic disciplines, the fields of study. But none of them must ever be thought of as complete or all-encompassing, developed as they have been to respond to particular kinds of questions posed at particular moments in time. Turned, as lenses or perspectives, on the shared world of actualities, they cannot but continue resonating and reforming in the light of new under-currents, new questions, new uncertainties. (p. 127)

This is a tough challenge, far harder than Anspach's public rhetoric would have us know. It would be folly to think that in 2 short years such fundamental transformation could take hold, especially given the frenetic pace of these teachers' days, their need to maintain equilibrium and balance in a workplace torn by conflict and burdened by excess. Anspach's move to a middle-school format was grounded in an ostensible desire to serve the "whole learner" more effectively, to honor the developmental needs of early adolescents; but how can teachers expect to create such conditions for kids if their own developmental needs are so steadfastly denied? An intersubjective space has begun to open for the Dynamos of Anspach, but it remains tentative and small. "I think it's working," says Steve, rubbing his head, segueing into his *Titanic* metaphor. The restructuring is "pretty good," say the students. The houses are "just the way they want to organize things," not "something that's going to change your life." Anspach is on its way, not yet arrived.

How to honor these teachers' needs as learners? How to ease their transition into this bold new way of doing business? The teachers' first answer is always the same: *time*, lots more time. Time to talk about every kid, time to plan interdisciplinary units, time to explore a problem or issue until they all feel satisfied, time, even, to have a conversation in which they finish all their sentences. But how much time would it take to build the sort of trust that would allow them to address their fundamental differences? How much time to lobby for a reduced student load? How much time to delve into the needs of even one of those kids in the middle—the kids who never get talked about because they're quiet, earn solid Bs, don't attract notice? Andy Hargreaves (1994) points out that administrators often think of time as an abstraction, forgetting the human urgencies and competing demands that crowd teachers' workdays. School reformers can be even more out of touch with what "having enough time" means to teachers. Judith Warren Little (1993a) notes that reforms often come at a fast and furious pace, typically with scant attention to real teachers, classrooms, and schools. "Complexity and ambiguity are inherent features of the more ambitious reforms," she writes, "making progress uneven and difficult to detect—especially given the relative absence of tested principles, policies, and practices" (p. 139).

Lasting, substantive reform involves whole schools, demanding cooperation across diverse sectors. Reforms are more complex than most reformers acknowledge, and the challenge of Anspach's new interdisciplinary houses is certainly no exception. Shelly also needed time—to get her administrative sea legs, to secure the trust of Anspach's veteran faculty, to gather a wider array of voices, energies, and material resources. Teachers speak of her as a transitional figure, an untried leader brought in as a change agent. The transformation she was asked to produce would be deep and sweeping, a small miracle made more elusive by overcrowding and tight finances. She is as much victim as villain here, but she tries to imagine her troubled leadership resulting in something fine, "the right thing for children."

Should schools be set up to promote disciplinary excellence, or to teach the whole child, as Shelly suggests? John Dewey pointed out a long while ago (1938/1963) the folly of thinking in such terms, of dichotomizing attention to content *versus* attention to individual learners, since we so obviously need to do both. Anspach offers so little opportunity to reflect on any of this, let alone risk a searching discussion that might reveal gulfs of difference and hurts that might not heal. This place is in a hurry, no time for public doubts. The argument has been cast in either-or terms, the old cast off in favor of the new, full steam ahead.

Administrators in Steve's district would no doubt wince to hear him compare his award-winning school to the *Titanic*. But Steve and his colleagues still hold out hope, and they want very much to play key roles in the navigational process. If they are to improve students' chances, their own must be improved, too, beginning with a reduced student load, greater input into school decision making, and adequate time to pursue shared possibilities. They have much yet to do—turning the lenses of their disciplines this way and that, imagining ways to meld their subject-matter expertise, identifying parts of the past they wish to conserve, setting shared goals and strategies. The path beyond "pretty good" is neither obvious nor easily negotiated, but perhaps there could yet be a will to try and circumstances that support the attempt. Their ambitious ship is in quiet trouble, but there are some determined people on board, managing in the face of hard odds. As Steve says, the Dynamos are doing what they can to save each other. Doom hardly seems imminent, but his metaphors send distress signals.

Chapter 5

Fortunate Lives:
Jo and Jane

Her stepmother said, "Well, I have thrown a dishful of lentils into the cinders. If you have picked them all out in two hours you shall go with us." The girl went through the back door into the garden and cried, "Ye gentle doves, ye turtledoves, and all ye little birds under heaven, come and help me"—
"The good into a dish to throw,
The bad into your crops can go."
(Grimm Brothers, 1945, pp. 155–156)

The interstate is bright in the noonday sun, undulating farmland extending toward far horizons. Last winter's frozen moonscape is cartoonishly leafy now, broad expanses of corn already knee-high in the late-spring heat. On this last day of May I am visiting Jo Jamison and Jane Clifton, two first-year language arts teachers who will soon be team-teaching a pair of summer classes for kids. They are former students of mine, energetic young educators uncharacteristically weary just now. There is little rest in sight—a day or so to figure grades, then next week the month-long session begins. I am here a few days ahead of the new beginning, catching a glimpse of Pioneer Junior High, the school where they have launched their careers.

THROUGH THESE DOORS

I turn onto a county road, dense green on all sides, tidy farm houses and crumbling barns dotting the landscape. At close range this place looks almost surreal, more like a too-bright postcard than the site of the bustling school Jo and Jane describe. Then Pioneer Junior High appears at the edge of a cornfield, its brown-brick gymnasium jutting above the flat expanse. The edge of a small city is nearby, but I am told that this is very much a rural school, virtually every student bussed in from the encompassing patchwork of farms and tiny towns. Burned into the grassy berm in front of Pioneer is the district name, "Grant Wood"—for the junior high sits at one end of a consolidated campus, a sprawling turf that is home to three elementary schools, a high school, athletic fields, district offices, a bus barn, even a groundskeeper's residential trailer. Kids start here as kindergartners, the move into junior and then senior high but a succession of walks next door.

The surrounding countryside has its share of rural poverty, a smattering of modest affluence, and a predominance of solid middle-class people making do; but Wood schools are clearly places of pride, kept clean and freshly painted, invested in and well used. The parents I will meet here are tough and caring, focused on community and family, full of insistence that their kids maintain decent manners and habits of hard work. The parking lot is filled with American-made pickups and campers, often sporting flag decals or bumper stickers touting country-western stations. Kids at Pioneer Junior High learn line dancing in physical education, entertain in a lavish performing-arts center, and enjoy ready access to state-of-the-art computing facilities. This is a place of cultural conservatism and pedagogic innovation, of patriotism and generosity, of sports enthusiasts who also attend school plays.

Jo and Jane have liked it here, but their descriptions have sounded more like balanced appraisal than boosterism. They know which of their kids are really poor and perhaps even hungry, which live at a local family crisis center, which have been deemed to have "behavior disorders" or "special needs." They tell me that diversity at Pioneer is primarily socio-economic, the difference between kids who live on horse ranches and kids who live in low-rent Victorians in defunct farm towns. The district is marked by a strong athletic tradition: Parents and kids alike regard games as big events, and many of the district's administrators and senior teachers are past or current coaches. Pioneer's principal was hired out of the teaching ranks not long ago, and it is easy to peg him as the coach he once was; but he's a vast improvement, some will tell me, over the "family dynasties" of male administrators who long ruled this place.

Both Jo and Jane have worked closely all year with their interdisciplinary house teams, Jo at the eighth-grade level and Jane at the seventh. Each team has slightly over 100 students, a daily planning period, its own meeting room, and lots of coordinated activities, including forays into what the teachers call "integrated interdisciplinary curriculum." Jo and Jane explain that Pioneer is really a middle school, not a junior high at all, that the transformation had taken root several years before they arrived here. "Other places are middle schools in name only," Jo once told me with a laugh;

"we're a middle school in every way *but* our name." Jane added that if Pioneer were a middle school, its initials would be "P.M.S.," and district administrators decided that was out of the question—what to do about those letters staring back from the wrestling mat, after all? "Yes," Jane insisted as I laughed in disbelief, "I'm *serious*." A senior faculty member tells me that city kids already call the place "Cowpie High," and "the P.M.S. thing, well, that just seemed too much to ask."

Pioneer Junior High looks as though it could withstand any tornado that might come its way, sturdily built after World War II and remodeled a couple of decades later. "Through these doors," reads a proud sign over the front entrance, "pass the finest students in the world." It is easy to see that lots of kids have passed here, but the inside of the building looks well maintained, most walls a clean white enamel, shiny red tile in the entry foyer, the floors well-swept beige linoleum or commercial berber. I note the usual tokens of school pride: a state citation for educational excellence, a modest glass case with various trophies, a display devoted to "Mud, Bugs, and Learning: Outdoor Education at Pioneer." This is a place that respects the past and looks to the future, striving, in the words of a school slogan, "to ensure quality learning today for tomorrow." The district mascot is the falcon, and a stuffed specimen is perched between the state and national flags that hang over the school's central stairway. Further down the hall, just beyond a big poster detailing "when to salute the flag," a smaller falcon stares lifelessly down the bustling corridor.

The secretary buzzes Jane, and a few moments later she greets me with a broad grin. We walk to the meeting room where Pioneer's two seventh-grade teams—designated "gold" and "red" after the school's colors—are finishing a combined meeting. The team room is windowless and cramped, but equipped with phone, computer, printer, coffee-maker, and a big square table. The only woman besides Jane is Amy, her student teaching mentor and key source of counsel over this past year. Jane has told me that they have become close friends, and Amy smiles as we are introduced, murmuring her eagerness to chat. Amy is in her early 30s, not much older than Jane. The others are all middle-aged men, most splitting their work between teaching and coaching—the school's wrestling coach, the track coach, the baseball coach, the football coach, and so on. Science, math, and social studies, their academic subjects, fade to the background; as the meeting winds down they banter about sports, their voices booming, their presences large and imposing. The two women are assigned to different teams, and I identify the men who meet daily with Jane, all of them wearing T-shirts boosting the school's athletic programs. Jane and Amy seem small and reserved by contrast, but they exchange knowing glances, and as Jane and I rush off, Amy squeezes my outstretched hand, her gaze warm and direct.

A GOOD PLACE TO BE

We find Jo hunched over a keyboard in the school's computer lab, and as she looks up a continuous tumble of talk and laughter begins. My brief tour of the school starts right here, a bright room crammed full of new machines, including a multimedia station where Jo and Jane produced a school literary magazine this spring, cheerfully ignoring warnings that the publication had failed many times before. They demonstrate writing software they use in their classes, programs that allow kids to make words into funny shapes or add drawings and photos. This is the most lavish school computing facility I have seen, and Jo and Jane say they are still learning about the instructional options it holds. Meanwhile, a computer-printed sign offers a stern note of caution: "If you think this equipment isn't expensive," it reads, "a new mouse roller ball costs $9."

The school library is also equipped with several new computers, but despite its CD encyclopedias and automated checkout system, it is a less impressive place. When Pioneer became a middle school 5 years ago, all the ninth-grade books were moved to the high school, leaving a skimpy collection that barely lines one wall. Jo and Jane say that the library is over-committed technologically while falling behind on book acquisitions. This worries them, especially since the nearest community library is inaccessible by local bus, and many of their kids cannot afford to buy books of their own. To make matters worse, their school librarian is grouchy with students. "There are two places where kids should feel absolutely safe," Jo says; "one's the counselor's office, and the other is the library." Jo and Jane regularly submit book requests, but they have meanwhile become garage-sale enthusiasts, accumulating small classroom collections, lugging in bean-bag chairs to make reading corners.

They are quick to point out that the cantankerous librarian is a real exception to the rule here. Pioneer is a good place to be, they say, the best of the Grant Wood schools as far as they can tell, the one with the finest facilities and most professional treatment of staff. The corridors seem spacious even during passing periods, the air quality good even on these warm days. Pioneer offers eager support and mentoring—in-services on authentic assessment and technology, individualized help from senior faculty members, lots of encouragement to try new things. "To risk creates the possibility of failure," reads a sign in Pioneer's school office; "Not to risk ensures it." It is a word that comes up often here: When I asked the superintendent why Jo and Jane were hired, his reply—"because they're willing to take a risk"—came without hesitation. He still brags about the program Jo's kids broadcast from the district's low-frequency station this year. Jo and Jane represent the kind of "fresh blood" the district needs for such projects—a radio station, maybe even television broadcasts one day. "In a nutshell," he added, "the district's philosophy is that 'we' is better than 'me.'"

The superintendent is especially proud of the new industrial arts facility that Jo and Jane show me next. Computer-driven work stations allow kids a host of high-tech opportunities—programing a lathe to carve a wax figure, telling a robot how to repair a model car, designing a water-management system for an imaginary town. To the superintendent, this is exciting "hands-on stuff—to give them a chance to see what a robot does. Pneumatics and hydraulics, all those things. For that age, with the hormones flowing, they need something to put their hands on, rather than the other person." Jo and Jane are glad for anything that engages kids, but as we walk through the facility their talk is mainly of the industrial arts teacher, how hard-working he is, how nice to everyone. He had to learn all this new technology from scratch, Jo says, a challenge even to this "techie kind of guy" who "learned as he went." They proudly show off the big tables their colleague built one weekend, just he and the superintendent with lumber and a few power tools.

Our tour ends upstairs in the teachers' lounge, one of the nicest I have ever seen—lots of space, a collection of round tables, a small kitchen, and two walls of windows that look out over grassy meadows and playing fields. There is light and air here, space to breathe. Jo and Jane say that the room is so inviting that most teachers and support staff eat here every day. I notice in the weeks to come that while the room is packed each noon hour, gender segregation is strictly observed, the male teachers and coaches boisterous in the center of the room, the women holding quieter conversations off to the side. Jo and Jane open their health-food lunches and settle to their accustomed habit: hurried talk about class, kids, and how things are going. They pause only to explain to me the meaning of the various acronyms they drop in from time to time, labels for various innovative efforts staff committees are trying this year.

Jo and Jane are full of enthusiasm for this place, but both admit to feeling tired and strained, to wondering where they will find the energy to start all over again next week. They don't say this to senior colleagues or administrators, but they confess it readily to one another. Two girls got into a fist-fight as they left Jo's class the other day; her colleagues have told her it wasn't her fault, that she should "take a shovel, dig a hole, and bury it," but she says now that it's still on her mind, and suddenly her smile is gone. Jane's eyes look tight as she talks about her struggles to connect with her male colleagues this year, the guys who sit now around a center table, talking loudly and gesturing expansively. She is glad for a chance to collaborate with Jo this summer, she says; they both are—they just need to move through the next few days and put the academic year behind them, to clear out a little space for fresh thoughts. They enjoy lots of opportunity here, and one of the key challenges is knowing how to manage it all.

ROOKIES

They grew up within a few blocks of one another, and their mothers, both teachers, were casual friends. For some reason Jo and Jane traveled in separate circles, and they find it a bit eerie that they are together now, several hundred miles from their childhood homes. They go way back, but their close friendship is something new, beginning when they went through the same teacher-preparation program and deepening over the last year. "This is a very interesting case you're dealing with here," Jane tells me. "It's weird. There's a purpose to things in life. And the fact that we're sitting here is bizarre." Readers will come to this chapter, Jo adds, and think "this is *so twisted*." Will people think I made their story up? "Exactly," Jo responds. "They will."

Jo and Jane both come from large families, and they often say that their new intimacy feels somehow familial. "Sometimes I just look at Jo and I think, 'we're like sisters, practically,'" Jane says. "I know, I know," Jo responds. "In a past life, maybe." To their male colleagues they are "the rookies," two young women with little experience, lots of enthusiasm, and backgrounds that set them apart from the school's old-guard traditions. Their connection is both emotional and pedagogic, a bond born of an appreciation of difference as well as the ease of similarity.

Jo

A life-size plywood likeness of Jo stands watch at the front of her classroom, a cartoon bubble captioned "Ms. Jamison sez . . ." bearing the day's announcements. The figure is easily recognizable—the artsy purple dress is something Jo might wear, the expressive face a perfect oval. But the hair beneath the beret is green, and kids often ask about that. She explains that the figure was created by her mom, who remembers a time when Jo dyed her light-brown hair green for a school play. Kids call the figure "Ms. J.," and there was much consternation when a boy accidentally broke off one of its upturned green shoes. "I made him write a letter of apology to my mother," Jo recalls with a smile.

Lots of mentors have come Jo's way, but she talks most eagerly about the influence of her mother, an artist and art educator. Jo has her sense of humor, her love of kids, her ability to connect with those in various kinds of trouble, and, beneath the surface whimsy, her steely strength. Jo has watched her mother teach and has even taught with her, a vacation Bible school class years ago. There are so many teachers in Jo's family that she always thought she would find another career, but those weeks beside her mom changed her mind, the two of them with a roomful of kids, making connections and having fun. "It was hilarious," Jo says now, but she also remembers it as a formative experience, her every collaborative relationship evocative of this first one. Jo and her student-teaching mentor often team-taught together, what they called "doing the dance," what Jo calls now a "beautiful movement." "She stepped into my mom's shoes in a lot of ways," Jo says; "they're very much alike." Their classroom collaboration recalled something she had known long before teacher training, something intuitive and natural, what she was seeking as she made the decision to work at a middle school.

Jo is in her mid-20s, just a year older than Jane, but she already knows a lot about who she is and who she will be. She married her college sweetheart 2 years ago, and says she'll always teach, although she also dreams of one day gathering the necessary credentials to take over the school's library. She already imagines the mural she and her mom would paint on the white walls near the entrance, images that would draw the eye and heart, inviting and welcoming. For now, she has plenty to balance—time for her husband and extended family, time for her new colleagues, time to plan instruction and help with Pioneer's drama program. Somehow she manages to find lots of time with Jane, too, whether in carpool chats, quick lunches, or on weekends and evenings. They try not to talk shop after hours, but there is so much to explore. "Okay," their conversations often begin, "I'll just say this *one* thing."

From the first moments of her interview, Jo knew that Pioneer would hold some challenges: She had no sooner walked in the door than one of the male teachers, now one of Jane's seventh-grade colleagues, asked Jo if she was married. She saw that the question crossed a legal line, but her response was tactful, her manner firm but friendly. Jo says she comes by her peacemaking ways naturally, having grown up a middle child in a large blended family. She worries about this a little, wonders if she sometimes smooths over conflicts when she needs to speak up. Her colleagues brush this aside: There are lots of strong personalities on her team, but they agree that Jo brings a fresh perspective and the talents of a born mediator. They have already named her next year's team leader, something else to juggle. "She's a keeper," her colleagues tell me again and again, "we knew it from the start."

Jo completed an internship at Pioneer as part of her teacher training, so she arrived last fall already knowing a bit about the school and its staff. She understood that male coaches hold a lot of power here, but she knew some of the strong women, too—Erma, the forceful social studies teacher who leads her team this year, and Pam, a language arts teacher who is Jo's official mentor. Several senior colleagues stepped forth when Pam went on maternity leave last fall, taking Jo under their wing and keeping watch. She and Pam talk periodically now, but the relationship is not as close as Jo expected, and her voice registers regret as she wonders why. For talk about language arts, she also has Amy, Jane's seventh-grade mentor. And, of course, she has Jane.

A prestigious high school was about to offer Jo a job when she got the call from Pioneer. Jane was hired the next day, cinching it for Jo. "That was a big factor," she admits. "I thought, how ideal!—that right hand next to me, and the same for her. I mean, a built-in support person with me. How could I go wrong?" Eager to explore the workshop pedagogies they learned about in teacher-education courses, they turned to one another for advice. Jo was drawn to the thematically guided activities described by Linda Rief (1992), Jane to Nanci Atwell's (1987) more open-ended approach, a difference that Jo sees as indicative of contrasts between their personalities. Still, they faced many of the same challenges: how to focus their brief "mini-lessons," and especially, how to help kids get accustomed to this rather different approach. Jo and Jane had lots of freedom to design their curricula as they wished, but no fully realized models, no precedent to build on. Jo looks forward to next year, when many of her eighth-graders will come fresh from Jane's seventh-grade class. "Jane's the one that trained them," she beams, "and they'll be all ready to go."

Jo also turns to Jane when she needs to talk about issues with kids. Often she brings concerns to her team as well, but she worries that "they're going to think I'm a wimp," or that her youth has a way of eliciting their "nail-'em-to-the-wall attitude." Sometimes the carpool seems "a safer environment to share those kinds of things," an easy place "to kind of unload, just to help each other through the bad days." Jane is in the same boat, wrestling with similar issues, another first-year teacher sometimes mistaken for one of the school's students. Both are a little "burnt out," Jo admits, needing more of a break than the next few days will provide. But without one another, she quickly adds, the past year would have been much harder.

An added challenge for Jo is managing the demands of Pioneer's fledgling drama program. Jo participated in various productions throughout high school and her undergraduate years at a small liberal-arts college. "These drama things sort of run in my family," she explains—there was the surprise belly-dancing skit her divorced parents did at her wedding ("here were these people with *no rhythm* . . ."), and then she learned as a senior in college that she too could "put together stuff that was pretty on target, pretty funny." She knows the fundamentals—how to build sets, how to operate stage lights and curtains, how to work with beginning actors and actresses. She is good at this sort of thing, and she and the kids have lots of fun. But Jo's talents are bringing extra pressure, extra time, more issues to talk through on those car rides home.

Jane

Jane's father is a college professor, her mother teaches high school, and her four older siblings have all gone on for advanced study. Hers is a family of highly focused academic stars, and while I think of Jane as both able and confident, she describes herself as a shy person of modest accomplishments. Jane is physically small, her features finely chiseled. While she has already found some firm places to stand, her mind remains open and a bit restless.

Jane spent an undergraduate year studying in Scotland, a time that helped her "to always look at things in a different light," to understand that instructional approaches are as different as learners' needs. Another shaping experience involved a struggle to learn high school French: Somehow she lost her stride, returning for further study only several years later, when her college English major demanded it. Jane was surprised to find that after all that time of "feeling like an idiot," suddenly it "clicked, like magic" during a summer intensive program. "It's something that teaches me that there are a lot of kids who, maybe I can't get them to see it, but they are *going* to see it," she explains. "Not everybody's going to be ready at the same time, and there's nothing like personal experience to teach you that."

Jane has often sought her parents' advice about her new professional life. She and her mom laugh now about Jane's first meeting with Amy, the night she called home, nearly in tears: How could it work?—how could she student teach under a woman who wears mini-skirts, fishnet stockings, and spike heels, who has such big hair? Jane soon learned that a kindred spirit rested behind the off-putting persona, and her weekend calls gradually turned to more lasting concerns. These days she talks about finding the right balance in her workshop classroom, about stepping back but not too far, about promoting a sense of student engagement while preserving teacherly authority. Jane looks even younger than her 24 years, so slight and soft-spoken that she seems a bit vulnerable. Her parents want Jane happy as well as successful, and they are glad for Jo's presence at Pioneer, someone to remind her that putting off lunch means going through the afternoon light-headed and shaky.

Jane knows that Pioneer is in many ways a good place to start out, but she thinks often of moving on. She would like to work in a more ethnically diverse setting, for one thing. And she is hungry to be part of a team that regularly plans interdisciplinary curricula and reflects together about teaching and learning. Her all-male team may not be what she hoped for or expected, but the men advise her about school procedures, what paperwork needs filing when, even take her class from time to time when she needs to be somewhere else. They have also taken an interest in Jane's car-insurance needs: "They *adore* Jane," Jo explains, "and that's something they can do."

"Here's a typical team meeting," Jane begins:

> After class I'd go drop off my stuff in the team room, and nobody would be in there yet. Everybody would take time to wind down a little bit. Every day Rob would have a call. So, we'd sit there, kind of talk for a while, wait for Rob. Normally, like I said, it's just the four guys and I'm in there with them. And Al is our team leader, a football kind of guy. With a deep voice. He's the team leader. He has all the information that we need for the day, usually. And after he's done, he'll usually say, "Does anyone have anything they want to talk about?" And so we do. And it's really laid back.

Why do Jane's female colleagues take her aside periodically and ask "how can you stand those guys?" "The guys on my team are pretty intimidating," she admits. "I felt a little frustrated at times." While she would love to see them talk about interdisciplinary curricula, her teammates have other interests. "Usually," she observes, "the talk does turn to sports. They're all coaches, and they all want to know what's going on." Jane is "pretty sure" that the guys are good teachers, "although they're pretty private. I don't talk to the men on my team about academics, about the theories of how to teach something. Period. That doesn't get discussed."

She has learned to hold her own amidst her team's rough-edged banter, although one recent incident warranted particularly close attention in her carpool talks with Jo. At a Monday-morning team meeting she mentioned seeing the AIDS quilt over the weekend. "Oh," said Rob, the colleague who had been trying to get her goat all year, "you are *so* cultural." Jane tensed as they began probing her feelings about homosexuality and made their own unanimously known. Jane stood firm, finally saying that on some issues they may just have to "agree to disagree." Later she would say to Jo that she could hardly believe she found the courage to be so direct. "I figured," she recalls, "that I had to live with myself."

Administrators thought her team needed a woman, Jane surmises, and she must have seemed like someone who could manage. Their meetings can be hard, but she is realizing that she indeed can. Jane says she never thought of herself as brilliant, but she does "get along with people pretty well." Increasingly, she finds that when would-be sympathizers ask about her team, the first thing out of her mouth is, "Oh, they're not all *that* bad." Jane is learning things:

> I've learned what real people are. Because university life is like a dream, and not a good dream all the time. I admire the way that they are. They're just real people. They don't have glamorous lives. They care about their families, they like to go play softball on the weekends, have a barbecue, drink some beer, watch the TV. This is life to much of America, and it's time I wake up and face it. And it's really taught me that they're good people beyond the racist or sexist comments that not all of them make, but some of them make. And I've had a real hard time being comfortable with the fact that I can like them.

They are "worlds apart" on most issues, but Jane has come to feel an unlikely bond with her team just the same. "Most days we genuinely look forward to seeing each other," she admits, "which is bizarre." Jane has tried to approach her team as another opportunity rather than a simple piece of bad luck. As she talks about her new colleagues, she is reminded of a summer job back in college:

> It was a bunch of guys. I was the only female there. And they were foul-mouthed, you know, drinking beer on the weekends, making comments about women. And I *liked* them. They were caring, kind people underneath all of that exterior. And they liked me—it was evident. We had a relationship at the end of the summer where we sent postcards, I visited, and my mom said some guy pulled up on a Harley one day at our house, knocked on the door, asked for me, and gave her a city hat for me. And it's the same kind of feeling I get with these guys. Yeah, there are things that we disagree on, but I feel fortunate.

Still, something is missing. "My collaboration with Jo is not comparable," Jane admits. "There is a different sense, I mean, Jo and I were trained together, we like to talk about learning styles, more general issues. Like, 'this worked well in my class today, have you tried it?' I've asked the guys maybe once or twice for advice on how to go about doing something, but very rarely." Even at the end of a long year, the chance to work with Jo was something she couldn't pass up. "We thought it would be fun, you know? Something to do. Insanity?"

PLANNING

The superintendent asked Jo to teach summer school when a fellow teacher opted out of two scheduled classes. One was a drama workshop, the other a musical production class, and Jo seemed a logical replacement. But it would mean lots of work—all morning in class for the whole month of June, with a big public performance at the end. Doing it alone seemed too much, but on a whim she asked Jane if she might be interested in team-teaching. "She said no right away," Jo recalls. Jane remembers thinking the whole thing crazy: "Me, in drama? Yeah, right. I wouldn't know what I'm doing."

But when Jo called to decline, the superintendent threw her for a loop. "He said, "'well, what if?'—and I totally was floored by this—but he said, 'what if I paid you $12 an hour and you and Jane did it together?'" It was several dollars less than the solo offer, but still more than either could make doing clerical work. "Well, that certainly changes things," Jo remembers saying. "I wrote it down on a little sheet of paper and walked into Jane's room in the middle of her class—I came in to her and said, 'Look at this! This really changes things!' And then she said . . .'" "I didn't say anything *then*," Jane interrupts. Instead, she talked to Al, her team leader and a known expert on district politics, who told her she would be crazy to snub this offer from the boss.

They had to decide within two days. "We said 'we'll do it,'" Jo remembers, "and then we didn't do *anything*." "We just ignored it," Jane adds. "We set it aside, on the back burner." They turned in grades on a Friday afternoon, then celebrated at a colleague's house, drinking beer and laughing around a bonfire. Jo stood up in church that Sunday, her voice trembling as she talked about the year and how glad she was to be a teacher, taking her husband's hand as she sat back down. Jane enjoyed a brief respite with family and her boyfriend, little more than a half day's breathing space. And then, finally, with just a day to go, they met in a deserted school workroom to think about the summer class.

They had received their class lists just a week earlier—twice as many students as anticipated, the superintendent's fourth-grade son among them. "It was last-minute planning," Jane admits. "I was not a fun person to be around until after we had that first week planned." But they grin broadly in the photos they snapped of one another that afternoon, holding my tape recorder aloft in the temporary stillness. By evening they had the first week's plans in order, largely icebreaker activities they remembered from summer camp, things that would help them get to know their students. The kids would have a "snowball" fight with crumpled pieces of white paper, unfolding them to find information about a classmate; act like cogs in a machine, moving in coordinated syncopation; sing "Jingle Bells" again and again, first as Elvis Presley, then as a high-society snob, then as a Valley girl. They talked about ways that one activity might build on the next, leading the drama kids toward an appreciation of what it means to be in character, the musical kids toward work on a production.

In a way, it was nice to have a concrete goal: end of June, high school auditorium, kids on stage, parents and friends in the tiered rows. But that was only 4 weeks off, and they were still undecided on the question of *what* would be performed. Jane recalls the moment when Jo hit on the idea: "'Well,' Jo said, 'let's write our *own* play.' And *Jane* said, 'you're insane! You're even more insane than I thought you were!' I'm just thinking, 'O God, I really don't want to waste my *entire* summer.'" Jo was remembering a graduation performance she and some classmates did back in college; first they developed a series of improvisations, then a script. "She had all this in her head," Jane recalls, "and I didn't know what the heck we were going to do. So that's why it seemed so overwhelming to me." But with the first week planned, things began to feel a little more secure. "We had a really successful planning period where things just fell together," Jane says. "It proves to me that our delivery may be different, but our teaching ideas are very close." "The more the merrier!" Jo exclaims. "Double whammies is what we are."

The week before, Jane had talked to one of Grant Wood's elementary librarians about getting a copy of "Cinderella" to use in the musical class. She sent over a familiar-looking volume, but also *Yei Shen* (Louie, 1982) and *Ash Pet* (Compton, 1994), Chinese and Appalachian versions of the story. "All I had said to her was that we would like a book of 'Cinderella,'" Jane says. "We wanted the original story to look at. That's all I said, and then Paula sends over these." "It was exactly what we wanted!" Jo adds. "We didn't even *know* what we wanted," Jane reminds her. "And then there it was, a gift to us, and the idea just went like that. From the minute we saw those books, it's like, 'of course.'" The play would be based on the Cinderella story, but the particulars would come from the kids.

WE'RE DOING THIS TOGETHER

This first day of summer school is humid and hot, but the kids who stream in from the bus stop show no signs of slowing down. Lots of impossibly skinny legs jutting out of colorful shorts, lots of out-of-proportion dark glasses and new sunburns. I wait in Jo's classroom while she and Jane round up the kids who have gone next door to the high school auditorium. They were to have met there all month, but the high school drama director nixed that plan at the last minute. They need to win her trust, and Jo takes on the role of ambassador and diplomat. For now they agree to use the performing arts facility only as they begin regular rehearsals, and only with the strict understanding, as Jo tells the kids again and again, "that it isn't a gym."

The principal comes looking for Jo and Jane, a burly, terse guy, yet another former coach. I explain that I was once their teacher, that I'm here now to watch them work together. "Well," he says, "you guys must have been doing something right." Then he notices something on Jo's wall, little pieces of the gummy stuff that attached last year's posters. He murmurs his concern that maybe it won't come off, then his relief that it does, referring to Jo as "she." He seems glad for Jo and Jane's presence, but a little distrustful of their youthful friskiness, not quite sure that they can be counted on to take proper care. I am reminded of the gamble this class is for them, another test, another chance to establish a reputation for reliability as well as innovation.

Kids meander uncertainly through the door, most considerably younger than the eighth-graders who ordinarily inhabit this room. Many seem visibly nervous, and only when Jo and Jane bustle in with another crowd does the tension lift. Everyone should wear a name tag, they explain, so that they can call the kids by their first names, and oh yes, they need this information sheet with everyone's bus number and the name of an emergency contact. An air of purpose fills the room, and then it is time to begin in earnest.

"We're doing this together!" Jo begins, grinning brightly. This is the first-hour drama class, and she talks about how they will help produce the musical at the end of June and put on their own brief performances, too. "There's something called one-acts," she says, "but you guys probably know about that." They engage in a bit of back-and-forthing, Jane adding details or inviting their input. Then the baton is passed and Jane takes the lead, asking what they know about rules. They generate a list: no horse-play, no food or drink in the auditorium (but it's okay here, Jo quickly adds), and no making fun. "With Ms. Jamison," Jane explains, gesturing toward Jo, "we'll have to do some stuff that's pretty wacko, that you wouldn't do just hanging around with your friends." They detail their system of warnings and time-outs, checking to make sure the kids understand, asking for their input. Jo and Jane are dressed in casual summer clothes, shorts and T-shirts that the kids might wear, and they seem more like camp counselors than teachers. By the time they ask the kids to leap to their feet and practice making funny faces, the tension has begun to ease.

The musical class finds Jo and Jane already warmed up, again shifting roles and responsibilities, this time with a heightened air of fun. They ask the kids to write down their favorite movie stars, places, and foods, then crumple up the sheet of paper and throw it at someone. "Ms. Jamison's been *bugging* me," Jane exclaims, "so I'm gonna get her!" These kids are really young, most just out of third grade, and they struggle to find their voices, their teachers nodding, smiling, praising. I am struck by how many say they long to go to Hollywood, "to see the stars." Again Jo and Jane talk of the need to respect one another: "Now say Ms. Clifton's been making fun," she begins; "how would that make other people feel, do you think?" Jane hangs her head in a show of mock remorse, muttering apologies. Then they order more face-scrunching and shoulder rolls: "Gotta do this!" Jo explains, "*every* performer does this. We're gonna get in the habit right now. It's a little like you're going out for track, 'cause acting can be real physical sometimes." They curl into little balls, then reach high, then run in place. "Ah," says Jane in mock distress, "I didn't know *running* would be involved." Jane keeps explaining that she was always afraid to look silly when she was a kid, and Jo promises they will all look silly together.

"Today was a really fun day," Jo says as the 2 hours come to a close, "did you all enjoy it?" As we walk the kids out to the bus stop, Jane whispers that she was really nervous this morning, but that she is already charmed by these kids. What makes it so good is that she and Jo are friends, Jane adds, their shared presence so natural. "Why are we playing all these games, having all this fun?" a kid asks. "Well," Jo replies, "it's *supposed* to be that way."

DANCING AGAIN

The first days pass, Jo and Jane balancing their continuing desire for summer-camp fun against a gathering sense of urgency. The musical kids will be putting on a performance in a scant few weeks, and the drama kids will help advertise, build sets, and work as stagehands. Jo and Jane are paid for a half-hour's planning time each day, a running joke as their afternoons together stretch into evenings. They drive to a costume shop, then make field-trip arrangements at a local theater, stopping at a hardware store for nails, lumber, paint. They want to keep parents informed about the month's activities, so there are letters to write, too. "Dear Parents," they begin,

Jane: We have just completed our first year of teaching language arts at Pioneer Junior High . . . and are very excited about spending the summer working on . . . We are very excited about um, spending the month of June exploring dramatics with your child. That's good.

Jo: Oooh-hoo-hoo.
Jane: We have a lot of good activities planned . . . um, which
    explore all aspects of theater.
Jo: Which explore . . .
Jane: Which um, look at the diverse aspects. Here [uses thesaurus]
    explore, explore, discover . . . um, expletive [laughs], investi-
    gate, research, inquire, search, which delve into, I love sayin'
    that. Which delve into the many aspects of theater. Um, colon,
    acting . . .
Jo: Scriptwriting.
Jane: . . . scriptwriting . . .
Jo: Makeup.
Jane: . . . makeup, props, and set production . . .
Jo: Lighting.
Jane: . . . lighting . . . publicity, and others . . . The focus of our,
    should we say, let's say the focus of our course or . . . we have
    that written down too, where we talk about goals [flips through
    papers] . . .
Jo: We hope to create an environment . . .
Jane: Where your son or . . .
Jo: All students feel comfortable experimenting.

Increasingly, they act as one, two minds working like the coordinated machine the kids enacted in one of their exercises. In class their ease and intimacy are even more apparent, as they pass off the lead role in whole-class activities, move among small groups, or take turns running down the hall to make hasty photocopies or phone calls. Some of the class activities are primarily Jane's, others Jo's, but they all bear the imprint of both. Together they imagine where they want the classes to go and how to get there: first trust-building and comfort, then risk-taking and creativity, finally closely cooperative work on the final production. From day one, Jo tells me, "I thought, we're doing that dancing thing, we're dancing again."

Early on in the drama class, Jo and Jane show videos of various television commercials, calling the kids' attention to props and setting as well as manipulative ploys. Then the kids imagine products ("Sun Soda," "Dr. Zuper," "Rocket Skis," "Too-Tall Taffy"), and write commercial scripts; first they are videotaped acting out their own; then, to test their degree of detail, the scripts are passed among groups. By week's end the kids have thought about advertising gimmicks, watched their own ideas move from imagination to production, encountered a motivating writing task, and sorted through some of the challenges of collaboration. Interspersed in all this are games designed to build confidence and community—pairs say tongue twisters faster and faster ("which is the witch that wished the wicked wish?") until someone goofs up, or groups perform charades (a McDonald's drive-through, building a campfire, a tornado) until someone guesses correctly.

Meanwhile, in the musical class small groups are drafting their own versions of the Cinderella story, and Jo and Jane circulate as they brainstorm, write, and sketch. "We have mice in our story!" one boy tells Jo; "*Lots of mice!*" seconds a teammate. They have cast Michael Jordan as the fairy godfather and decided on a stretch limo as a coach. The kids chime in one by one, each adding new details: Cindy, the story's main character, is cursed with mean stepsisters, including a particularly rotten one named Ethel who is forever telling her what to do. She's having a hard time finding something to wear to the prom, but then Michael makes her old dress "so much prettier." Jane remarks that Michael Jordan has studied ballet, evoking much giggling about appropriate costumes.

Another group is writing a script called "Stacey Goes to New York," in which a "nice," "sweet," "softhearted" Oklahoma girl gets a chance to attend the big-city concert of a rock star who happens to be named Prince. "He doesn't like New Yorkers," one of the kids explains, "so he's inviting Oklahoma." "Oklahoma?" Jo asks. "The whole state?—everybody? So he can check out the women?" The kids nod solemnly, then start in on the stepsisters, Bubelia and Bertha, who have lots of power around the house because the father and stepmom, Big Mama and Big Papa, like to go out of town.

They call a break, and Jane puts on a tape with snippets of various kinds of music. Jane talks briefly about how music affects a person, and how they will probably feel like moving around in different ways as they listen. "We're gonna do this," she says, kicking off her shoes, "because we're not afraid of looking silly." It begins with a peppy rock number, and the kids bop around like mops. Then a slow jazzy sax: "Awright, we're groovin' now," Jane murmurs. A bluesy guitar is next, Jo moving her hands like a cartoon Cleopatra. Then a symphony: Jo exclaims "pirouette!" and students twirl around, crashing into one another and nearby chairs. Jane gives permission to sleep through a soulful new-age instrumental, because she plans to. "What does it sound like?" Jo asks. "Dead dogs," says one student; "waves," says another; "wind," yet another. "Yeah," Jo says, "You *look* like the wind. This is kinda weird, but that's what creative people do—they act weird!" It ends with Jane playing the air guitar and kids forming a human chain, dancing around the room until the music ends and everybody collapses on the floor.

But serious work is going on here, too, something Jo and Jane realize again as they read through the kids' play sketches. Every group had good ideas, and the trick becomes how to work them all into a final script. Jo and Jane hit on an idea: While each group performs its sketch, the others will fill out checklists indicating what three things they liked best. When Jo and Jane sit down to write the script, they will incorporate something from each group, using the kids' preferences as guides. For now, Jane tells the kids that the groups' stories were "wonderful." "Ohh," adds Jo, "they were *wonderfully* creative!" Just halfway through the second week, the class has come together, everybody eager to toss out ideas, fun and hard work fast becoming one.

There are snags, as when Amelia, a moody fourth-grader, has a gradual falling-out with her group. Amelia has little taste for collaboration, and at first she feigns illness—a headache, perhaps the flu coming on—to beg off. Things come to a head as the small groups are writing their play sketches, and Amelia insists on ideas the rest of the group rejects. Suddenly she is gone from the room, and when Jane finds her crying in the hall, Amelia refuses to talk. Meanwhile, the group complains to Jo: Amelia won't cooperate, she's temperamental and difficult. The next day Jane takes them outside in the sweltering heat. "Now I understand you guys have been having some troubles," she begins. "Let's talk about it." "It was hard," Jane tells me later. "I'm not sure that they're going to be able to fix it today, but maybe they've learned something from being able to talk about it." The group comes back to class ready to participate, but Jo and Jane worry about Amelia and wonder how to play to her strengths.

Jo and Jane have their own moments of tension, too. One Friday Jane sits down to write yet another letter home to parents, and as Jo looks over her shoulder, offering repeated suggestions, they have what Jo describes as "our first tiff." They learned in the process "what *not* to do," Jo explains. "We got on each other's nerves," Jane admits. Jo says she has written lots of letters for "other jobs," so she can "just write one cold," but Jane tends to regard first attempts as drafts to be revised. "*I've* written lots of letters, too," Jane puts in. "But that was social," Jo responds. Jane, a bit coolly: "Not necessarily."

"It's like she's one of my sisters," Jo says. "She's transcended the friendship status, and she's like a family member now—we can bicker together and be grumpy together, and still have a lot of fun together. We both feel the absence of our sisters strongly—and missing them." They have known each other a long time, understand one another's histories, sat side by side in methods classes as they began to articulate their pedagogic visions. But if their bedrock beliefs are similar, their ways of enacting them are sometimes different, and this is a source of challenge as well as excitement.

Always the extrovert, Jo is nudged by Jane's reminders to watch and wait. Jo and Jane laugh as they remember how one morning a shy student told them of a game she knew, and Jane invited her to teach it to the group. Jo remembers "trying to interrupt, because she wasn't explaining it as *I* would have done." Jane gave her a swift look and pantomimed zipping one's lip. "I'm sure the student's explanation wasn't understood by a lot of kids," Jane allows, "and then I said, 'Is this what you were trying to say?'"

Jane is learning this summer, too. Next year she plans to use more games in class, to introduce lessons and to help students ease into working together. She suspects that she will never be as flamboyant as Jo, but Jane is considering ways to be a little bolder. Public relations is something that comes naturally for Jo, whether asking parents to supply daily treats for class, or letting her principal know when something unusually creative is going on in one of her classes. Jo tends to be noticed more, and especially in this male-dominated environment, Jane needs to help others see her strengths. On several occasions this summer her male colleagues stop by to say hello, sun-tanned men who lounge in the doorway, seeming singularly unimpressed as she talks about the summer classes. Jo accompanies Jane to their baseball games, helping her friend see the political mileage to be had.

"I'll tell a little anecdote," Jane begins. Just a few days ago they were leaving school, late as usual, when they saw Kent Yankovich, Grant Wood's superintendent:

> Jane: And we were at that stop sign just as you get onto Sixth Street. And he was there, and outside of his van he had this trailer hitch thing. He was standing there, obviously trying to get it to work. He was having car trouble, basically. And I pulled up and we go "Kirk!" you know, and . . .
>
> Jo: Kirk?
>
> Jane: Kent! (giggles). This is a continuing problem. Anyway, I said, "Kent, what are you doing?" and then he kind of looked and I said "do you need some help," and blahblahblah. So, anyway, we saw him. So then we turned left, we're driving along and Jo's like, "it's a good thing we saw him there." I'm like, "why, that he saw we stayed late?" And we cackled and I don't remember exactly what I said, something like "I don't think he thought about it." Something to the effect that Kent wouldn't have thought twice about the fact that we were there late. He's trying to fix his car!
>
> Jo: But in the back of his mind . . .

Jo has a weekend potluck at her apartment, inviting "professional friends, personal friends, family." "Well," she adds, "Jane sorta spans categories." Jane brings a colorful salad in a beautiful ceramic bowl, settling comfortably into conversations about food and old friends. But there are only 2 weeks left, and Kent the superintendent will be in the audience when the curtain lifts that final Thursday night. It will happen, they know that much, but for now they turn to the challenge of producing a script.

AUTHORING

They write the script on a laptop on loan from school, passing it back and forth as the afternoon stretches into night. Seated on separate couches in Jane's air-conditioned apartment, they strictly observe the ground rules they set after their tense letter-writing experience last week: no peering over one another's shoulders, no commenting on new text until the writer is ready to say it back, no interjecting suggestions while the other is still writing. They laugh now about last week's run-in, admitting that they were "quite irritated with each other." Their mutual trust made it possible to get openly mad, then to talk through sensible strategies for next time. Without that conflict and its resolution, Jane suspects, the scriptwriting "would have been a more harrowing experience," and she would have missed the implications for student work:

> We were nasty to each other that day, and it taught us that I could say "this is how I write," and Jo could say, "well, this is how *I* write." And you forget that you might need to say that. That is something that I really want to use in my classroom next year—to say, "Okay, everybody has these different kinds of writing." It's a perfect anecdote to share.

As they begin work on the script, they remind one another of the rules, then Jo summarizes the kids' preferences:

> Fairy godmother is a Michael Jordan–type figure and therefore the basketball equals the pumpkin, which turns into a sort of a coach. It turns into a limo. Then the famous glass slipper will be a sandal, and instead of going to a ball they're going to a rap concert, which will give us an avenue to put on a song, a rap song. Which is very easy, to write raps. And dance. We're going to invite the entire state of Oklahoma. Maybe not.

Jo and Jane had imagined a prairie Cinderella, but their students have set the story mostly in New York City. They face tough calls: Jo and Jane want the kids to feel ownership, but giving up their own preferences is hard, especially when it means a whole state at the rap concert and props for a luxury hotel suite.

In the end, they hammer out compromises. Cindy, a sweet, beleaguered Iowa girl, enters a radio contest and wins tickets to see the famous rap group, Braxton and the Boys, in New York City. When DJ Jazzy Joe calls to announce Cindy's good luck, her obnoxious stepsisters, Bunny, Bertha, and Blanche, proclaim themselves the real winners. The stepmother, Big Mama, is a little passive but not a bad person, and she ensures that Cindy is able to go along. Enter Michaela Jordan in a ballerina get-up, speaking lines the kids proposed and some new ones besides: "You wish it, I dish it!" "Abracadabra, Cindy was gypped, get her to the show lickety-split!" With a toss of a basketball, a stretch limo awaits. "Oh, my gosh," Cindy exclaims, "is that for *me*?" "Ready, waiting, and fit for a queen," Michaela responds. "But you don't quite look it yet. We need to get you some real threads." Another toss of the basketball and a collection of clothes flies on stage. "Cindy's no fool, she's got to look cool," Michaela chants, "whip up some duds from those leftover grubs!" Cindy appears in a new outfit, incredulous. "Wow!" she exclaims, "this is killer!" "There's one catch," Michaela warns. Cindy must leave the concert by 1:43 A.M. "This game *can't* go into overtime."

Bunny, Bertha, and Blanche have pocketed Cindy's backstage pass, but Braxton spots her at the concert and falls immediately in love. Then they just happen to bump into one another in an empty corridor after the show, and Cindy offers a helpful performance tip. "Wow," Braxton exclaims, "you really know your stuff. Are you a New York musician too?" "No," Cindy answers demurely, "I'm from Iowa. Besides, it was just a suggestion." Braxton invites Cindy to a private party, but the clock reads almost 1:43 A.M. and as she hustles offstage, the rap star in hot pursuit, she loses a sandal. "This isn't an ordinary groupie," a determined Braxton tells his assistant. "I'm goin' after her." True to his word, he shows up at Cindy's Iowa home, just as Bunny, Bertha, and Blanche are complaining to Big Mama that Braxton never showed up backstage, that he was "out all night looking for some dream girl." "Well I know of some pretty eligible girls *right here*," Bunny remarks, and the fateful knock is heard at the door. This is the last house on Braxton's list, and he looks dejected as the three stepsisters fight over the sandal. Then Braxton's assistant has an idea: "Didn't the station say they gave *four* tickets to each winner?" Big Mama starts to say "Well Cin . . . ," but Bunny slaps a hand over her mouth. Then a stray basketball rolls across the floor, the crucial clue. "If no one else lives here," Braxton inquires, "then where did *that* come from?" Enter Cindy: "Oh, sorry," she apologizes, "I was daydreaming and dropped my limo, I mean my basketball." Then, looking up, "Braxton!"

The task of scriptwriting spotlights not only Jo and Jane's working relationship, but the ones they have formed with students as well. Even as they incorporate key ideas from each group, Jo and Jane wrestle with the question of where and how to provide guidance. They think of the audience—an audience for them as well—and hope the kids will not be terribly disappointed that a few ideas were sidestepped: Cindy in a risqué red-satin halter top, controversial rap songs during set changes. Perhaps most notably, Jo and Jane assign parts. "I think we have to be real careful to let them know that these are decisions that *we* are going to make," Jane tells Jo, "because we aren't going to argue about this." With only one boy in the class, girls will play most of the male roles, something Jo and Jane have stressed from the beginning. They cast the moody, individualistic Amelia as Braxton the rap star, a pretty girl named Kelly as Cindy, but they save the stepsister roles for the most gregarious of the bunch. The other kids will fill in the rest—their only eighth-grader will be cast as Big Mama, a dancer as Michaela, and then there's the audience at the rap concert as well as the "boys" who will sing and dance with Braxton.

Sleep-deprived and a little nervous, Jo and Jane come to class the next day with photocopies in hand. "We tried to pool your ideas," Jo begins. "We don't want you to think that because we typed it, they aren't your ideas. We both said that we couldn't have come up with anything this great if we'd tried to just sit down and do it." They sound more open to negotiation than they did late last night: This is just a working document, they emphasize, adding that they were especially punchy when they wrote the ending, and role assignments are tentative, too. They invite the kids to provide suggestions in writing, and to talk to them privately if anyone is unhappy about a role. "None of this is etched in stone," Jo explains. "We want you to know that this is very much a team kinda thing." "It's not competition," Jane puts in. "Every part is important," Jo adds.

By Friday the script is in final form, complete with suggestions the kids have added (the nasty stepsisters get their just desert—a future spent baby-sitting Cindy and Braxton's unruly children). Chris, a gangly sixth-grader cast as Blanche, went home after she saw the initial script and wrote a rap lyric for the concert scene, entitled "Dreamgirl":

Girl, dream giiirrrl, girl, dream giiirrrl,
Lookin' far and wide
For my future bride
Girl I knew it was you when you tried on that shoe!
Girl, dream giiirrrl, girl, dream giiirrrl.

There's a full page of lyrics that Jane sets to music, using a background tape her boyfriend supplies. In the days ahead, Jane helps the kids choreograph a brief dance that has them leapfrogging over one another as they appear on stage. The rap becomes the play's centerpiece, and Jo and Jane will long remember the day when Chris shyly passed it their way. But it becomes harder and harder to remember where the other parts of the script originated—who wrote a particular line, which idea came from which group, what the kids proposed and what was added as Jo and Jane passed the laptop back and forth. This collaboration has blurred creative boundaries, and everyone is invested in both process and product. A hush descends as the kids do the first read-through, and when Jo and Jane call a break, the class insists on continuing. The room is filled with purposeful concentration, with the sense that everyone's energies are needed here.

Jo and Jane wonder what I am making of all this, what I might find to say about it to anyone else. It is, they keep reminding me, an ideal situation: two classes, around 30 kids total, all there by choice—and two teachers who have known each other from childhood, who share a common teaching philosophy, who have become close personal friends. They are able to collaborate so well largely because of this, they surmise—but, on the other hand, maybe this summer would have made or broken their relationship. "If we weren't friends before this," Jo suspects, "we would be friends now, because it's just very intense." "You have to be best friends or worst enemies," Jane adds with a smile. "That's right!" Jo responds. "One or the other! That's true enough."

TEN DAYS OF REHEARSAL

Jo and Jane walk the kids over to the high school's performing arts center in the steamy heat, ready to begin work in earnest. Beyond the glass doors is the cool foyer of the new theater, and we gather there briefly, Jo and Jane whispering instructions. Today the high school drama director will take them on a tour, and Jo and Jane remind the kids of the "no pop/ no snacks" regulation. This place is huge and luxurious, the stage trimmed in oak, the walls soft gray, the stage curtain burgundy velvet. The drama director notes that each of the cushioned mauve seats cost $200, stressing the importance of keeping everything "lovingly preserved for your younger brothers and sisters." She shows them how the surface of the stage can be removed to reveal an orchestra pit, points out the massive speaker system and glassed-in sound booth, how the lights suspended from huge ceiling bars can be used to create different effects. Most of the kids have been here for district assemblies, but today it takes on new significance. A collective hush marks this moment of transition, and the giggly fun of the first 2 weeks gives way to intensive work.

"You are the authors of this script," Jo says as she hands out final copies. "You guys should feel really proud. And because it's ours, we can decide how we wanna do it." But, she adds, "What we're dealing with at this point is 10 days of rehearsal," and the scripts should be "glued to their bodies." They do another read-through, a much smoother one, Jo and Jane whispering to each other, troubleshooting and comparing notes. They call the kids' attention to stage directions, occasionally explaining how the set will be designed, how actors will move on and off stage, where music will be added. Together they face the work of memorizing lines and much else besides—set design, costumes, choreographing, stage directions. Jo and Jane begin making lists of things to do and people to contact: Who has furniture, who can help with lighting or sound, who can provide costumes or set accessories. "Whoa," Jo exclaims at one point, "what if we had to do this alone?"

They expect help from everyone—colleagues, friends, most of all the kids—and they get it. Tattered furniture from the special-ed room becomes the luxury furnishings of a New York hotel suite; the drama kids make posters and paint background scenery; and parents loan materials for makeshift costumes. "You should see our cherubs!" Jo exclaims as I arrive late one morning. "They're coming to class in character!" Indeed, the stepsisters arrive elbowing one another, the concert audience dances, and Amelia struts down the aisles, her hair concealed under a backward baseball cap. Only Kelly proves a problematic choice: Slow to learn her lines, she remains wooden even after repeated queries from Jo and Jane: "Now what do you think Cindy might have been feeling at that moment? What facial expression or body language seems right? What tone of voice?" Jo and Jane worry that she is too pleased with her role, a little smug, not challenged to work hard like the others. When I announce to the class that I would like to talk with some students, Kelly is quick to come forth. "You'll want to interview me," she points out. "I *am* Cinderella, you know."

Jo and Jane lean on everyone, worrying later about pushing too hard. "You were a maniac today," Jane tells Jo after a particularly intense session; "*I* was a maniac yesterday, but *you* were a maniac today." Jo and Jane take turns walking the kids through their parts, giving suggestions on how they should position themselves, how to add gesture and feeling to their lines, how to move smoothly on and off stage. Sometimes they catch themselves telling kids different things, and they stand together, taking extra care to build on one another's comments. They have upped the ante: Two weeks ago the kids' every effort met with effusive praise, but now a halt-

ing run-through gets a qualified "Okay, pretty good, let's try it again."
"Ms. Clifton and I aren't gonna be quite as much fun as we have been," Jo
warns.

In interviews the kids acknowledge that they are working hard, but
emphasize the fun and learning too. A few note that having two teachers
giving instructions can be confusing now and then, but all stress that the
benefits far outweigh any drawbacks. "If we only had one of them," a student tells me, "it wouldn't be as fun, because they work together." "With
two of them," says another, "they can share their ideas, and just be smarter,
because there's two brains on everything." Many of the kids talk about the
efficiency of having two teachers on hand, allowing Jane to work with one
group and Jo with another: "They can take a group of people over to the
middle school like they did today," one girl observes, "and then have the
other people stay here and paint or something." The kids see Jo and Jane
bringing balance and complementarity, "different ways," "different points
of view," a good model of how to have an argument and wind up the richer
for it. They talk about learning to work with others, to "not be as quiet
and stuff," to speak up before a crowd. "You can't hide from them," one
shy girl explains, "because then they'll just say, 'come on, get in here,'
whatever."

Jane stands center stage, reminding Braxton to hug Cindy's sandal,
Cindy to put more feeling into her lines. "Too noisy backstage!" Jo hollers
from the sound booth. "Okay," Jane says to a group coming on. "Remember where you go? You'll go down by the couch—doesn't the band stay
behind the couch? Wait a minute, let's do that again, that's kinda screwy.
Band from the back door—where ya goin?" She supplies forgotten lines,
half-absently responding when a kid announces a trip to the restroom or
water fountain. Both she and Jo are more muscular in their nudging as the
days go by, ordering kids about, sometimes physically rearranging them
on stage. In idle moments the kids twirl and sing, still having a wonderful
time even as the performance date looms ever closer.

The kids begin rehearsing in costume—a sequined dance outfit for
Michaela Jordan, sunglasses and flannel shirts for Braxton and the boys,
Cindy's "killer threads" a conservative two-piece cotton-knit outfit more
evocative of a Lands End sale catalog than a New York rap concert. There
are lots of visitors these days, old friends that Jo or Jane greet with warm
hugs, their focus returning immediately to the kids. A childhood friend of
Jane's tells me that seeing all this is "bad" for her: She always wanted to be
a teacher, she says, and watching the rehearsal makes her realize what she
is missing, makes it harder to face the job she has. Despite the intensity of
these last days, Jo and Jane's enthusiasm is undeniably contagious. Everyone is needed, everyone swooped into the collaborative circle: Visitors are

probed for feedback, and day after day the drama kids lug over props and supplies, laughing in the sweltering heat and brushing off my offers of help. I wind up hammering so many nails and running so many errands that when Jo finds me sitting alone one morning, finally catching up on field-notes, she is momentarily concerned about my feelings: "Just because they don't need you this moment," she assures me, "doesn't mean that they won't need you later." Only when the superintendent stops by do Jo and Jane feel their pulses race, but this, too, passes, his applause hearty as the lights come up on yet another bumpy run-through.

As the first week of rehearsal ends, Jo tells the kids that they have "come a long, long way" and their growth is "astronomical." But there is still more to add—smoothing out the set changes, working with the drama kids to orchestrate the complex array of switches and ropes backstage. She and Jane insist that the kids practice their lines over the weekend. "I can't," says Big Mama, explaining that her family will be off on a car trip. "You must," Jo responds, not skipping a beat. "Take the script with you." As the kids leave, Jo and Jane go off campus to work, hungry, despite the suc-cesses of these first three weeks, to get away. This weekend Jo and Jane will take a bit of time to read, to talk to friends, to hang out. On Monday morning the kids will tell them they look tired and ask if anything is wrong, and Jo and Jane will once again pull one another into a new week, together finding laughter and balance for the final stretch.

RAP ON

It is the night of the big show, and the woman who pulls into the park-ing lot beside me could only be Jo's mom. Her white hair is cut short on one side and longer on the other, her earrings are purple hands, her dress a calf-length T-shirt tie-dyed all the colors of the rainbow, her oversized eyeglass frames hot pink. We chat about Jo—how nervous she is tonight, about her opening-night jitters when she performed in school plays, about how drama goes "way back" in their family—skits at family weddings, that sort of thing. "Oh, come on," Jo's mom told her tonight, "we've been through this so many times!" The line, the inflection, the smile: Jo all the way, could be Jo giving the kids one last pep talk even now.

Just ahead of us the superintendent pops out of his van along with his wife and younger child, all of them dressed for a casual family outing. He laughs and chats with other members of the audience about needed school repairs, rototilling, and vacations. Lots of these people know each other, and I am reminded that many of Jo and Jane's students this summer were teachers' kids. The crowd tonight is largely couples in their 40s, but there are a few grandparents, some younger brothers and sisters, and an enthusiastic crowd of Jo and Jane's friends. The drama kids stand beside the doors to the auditorium, handing out the programs they produced over at the computer lab, their nervousness incongruous beside all these relaxed and smiling grown-ups.

Finally Jo and Jane appear on stage. Jo tells me later that anxiety makes her talk too much, so Jane was appointed to go first. "Our faces are probably brand new to a number of you," she says to the hushed audience, "because we're first-year teachers here." She seems as poised as ever, they both do, but later they tell me their knees were shaking. They take turns explaining that their goal was to make the summer workshops as student-centered as possible, that they were more facilitators than teachers. Jo talks about how the play came to be written, how the kids suggested plot and even specific lines, that it was the process of putting this all together that really mattered more than the product, "the performance you'll see tonight." They thank a long list of people, all of us who carried supplies, gave feedback, or loaned facilities or props.

Then the show begins, the audience laughing uproariously at lines that never seemed funny before. Bunny picks up the phone, her voice rich with snottiness: "Hello, DJ Jazzy Joe?" Somewhere in the audience a friend of Jo and Jane's, a former disk jockey, cannot stop laughing at this, and giggling proves contagious. There is laughter at Michaela's ruffly, sparkling costume, a hot-pink sequined heart over her own; at the pumpkin turning into a stretch limousine; at Braxton, all long, sinewy legs, strutting like a mega star, then rocking out with Cindy; at the stepsisters, screeching as Cindy drags their luggage across stage ("What if the plane crashes?" "At least we'll die beautiful!"). The rough spots tonight are not the usual ones, the ones Jo and Jane targeted again and again during rehearsals. These snafus are new: Bertha and Cindy giggle uncontrollably through their lines; Michaela falls down during her grand entrance; Jo accidentally plays the sound of fireworks where she meant to put on an M.C. Hammer rap; Bunny appears at the rap concert in a blue satin robe, having forgotten to change after the hotel-room scene. Gone are the velcro-fastened sandals Cindy wore in rehearsals, replaced, much to Jo's horror, by oversized beige pumps. "Get those shoes off her!" Jo hisses over the headset, but Jane is busy backstage and does not hear. The show goes on, Braxton yanking off the shoe with grim determination, setting off another roar of laughter. The curtain descends on the final scene—but not quite far enough, and the audience studies the performers' fidgety feet, the beige pumps a real standout. Jo and Jane's principal misses the performance, but the next day he will tell anyone who asks that he "keeps hearing about it—that it was *funny*."

I arrive the next morning to find the auditorium stage cleanly swept, the furniture and flats gone, the drama kids standing around chatting on the empty floor. Jo and Jane are in the control booth, signing certificates for everyone ("Good 4 You"), and writing a letter to parents explaining that for $5 they can purchase a videotape of the performance, captured on film by the drama class. They came up with these notions at the last minute, in the car—and this time the letter home to parents will be scribbled and hastily photocopied, not thoughtfully composed and word-processed on Pioneer letterhead. Jo and Jane say that the superintendent keeps remarking, "Good job, ladies." "He's been very complimentary," Jane says.

The kids are winding down, too, saying good-byes and recounting last night's events, loading supplies into Jo and Jane's cars for the brief ride back to the junior high. Once there, they unpack and put away, an amicable army of practiced workers. Then Jo and Jane find a vacant classroom where they watch the performance video and eat treats the kids have brought—dense chocolate "mud" mousse with green-and-red gummy worms, huge sugar cookies, grab bags of candy. A little while later the musical students come in to watch the tape, too, a few expressing concern at their mistakes or the audience's unanticipated laughter. Jo and Jane are relaxed and positive, insisting again and again that the performance was just great. "Some of these snags you have to expect," Jo explains; "it's okay."

Mostly the kids find the tape extremely funny, from Jo's opening remark that this would be the "international debut" of the play. "Doesn't Ms. Clifton get to say anything?" one youngster asks, studying her teachers on the screen. Sure enough, Jane is staring at her feet as Jo rattles on, "kinda like Michaela, while she was waiting for Cindy to change clothes," another student remarks, and everyone laughs. Then, just as Jane makes a few closing remarks, the camera pans away. "Oh, great," Jane says as she watches this, evoking another explosion of laughter. Jo provides a running commentary while the tape continues to roll, mostly applauding and praising. The very things Jo and Jane would have leaned on vigorously a few days ago are occasion for relaxed reassurance now. As the two girls dissolve into nervous giggles, Jane says "that's my favorite part." Michaela falls down, and Jo observes with gentle sincerity, "That works so well!" There is a moment where the three stepsisters lean together in sync: "Now wait," Jo says to the group, "this is good." One girl's mom has said that the scene changes took too long, but Jo explains that most productions have people to do the acting and bigger crews to manage the stage. "You guys had to do both," she says, "which was amazing. It's okay that it took awhile." Braxton comes out and the kids laugh again. "Awright, this is so cool," Jo exclaims, "rap on, rappers!" The kids snap their fingers and clap, chanting along with the second verse. Finally they watch themselves taking a final bow. "A smashing success," Jane exclaims.

It is time for the certificates—"our own academy awards," Jo says, a star on each one "because you guys were *all* stars." "I can't believe what you pulled off in 4 weeks," she tells them. "Anything you can have in rehearsal for just 2 weeks—you guys should be so proud!" Each child goes to the front of the room to shake Jo's hand, then Jane's. Finally, they file out, hugging their teachers and each other, saying good-byes, reluctant to go. Jo and Jane bustle about, finishing off last-minute put-aways, impatient to be off. They hurry downstairs, fielding stray questions, giving yet another hug. "You know what my dad says?" one girl asks. "No, really—he says you guys don't look *old* enough to be teachers." One kid promises to write, others to take the class again. "Now this finally feels like the end of school!" Jane says as they hustle toward the door, waving to the group still lingering. "I'll miss these kids," Jo murmurs as they walk away, "but not today." They find their principal outside and exchange greetings, Jo and Jane telling him that he missed a great show. "I heard it was funny," he says yet again. Jane playfully taps his shoulder, then, as she and Jo walk off to the parking lot, she pauses. "I can't believe I just punched my principal," she says.

Finally they pack themselves into Jane's car, off to meet Jane's boyfriend and Jo's husband for a weekend away. We watch them drive off, down the curving road past the bus garage, onward to a break, upraised arms waving backward good-byes.

PARTINGS

Jo and Jane will be back at school in mid-August, and they have encouraged me to come talk to their colleagues and observe their regular classes. I am not expecting to hear from them until then, but at the end of July I get a call from Jane. Home for just a few days, she has received some bad news from Jo. Jane tells me that her "friend Amy" has been diagnosed with leukemia, that she will be in chemotherapy until the end of December and out for the year. The shakiness in Jane's voice throws me, as does the designation "friend," so I only slowly realize that she means her mentor and colleague. Amy is only 34, and her symptoms are not obviously acute—bleeding under her fingernails, fatigue, strange bruises. Jane is stunned, then stricken, letting only Jo see her fear and sadness. They will spend as much time as possible together during these last days of summer, counting all the ways that Amy has become part of who they are, telling stories that make them laugh and cry, assuring one another that it will all come out okay.

Jo and Jane still talk once the regular school year begins—in the car, on weekends, during the 15 minutes that their lunches overlap—but the pace is much faster, and they feel strange about going on, swept up in the blur of events while Amy fights infections and loses her hair. The teachers are taking turns doing short interdisciplinary courses, and Jane offers "Gender Issues," a workshop Amy introduced last year. Jane tells me about the day she had the kids read a play about a young guy going out for ballet. "If you don't get hurt and it doesn't make a lot of money," one boy remarked, "then what's the point?" I walk in one day as she is showing a segment of an Oprah show Amy taped last year. The focus is male teachers' sexist treatment of girls, and Oprah keeps acting puzzled, exclaiming that she never felt oppressed this way, "and I've been a girl my whole life!" Some of the boys in the class laugh derisively at this: "Oh yeah, right," one remarks, "and I thought you were a *boy*." Jane fastforwards the tape through a commercial, but not before the kids catch a glimpse of women office workers admiring a construction worker drinking Diet Coke. "You know what's sexist?" a boy comments. "That commercial." Jane is alone before the crowded classroom, thinking on her feet. These kids have to be here, and they test limits, posturing.

As the class clears out Jane wonders aloud how Amy would have handled the discussion, then suddenly stops. "Here I am living my life," she says heavily, "and look what Amy is going through." Jane has been visiting Amy often in the hospital, but she gets stuck for topics besides work—work, she says, or their health-food lunches, another familiar focus. Jane's days are full of abrupt transitions in and out of this dark pool of worry, and now, time for a team meeting, is one of them. As we stroll down the hall she tells me that the guys are sending Amy a card, but they don't talk much about her illness, don't seem to know quite what to say.

Al, Jane's team leader, keeps the meeting affable but businesslike, making sure Jane's concerns are heard in the press of deep male voices. Jane hands out written guidelines for the book reviews she requires in language arts, explaining that kids can write about books read for any of their classes. "Can I make a suggestion?" one asks—a hint, Jane tells me later, of their efforts to be more tactful this year. Maybe she should provide full instructions in her class, he says, so the rest of them can just issue reminders. Jane responds with calm matter-of-factness, but there is an undercurrent of mutually understood humor here. "Okay," she says as this discussion comes to a close, clasping her hands on the table, "what can I do for you guys?" After brief talk about an upcoming standardized test, the conversation turns to weekend trips and where to go for pizza before tonight's football game. As I leave, one of the guys calls out to me: "I'll tell you about Jane sometime!"

While Jane holds her own with understated humor, Jo plays the diplomat at her team's daily meetings. Jo, too, is something of a pedagogic oddball here: While a poster in Jo's room proclaims that "imagination is more important than information," her colleagues emphasize transmission and recall of facts. "We've just one year to get them ready for high school," says a senior woman on Jo's team, a challenge that she sees as a combination of imparting background knowledge and insisting on high standards of behavior. Here team meetings are frequently marked by tough talk about kids: "I talked to him in a way he could *understand*"; "We're not doing them a favor by stepping aside." One day someone raises concerns about all the kids who "can't seem to write a complete sentence," who "don't know about paragraphing." Jo describes how she addresses this sort of thing in her classes, and the others insist that they hang firm—"so they'll realize it's all of us, not just language arts," someone says.

When stern talk about kids becomes a kind of venting, Jo deftly changes the subject, never saying outright that this kind of thing bothers her. She emphasizes all that she has learned from them about the workings of the school, how she appreciates their generous support. Meanwhile, Jo's veteran teammates call the recent wave of new hires "the best thing that's ever happened to us." Here, for instance, is Erma, who has been at Pioneer longer than most anyone:

> It jacked the rest of us into thinking we may be old-timers, but we've got an awful lot to learn. They keep saying they learned a lot from us—well hopefully they have, hopefully we've given them shortcuts and taught them some tricks of the trade, but more importantly, I don't think they realize how much we've picked up from them—new ideas, innovative ideas, a feeling toward kids. Age has got to make a world of difference—when you're looking at a couple of 25-year-olds, you know, how much closer they are to the kids.

More than one senior colleague tells me that newcomers like Jo have been a "shot in the arm," a "reason to stay in teaching." Her meetings with her team may require perseverance and tact, but Jo is visibly warmed by their praise and lifted by their support. As with the kids in the summer classes, she knows she is needed here.

Near the school's front entrance is a display case with photographs of the faculty, and attentive observers note that Jo and Jane are wearing identical clothes. Jane tells me with a smile that she forgot to dress up that day, and so they swapped shirts and vests for a few hours. They scarcely see one another in a typical school day, and in the midst of this hectic time the photos are a marker, a reminder. The new year has brought unexpected strains and sorrows, but both describe themselves as more relaxed and confident, more fully a part of their teams. They remain close friends, sources of diverse and mutual support, but they agree that this time they are fully launched, active members of a whole faculty.

COME ON OVER

On occasion Jo and Jane look back at the summer's successes. They give a talk ("Two Rookies Collaborating") at a district staff meeting, then at a local university, then at a state language arts conference. It is always a smashing success, giving rise to a proliferation of student-authored Cinderellas in far-flung classrooms, but Jo and Jane have little time to dwell on past triumphs. Both are taking on added responsibilities in their separate worlds—Jo as leader of her team and drama director, Jane as a member of a schoolwide site-based management group. As the year stretches on, the summer seems distant, another time.

Jo and Jane enter the faculty lounge at different lunch periods, sitting down with circles of colleagues who come and go with the changing seasons. At first Jane has a hard time adjusting to Trudy, the long-term sub filling in for Amy. "She's okay," Jane tells me early on, "but I keep thinking, 'she's not Amy.'" Trudy sits munching Cheez-its, and Jane aches with memories of lunchtime conversations, all that talk with Amy about organic produce and tabouli recipes. But resistance to Trudy passes almost as quickly as her first impression of Amy, and soon they are using the lunch hour to talk shop and catch up on news. One day I watch as Trudy glances around the room, gesturing toward the table where Jane's male colleagues talk in booming voices. She jokes about trying some "gender integration." The others say that would be "risky," that gender segregation is "pretty pronounced" in the lounge. I ask what would happen if someone tried to cross boundaries. "You don't," comes the answer.

But just then Al calls across the room to Jane. She recently subscribed to a local newspaper, promising to pass the sports page along each day. Delivery has been unreliable, and she called the paper this morning to complain. "How'd it go?" Al wants to know. The room grows still. "Were you *professional*?" he asks. "What did they say?" Al leans back in his chair, arms stretched above his head, a big man with a big voice, smiling affably. "Come on over here," he says, and Jane rises so slowly from her seat, all eyes on her, that I wonder for a moment if she might be envisioning a scene from some old western. But this is no showdown, just a little something she has helped arrange, offering Al this friendly avenue of connection. This is a hard year for Jane and Al knows it. The sports page thing is an excuse to banter, to build a momentary bridge. They have a small conference, and both smile.

Back at the women's table, the talk turns to Amy. Someone saw a television show about death and dying last night and was suddenly overcome with anger. There is talk about friends who have died, of what, how long it took. Trudy recounts phoning her dad's apartment one day, an innocent call just to say hello; an ambulance attendant answered and told her that her father was dead. Someone else says she couldn't watch the program last night, couldn't bring herself to think about such things. But Jane tells them Amy is doing well, that she looked good when she visited school a few weeks ago. Not yet up to visiting when kids are present, she wears a wig anyway, just in case. She "didn't want to freak anybody out," Jane explains, and besides, "kids sometimes can be not so kind." Jane says the wig was gray, and it looked funny, since Amy's own hair was dark. "And she had nice hair," someone says.

The guys are talking so loudly—something about steroids—that the women lean in to hear one another. Then the men's talk turns to a recent sexual harassment settlement in L.A., how a woman at a law firm got $7 million. One of the guys calls out "come on, talk dirty to me!" to a passing woman. But someone else at the table says the woman's colleagues went too far, putting items in her breast pocket, that kind of thing. They shake their heads, then the buzzer sounds. Jo appears briefly in the lounge doorway, pointing impishly at Jane. She tugs at her vest, the same one they both wore in this year's school pictures, and their smiles hold private laughter.

A WIDER CIRCLE

Amy enjoys a brief period of remission, then come a lengthening series of setbacks and last-ditch efforts. A year away stretches into two, and finally she is in an isolation room, awaiting a second bone-marrow transplant. Jo and Jane bring her a series of Georgia O'Keeffe posters, colorful poppies and irises to enliven this room where real plants are not allowed. They chat over games of Monopoly, soothing her fears that this is taking too much of their time, demanding too long a distraction from the rest of their lives. Jo and Jane know how much she wanted to be back with the kids, back teaching again. They are upbeat and cheering, but they say privately that Amy's absence is an enduring sorrow, something that never quite heals. Jane gives the guys regular updates, trying to honor Amy and keep them informed, and most days she is matter-of-fact. Once she cries, the men falling into awkward silence. Another time, when a team meeting coincides with one of Amy's transplants, she asks for a moment of silence. "They couldn't believe I said that," Jane tells me later. Still, she speaks of her growing fondness for "the boys," especially Al. "He's just very special, very dear to me," Jane says, her voice full of tenderness. "Like a father."

Jo and Jane know that Amy is running out of chances, but still it comes as a jolt when their colleague Pam calls early one Friday to say that her remaining time can be counted in hours. Jo and Jane's principal meets them at Pioneer's front door that morning, offering assurance that substitutes are coming for anyone who would like to leave. But there is a slight delay, and they go for awhile to their classrooms. Jane gives her first-period class seat work, and sits looking out over the heads bowed over books and papers, sad for them, sad that they will never know Amy. Down the hall Jo has assigned seat work, too. She scans the room, her eyes resting on eighth-graders who were close to Amy. She wants to walk over and put her arms around them, to hold each one, and her sadness for now is focused on the fact that she cannot find the strength, at least not today. Like Amy, who longed to come back and teach, Jo and Jane are thinking first of the kids.

They go to the hospital with several colleagues from school, people who have known Amy since her first year at Pioneer. Pam is with them, the language arts teacher who has long been as close to Amy as Jo and Jane have become to one another. There is a wider circle, too, colleagues from social studies, art, special education. Amy squeezes back when Jo and Jane squeeze her hands, and they say they're here for her, for her family, too. Amy's friends and relatives are welcoming, and everyone waits. So much love in the room, Jo says later. It was 7½ hours, Jane tells me, Amy slipping slowly away. They all knew why they were there, but somehow when she was gone it was a surprise, a shock. Jane tried to go home but showed up later on Jo's doorstep. Jo's husband made tea and they stayed up talking.

Jo's house was a private beacon that night, but Pioneer, at least for now, is a more public home. "You know how great my school is," Jo tells me the next day. "We'll all be going through this together." Jo and Jane share an unusual bond, but both are open to the larger community, to the energy of a whole school moving together through loss. On Monday morning they will talk to their teams and lunch friends, and on Tuesday take separate turns at the microphone, reading poetry to the crowd assembled for Amy's memorial service. They understand one another with uncommon depth, but they turn as well to this wider network, letting colleagues see who they are, what they feel, what they have to offer. They will inherit possessions of Amy's—clothing, jewelry, books—and these become reminders of some-

thing bigger held in common. The memories of Amy that will become most
enduring are the times when she was, as Jane puts it, "so on your side,"
elated at a colleague's success, outraged at shabby treatment, saddened by
bad luck. Long after Amy's name fades from lunchroom conversation, Jo
will wear her colleague's old jacket to every performance of her drama
troupe. "Just wanted her with me tonight" she will say, patting the fabric
against her own arm, smiling again.

WE'RE VERY FORTUNATE

Pioneer is not a perfect place; the people here not always elegantly
matched. Sometimes Jo and Jane's colleagues are cranky, sometimes they
misfire, sometimes they have trouble crossing gulfs of difference or rising
above routinized ruts. Jo and Jane try to find where they fit, how they can
help, heartened to realize that their perspectives are increasingly heard.
They are here for each other, whether the occasion calls for advice on a
lesson plan or just a sympathetic ear, but theirs is not an exclusive relationship that fences others out. Jo and Jane try to approach their colleagues
much as they approached those two summer classes—knowing that a range
of ideas and gifts is needed, and accepting the human complexities that
inevitably attend such coming together. Collaboration like theirs has a way
of opening things up, sweeping in diverse talents and voices.

Jo and Jane are part of the bigger circle now, a circle that has helped
move them into full professional participation. New risks will be ventured,
new relationships forged, sometimes new friendships. They remain receptive to fresh opportunities, looking back on that summer together as an
instance of the kinds of learning communities they will work always to
create. They take care not to sit together at faculty meetings, and they trace
different paths at staff parties. Sometimes the storms that hit Pioneer do
not pull people together the way Amy's passing does; sometimes people
seem to be splintering apart, mumbling complaints in private meetings,
awash in resentment and mistrust. Jo and Jane rely on the diverse resources
their colleagues represent, but keep watch during troubled times, too.
Middle children from big families, they know about diplomacy and healing, how to repair broken ties. Connecting with difficult colleagues is a lot
like connecting with difficult kids, they find, requiring persistence, tact,
and an ability to listen.

Once in awhile connections are the deep and vital kind, the kind one
remembers for a lifetime. Maybe Jo and Jane are right, maybe their relationship is strangely rarefied, grounded in long acquaintance, shared beliefs, and crucial moments of mutual growth. In many ways, their work

that summer fulfilled the loftiest endorsements of teacher collaboration: "two brains on everything," as one of their kids put it, two teachers pulling together toward a common purpose. These two brains are enhanced by shared effort, but there is really more here, too. Jo and Jane can no longer trace the boundaries between their brains and hearts, their collegiality and friendship. In teaching together that summer, they modeled the sort of openness, energy, and trust that invites real conversation, real participation, real learning—not an easy thing to sustain in the daily grind of the school year, with its fragmented schedules, bureaucratic routines, and pressures to measure and rank. They know they cannot duplicate what they enjoyed over those weeks, but they try to carry a bit of it back to this bigger arena. The experience helped them grow in confidence, to become more attentive than ever to a varied array of colleagues, more accepting and persistent. This is largely because of who they are as people and as friends, but it also has something to do with the school they now play important roles in guiding and shaping.

Pioneer is a good place, they say, and it would be unfair to compare it too closely to that summer when hard work became such fun. Somehow the loss of Amy has thrown all this into sharper relief, but it has helped them understand the power of what they share together, too, this rare gift. "We're very fortunate," Jane says, her hand sweeping toward Jo. Her friend nods in accord, and their eyes shine.

Chapter 6

Moving On

Endorsements of teacher collaboration have become so commonplace that it seems we already understand what it is, what it can accomplish, and how to ensure its success. We forget a tradition that casts teaching as ruggedly autonomous, the effective few as self-sufficient as Natty Bumppo or Matt Dillon. Think of all those movies, from *Stand and Deliver* to *Dead Poets Society* (Ayers, 1996; Farber & Holm, 1994), all those news stories about teachers managing single-handed miracles. Solitary heroes appeal to the popular imagination for reasons that stretch beyond schools and teaching, into cultural values privileging self-reliance and personal accomplishment.

For all our talk about collaboration, we prepare new teachers in the same old individualistic ways, eventually certifying their capacity to function autonomously, lone adults in rooms full of kids. Teacher-preparation programs leave little time to explore the challenges of shared work or its potential for educational change (Perrone & Traver, 1996), and young teachers usually find still less opportunity for frank, searching talk with fellow adults in the public school workplace. Perhaps what is most remarkable is not the relative absence of collaboration among teachers, but the fact that it ever takes place at all.

The instances of collegiality described here represent a rather unfamiliar way of enacting careers in schools. Teaching has long been defined as transmitting information and learning as receiving it, both parties engaged in an essentially lonely, competitive enterprise. These notions are still very much with us, even as the professional-development literature touts the benefits of teacher collaboration and talk of "cooperative student learning" is pervasive. In practice, we are only slowly acknowledging that learning happens in and through relationships, by way of "instructional conversations" where teachers and students alike are engaged and mutually influenced (Chang-Wells & Wells, 1993, p. 85). Understanding collaborative teaching means understanding these relationships and their contexts, geographies both human and institutional.

Settings are particular and unique, and so too are the kinds of relationships they make possible. The word *collaboration* proves to be, as

Vygotsky (1986) said of all words, "a complex, mobile, protean phenom-enon," taking on new meanings in the institutional and relational situa-tions where people engage in shared activities and move toward new understandings (p. 245). I began with Judith Warren Little's (1990) defini-tion of "joint work": "interdependent professional activity involving con-scious structuring of time and task, as well as teacher leadership and ini-tiative" (p. 519). These words guided my selection of research sites, but they only begin to describe what I observed at the Self-Directed Learning Cen-ter (SDLC), Hamilton, Anspach, and Pioneer. Given all that makes them distinct, how can I characterize their connections? What do we talk about when we talk about "teacher collaboration" anyway?

COLLABORATION AND "PROFESSIONAL COMMUNITY"

Collaboration and *community*: two buzzwords traveling as a pair, talk about the former inevitably turning to the latter. The confounding confuses, especially since both words already mean different things to different people. What is a learning community, and how does one imagine its rela-tion to collaboration among teachers?

Discussions of educational community often begin with the distinc-tion between *Gemeinschaft* and *Gesellschaft* (imperfectly translated as "com-munity" and "society") posited by the 19th-century social theorist Tönnies (1887/1957). *Gemeinschaft* is the intimate connection of family members or citizens of small rural hamlets, marked by folk wisdom and a familial sense of roles and responsibilities. *Gesellschaft* is life in the public, commercial sphere, characterized by formal hierarchies, concern for public opinion, and norms of individualistic competition. Educators longing for a sense of car-ing connectedness find much to like in the notion of *Gemeinschaft*, some proposing that Tönnies's formulation become a guide to reconceiving schools (Sergiovanni, 1994). But Tönnies was describing not a set of well-bounded either-ors, but a continuum along which human confederations exist in a betwixt-and-between tension. As Merz and Furman (1997) point out, schools too occupy such a continuum, rendering talk of educational "communities" paradoxical and problematic.

Endorsements of teacher collaboration are informed by different values and goals, signaling conflicting notions of what close collegiality is or might do. Merz and Furman (1997) suggest that the common phrase "professional community" is a striking instance of such contradiction; for Tönnies, they argue, this would be an oxymoron, a "professional" life being tied up with *Gesellschaft* societal values (career advancement, making money), while "community" suggests the *Gemeinschaft* interdependence of a preindustrial farming town or involuntary blood ties. Recall, too, the oft-heard claims that "effective" schools are collaborative schools—the effective-schools literature highlighting measurable products, while collaborating teachers engage in an emotionally charged interpersonal process. Remember also the argument that schools must become more collaborative if they are to prepare students for the demands of workplace teamwork. Schools are to ensure economic competitiveness, this by the mechanism of people forging relationships: not an impossible combination, perhaps, but certainly riddled with tensions. Similar ironies surface in attempts to reform the evaluation of teaching with an eye to collaboration—the "peer coaching" movement (Joyce & Showers, 1982), and the National Board for Professional Teaching Standards, which seeks to identify a national cadre of elite teachers, partly for the purpose of establishing more collaborative school cultures (NBPTS, 1989).

We need systematic evidence that schools are doing their jobs, sensible ways to evaluate teachers' effectiveness and student achievement. But sometimes these concerns rest oddly beside Deweyan talk of democratic participation, or concern for promoting warm connection. For the tightly bonded teachers described here, the very idea of an individual career path would seem a little odd, let alone the notion that fostering economic competitiveness should be one of their prime goals. Endorsements of teacher collaboration keep one eye on the concerns of the marketplace, the other on the intimate rush of talk around a family dinner table—mixing desires as well as metaphors, and gesturing toward competing purposes and values.

In varying ways, each of these collaborations embodied something of the spirit of *Gemeinschaft*, certainly to a degree relatively uncommon in schools. These teachers engaged in small, closely connected working groups, but push far enough and we encounter borders and boundaries. Max and Bill's work at a small alternative school was enmeshed in a richly collaborative school culture, but the SDLC is increasingly at odds with district incentives to develop larger-scale, more cost-effective programs for at-risk students. Ada and Lou enjoyed a bond of friendship and shared values, giving one another courage to diverge from Hamilton High's long tradition of tracking. The Dynamos joined forces against a principal with a top-down management style, making the most of workdays beset by overcrowding and the demands of Anspach's new house system. Jo and Jane, though eager to work with a diverse network of colleagues, gathered courage and clarity through their early-career friendship. In each instance, teachers turned to one another, finding strength in numbers, and resources and resolve to face common challenges. In an ideal world, the network might stretch on indefinitely, mutual understanding and support limitless, rippling outward to encompass whole schools, school districts, municipalities, and so on. In this one, warmly bonded communities tend to be relatively small, intimate partnerships nestled within more impersonal institutions. As collaborating teachers look beyond their own circle, they often find themselves wondering how best to use their collective power—how to influence, how to resist, how to insist.

The place where spheres of influence meet is a political spot, and collegial communities have an important role to play there. If schools are increasingly *Gesellschaft* in nature, then a bit of *Gemeinschaft* might well provide needed balance (Merz & Furman, 1997). Each of these collaborations stood in contrast to existing norms, lending strength to stand firm and to propose new possibilities, different perspectives. These four collaborations provide a sense of mutual concern, but part of their goodness rests in a refusal to settle toward cozy complacency. The edges are charged, and while these teachers may not always experience perfect harmony among themselves, they have issues to address, stands best taken together. Their collaborations provide a way to talk back to the powers that be, bringing voices from the classroom into a still wider conversation.

COLLABORATION AS COMMON COURSES

Those advocating collaboration often cast it as a well-defined tool, something teachers everywhere can employ toward predictably efficacious ends. While the four collaborations described here could all be called productive, they are also dynamic and varied. How could one characterize these collaborations in ways that honor this variability and its relationship to the wider settings of school and community?

We have seen that talk of collaboration is laden with metaphor, mixing images of the marketplace and dinner table, corporations and families. Such metaphors are important windows onto tacit assumptions and values, our turns of phrase both signaling and shaping our ways of seeing (Lakoff & Johnson, 1980). That our metaphors for collaboration are paradoxical suggests that we hold conflicting beliefs about its nature and efficacy, too (DiPardo, 1997).

These cases suggest yet another metaphor for teacher collaboration, that of a *flowing stream*. Different streams hold certain things in common, but they are also shape-shifting and diverse, varied in terms of depth, width, speed, clarity, purity, and direction. Their course is shaped by the preexisting landscape, but streams can also chisel away at their surroundings, sweeping in new elements, overflowing their banks, transforming the context in large and small ways—usually slowly, starting as slow trickles, gaining force and direction over time. They are also remarkably fragile, vulnerable to a host of dangers, forces that can change the chemistry and direction in sometimes catastrophic ways.

The school landscape is professional and institutional, shaped by present urgencies and established traditions. And the stream is a human one, composed of people and efforts that change as a result of their mutual contact, contact that is itself in a continual process of transformation. These collaborations were ecological processes, instigated by well-defined initiative, but carrying on a less predictable existence than anyone could quite anticipate. Some were tributaries of a larger system—like Max and Bill at the SDLC, their work closely linked to the collaborative flow of a whole school, its banks charted by a school district concerned with instructional consistency and costs. Sometimes collaboration stood in turbulent opposition to the mainstream, as with Ada and Lou's "integrated" language arts course, their shared force a faint ripple, their influence sometimes felt as a kind of boat-rocking annoyance. At Anspach the banks were set by those who had restructured the school into its present house system, but here too was a provocative roughness, a collaboration that flowed through the system with a touch of impudence. Jo and Jane's collaboration was a kind of headwaters, a steady, purposeful current that found entrance into the larger movement of a whole faculty. For these two young teachers, as for Max and Bill, collaboration was both wide and deep, enriched by shared classrooms and school cultures that valued joint work. While these teachers' mutual loyalty was quite sturdy, their collaborations were more fragile, easily undermined by top-down directives or lack of time together. Even interventions intended to support their collaboration could all too easily obstruct the natural flow—as when the principal of Anspach Middle School presented sample goals to a skeptical faculty, or a district crisis team tried to help the SDLC's faculty manage grief.

For anyone who knows the force of moving water, these images suggest not only relationship, but also something of the countervailing forces that comprise the politics of public education. Various stakeholders come together in schools—as at Hamilton High, where parents, administrators, and teachers held conflicting beliefs about tracking, signaling different beliefs, too, about the value of ranking and sorting. Teacher collaboration carries a charge because schools are charged places, often mirroring conflicts in the wider society. This does not mean that teachers will always take the right stands, or that their joint work will somehow make political wrangling any easier to negotiate. Collaboration can, however, lend groups of teachers expanded influence, opening possibilities for airing a more balanced array of perspectives.

How can we judge the ultimate goodness of teachers' joint work, and provide supportive conditions? As we turn to these questions, it is wise to remember that collaboration will always mean particular things in particular places, and that fully realized answers are best charted on site. Fostering satisfying collaboration means attending to the complexities of relationships and schools—to basic questions regarding the depth and strength of human ties, and the role of underlying terrain in provoking speed or turbulence.

THE GOODNESS OF COLLABORATION

While these relationships supported worthy educational ends, collaborations can also founder, reinforcing bad habits or closed cliques, expending precious energy toward no useful purpose. Where group cohesion is carried to an unwise extreme, we find what Martin Buber (1965) called "collectivities" (p. 31), mindless confederations where individuality gives way to the will of a group. Togetherness can move us toward our better or baser selves, toward wider effects both good and bad.

These teachers maintained individual vision as they turned to colleagues, joining common enterprises with thoughtful deliberation. They emphasized that collaboration helped them better serve students, but they also spoke of how diminished they would be, both as people and as professionals, were it not for such satisfying company. If we conceive of teacher collaboration as an ecological process, we understand these virtues as influencing the wider terrain as well as what flows over and through. I turn here to three aspects of the goodness of these collaborations, benefits to individuals as well as collegial circles and schools—stimulating change, managing ambiguity, and promoting an ethic of care.

Stimulating Change

These teachers regarded their collaborations as personally transformative. They spoke of seeing themselves more clearly in relation to someone else, of recognizing in a colleague new directions for change and growth. Max and Bill at the SDLC pointed out that their differences might be best seen as *balance*, while each nudged the other toward greater internal balance, too—Max working to become more empathetic, Bill more persistent and frank. Over at Pioneer Junior High, Jo was learning from Jane's ability to listen and watch, while Jane was acquiring something of Jo's more extroverted, playful turn of spirit. These influences were reciprocal, born of continuing contact and mutual respect.

Collaborations helped these teachers toward more insightful reflection and trouble-shooting, too. As they wondered together about classroom events, they posed new questions as well as new strategies (Clift et al., 1992, 1995); in planning periods and hallway chats, a story of something gone awry could suddenly move into talk of possibilities, laying the groundwork for new and different narratives (Clandinin & Connelly, 1995; Clandinin, 1993). Lou came to Ada with frustration at a student who "just wanted an A," and within a few days they arrived not only at a clearer articulation of the issue, but a new plan of action as well. Even among the members of the Anspach Dynamo house, arguably the least intimate of these partnerships, teachers moved past frustration with resistant students and into new ways of framing concerns and responses. These were more than opportunities to think aloud about problems, as useful as that might be; in their more substantive conversations, these teachers established clearer understandings, new possibilities, and often new strategies.

Joint work can also present fresh possibilities for students. These teachers brought theory to life on multiple levels, practicing in their own professional lives the sorts of intellectual activities they hoped to promote in their classes. It has been pointed out that if we want learners to pursue collaborative reflection and debate, teachers must model such behavior, creating cultural environments that value and foster joint work (Kohn, 1996; Little 1993a; Maeroff, 1993; Meier, 1995; Sarason, 1972, 1990, 1971/1996; Tharp, 1993). If we want students to understand learning as a constructivist process (Clift et al., 1995), then we must display for them what it means to cooperate across boundaries of difference, to negotiate different constructions, to listen critically and find places to stand. Where teachers insist on being lone authorities, students are less likely to be moved to explore, risk, and argue. Not surprisingly, this benefit seemed to be most pronounced where students had a chance to observe their teachers collaborating, especially in the cases of Max and Bill at the SDLC and Jo and Jane at Pioneer.

The effects of these collaborations rippled into the wider contexts as well, stimulating the potential for larger-scale change in practice and values. Part of this rested in the sorts of conversations these teachers managed to start, touchy talk about kids at risk (SDLC), tracking (Hamilton), top-down management (Anspach), and gender equity (Pioneer). The very presence of debate and dissension raised the provocative possibility of shifts in focus and, perhaps eventually, in school policy and culture. Collaboration provided the strength that comes with numbers, encouraging argument about hard issues that might otherwise be set aside.

Sometimes these conversations spilled through doors, as in Ada and Lou's attempts to garner support for de-tracking, the Dynamo's parent-teacher conferences, or Jo and Jane's requests for support and supplies. Here, too, was potential for productive change, as collaborating teachers challenged traditional conceptions of educational boundaries.

Managing Ambiguity

Teaching is an ambiguous, uncertain business (Lortie, 1975; McDonald, 1992). Collaboration creates still more ambiguities, especially as it opens the possibility of new roles and responsibilities (Clift et al., 1992, 1995), but it can also function in ways that help teachers acknowledge and better manage the ambiguities of their work.

The issue of ambiguity figures prominently in psychologists' recent efforts to define a "post-formal-operations" level of adult development, what many are calling "wisdom" (Csikszentmihalyi & Rathunde, 1990; Kramer, 1983; Labouvie-Vief, 1982). In contrast to the well-defined sorts of problems commonly found on IQ tests, it is ill-structured, presenting "thorny" or "wicked" problems that are said to call up one's capacity for wisdom (Baltes & Smith, 1990; Kitchener & Brenner, 1990; Labouvie-Vief, 1990). The wise person is seen as possessing a complex, integrated grasp of the multiple dimensions of such problems (Labouvie-Vief, 1990)—as someone who, while knowledgeable, understands the relativity of all knowledge, and who therefore acts with a recognition of ambiguity and fallibility (Baltes & Smith, 1990; Birren & Fisher, 1990; Kitchener & Brenner, 1990). From a social-cultural perspective, such wisdom can be seen as jointly constructed, as people together confront the complexities and uncertainties of their environments, setting strategies and moving forward with an eye to ecological conditions (Hendricks-Lee & Yinger, 1995; Lee, 1993; Meachem, 1990).

These teachers suspended disbelief while they searched for potentially workable strategies, watching the wider landscape for clues and guides, sometimes just holding steady until conditions changed to make progress once again possible. Max and Bill's work at the SDLC was a particularly dramatic instance of this shared search for wisdom; in a school crisis with life-and-death implications, they studied the dynamics of classroom and school, working with the changing flow, always ready to alter their approach as the situation indicated (DiPardo, 1996). Ada and Lou also helped one another keep a sort of faith, moving with deliberate hopefulness through uncertainties in their classrooms, department, school, and community. The Dynamo team at Anspach Middle School awaited a day when they would enjoy better resources and more time; meanwhile, they together managed a trying situation, doing what they could to plant the seeds of change. Jo and Jane faced the uncertainties inherent in the first years of teaching, providing mutual support across a wide range of issues and occasions.

These teachers did not expect to resolve such problems completely or soon. The quest for certainties and solutions is imbued with the spirit of

Gesellschaft, a race for bragging rights where things go well and watertight defenses where they falter. These teachers were not afraid to admit to one another that what they were trying to accomplish was fraught with ambiguities that eluded their control. Together they moved forward, making adjustments as conditions warranted, helping one another read the local and wider terrain for signs and signals.

Promoting an Ethic of Care

Clearly the sorts of support these teachers gave one another were more than cognitive or pedagogic; clearly their relationships suggest that substantive collaboration can enlarge who we are as well as what we know. The intimacy of all this is challenging, they kept reminding me, "like a marriage." These collaborations were marked by interpersonal savvy, what a recent bestseller calls distributed "emotional intelligence" (Goleman, 1995). These partnerships both required and promoted an ethic of care (Gilligan, 1982; Noddings, 1992), an aspect of collaboration more easily described than measured. While it may not be the sort of thing that wins awards or finds its way into the administrative literature, this sense of interpersonal connection was a central part of what kept these partnerships vital.

Together these teachers wondered about the complexities of students' development, fretted over snags, pooled their resources in plotting helpful strategies. Students were the center, but they felt for one another, too, a care that existed for its own sake but also enhanced their efforts on the job. Sometimes this meant comfort in crisis, as in times of loss at the SDLC and Pioneer. But work in schools also involves lots of ordinary frustration—aggravating colleagues, misguided administrators, a class gone sour, inadequate material conditions, institutional rituals that interfere with learning. These teachers not only developed strategies and responses together, but also helped one another manage annoyances and stresses, providing friendship, laughter, a willingness to listen, and unwavering belief in a colleague's ability and goodness of spirit.

This sort of connection is hardly an inevitable consequence of people working together. Andy Hargreaves (1993) observes that a teacher's ethic of care can collide with an administrative "ethic of responsibility" emphasizing school improvement and professional obligation (following Gilligan, 1982). Hargreaves suggests that for teachers, caring about students is often intertwined with an aversion to intrusive administrative initiatives, including calls for increased collaboration. Top-down management can amplify desires for autonomy, and yet at Anspach Middle School, the most administratively controlled site of the four, teachers managed to combine concern for students and for one another. Here an ethic of care tended to discourage frank appraisal of differences, as teachers held back from discussions that might threaten their mutual loyalty. For Steve Rush and the other Anspach teachers, friendship seemed a necessary if not quite sufficient condition for collaboration; perhaps the rest would come, Steve hoped, through years of working together and deepening trust.

The caring aspect of these collaborations made them inherently satisfying, providing ample incentive to draw on one another's strengths and tolerate one another's weaknesses. In explaining how they had arrived at an ability to collaborate, teachers often referenced far-back experience and values acquired in childhood. Persistent habits of generosity and kindness characterized them as people as well as professionals, qualities not often mentioned in discussions of policy and school improvement. While we cannot mandate such modes of being, we can provide space and opportunity in which generative, caring connections might flourish.

SUPPORTING COLLABORATION

Like most people who work in schools, these teachers were concerned with local and immediate urgencies. Their collaborations were local and immediate as well, shaped by issues in classrooms, departments, and schools. What was good or successful in their partnerships rested in particularities and school ecologies, and so too did constraints and impediments. If collaborations are like flowing streams—dynamically changing, both shaping and being shaped by local settings—then "supporting teacher collaboration" requires a keen appreciation of the place and time in which a partnership is situated.

While they cannot be understood as separate elements or duplicated in cookbook fashion, these relationships suggest a few general guides for schools hoping to encourage fruitful collaboration among teachers. These can be seen as necessary but not sufficient conditions, starting points for strategies to be developed on the varied ground of classrooms and schools.

Have Good Reasons to Collaborate and Make Them Explicit

These teachers carried out various tasks together—planning subject-based or interdisciplinary curricula, buying supplies, addressing behavioral problems, managing field trips, and providing support in times of crisis. Consensus on goals and projects was hammered out most comprehensively at the SDLC, a small school with ample opportunity for contact and discussion. At the larger schools with less collaborative leadership, collectively owned reasons tended to be a bit more elusive. Many teachers at Anspach Middle School, for instance, regarded the move to interdisciplinary "house" teams as a symptom of higher-ups' hunger for awards and notoriety, what Andy Hargreaves (1993, 1994) calls "contrived collegiality." Over at Pioneer teachers had helped guide a less contentious shift to a middle-school model; but here, too, house teams tended to focus on logistics, setting aside the stickier challenge of co-planning instruction or exploring student learning. Caught in the press of daily demands, they found little opportunity to consider the possibilities of their joint work. How different it was that summer for Jo and Jane, with their looming deadline, firm commitment to students, and their own reputations on the line: pressure, yes, but a source of focus and purpose, too.

In the absence of thoughtful, clearly articulated purposes, collegial conversation can become unfocused, defensive, even factionalized or petty. Identifying purposes that go beyond nice-sounding slogans requires opportunity to reflect together, to honor the mysteries of teaching and learning, and to acknowledge the complexity of providing classroom environments that truly challenge and nurture all. It is a process that requires lots of talk, facilitative leadership, and patient exploration of what really matters.

Give Teachers a Real Say

Many of the teachers I followed emphasized that while the opportunity to collaborate is a necessary starting point, commitment must be voluntary, including freedom to formulate priorities and projects. Teachers inevitably find ways to avoid or dilute changes mandated from above (Sarason, 1971/1996; Tyack & Cuban, 1995). Where collaboration is instituted and guided by administrators, an essentially foreign culture may be introduced that undercuts teachers' attempts to fulfill their individual and collective goals (Cooper, 1988). Members of the Dynamo team often spoke of the move to a house system in this spirit, of missing their discipline-based departments and resisting administrative pressure to develop interdisciplinary curricula. "Have I grown?" asked Judy, the Dynamo's social studies teacher. "Yes, but I've also regressed."

The most full-bodied collaborations I observed were all freely chosen, self-monitored, and rich in human ways that must be supported but cannot be forced. Where teachers assume authority over their joint work and share in school decision making, conditions are set for the kind of open exchange Bill described at the SDLC: "We're not going to put in hours deciding something, give it to an administrator, and have it come down the pipe the exact opposite. We know that when we decide something, that's what we're going to do." Such knowledge is energizing, encouraging teachers' most spirited work and promoting a sense of mutual responsibility across whole schools.

Even the wisest teachers will sometimes choose to avoid collaboration altogether (Hargreaves, 1993, 1994). The possible reasons are not hard to imagine—incompatible colleagues, overwork, pressure to participate in ill-conceived efforts. It is important to realize that collaboration may not be the most attractive course all the time, and to promote an attitude of acceptance toward those who elect, perhaps even just now and then, to interact primarily with their students. The teachers I followed pointed out again and again that collaboration is like any other close relationship: Sometimes it hums along nicely for years at a stretch, sometimes it ruptures, and sometimes the key parties just need a little restorative time alone. This, too, should be approached with sensitivity and tact, and with a clear understanding that autonomy is not always such a bad thing.

Promote an Atmosphere of Interpersonal Safety and Trust

This concern is closely related to the kinds of tasks teachers will be ready to undertake together—some demanding a great deal of established trust, others providing less risky opportunities to get acquainted. If collaborative engagement is to deepen, so too must a sense of interpersonal safety.

For starters, collaboration should be kept separate from formal evaluation: As the SDLC's Max explained, people have trouble entering freely into such relationships where they fear "getting chopped." Virtually every teacher I interviewed made this point, grimacing as I described much-touted programs of peer evaluation or peer coaching (Joyce & Showers, 1982; critiqued by Hargreaves, 1994; and by Lytle & Fecho, 1991). Most teachers make this link in their minds, anyway, having long associated the presence of a fellow educator with supervision. Evaluation often proceeds as though effects can be readily traced to their causes, as though teachers alone are fully responsible for students' successes and failures. Frank attention to the complexities of teaching and learning requires the sort of interpersonal trust that is built over time—witness Max and Bill, Ada and Lou, and Jo and Jane. More typical, perhaps, are cautious teams like the Dynamos, who spoke of their 2 years together as a brief and harried time— a start, but just a start. One surefire way to bring trust-building to a halt would be to link the Dynamo's collaboration to administratively mandated evaluation, forcing them to confront their differences on someone else's timetable.

This is not to deny that disagreement plays a crucial role in collaboration (Little, 1990). Where trust is firmly established, conflict is often a key feature of joint work, evidence that multiple energies are fully engaged, together generating better ideas than any one person could alone. This was most emphatically the case at the SDLC, where conflict was widely regarded as key not only to teachers' professional development, but to student learning as well. Multiple teachers may be better for students than one alone, but only if collegial bonds are sufficiently strong to bear a bit of testing. Building relationships that can withstand conflict requires persistence, commitment, and the understanding that collaboration is equal parts participation and receptivity.

Personal contrasts were often a source of stimulation to these teachers, but differences can also be difficult to negotiate, especially where a partnership has not been freely chosen. While Jane was able to address her male colleagues with considerable aplomb, many young women might find the gender issues at Pioneer Junior High impossibly difficult. Recall, too, the 10th-grade book-buying team at Hamilton High, a committee of teachers pulled together by mandate, their noon meetings rushed and tense. Where a partnership is inescapable, teachers may feel less willing to address conflict in the forthright manner of Max and Bill—who had chosen to work together, wished to continue, and faced conflict squarely and constructively.

Because collaborating teachers are often breaking new pedagogic ground, they confront the risk of instructional failures as well. Many school districts proclaim their commitment to risk-taking, but building school cultures that truly promote it is another matter. Intent on retaining a reputation for excellence, Hamilton High tended to resist even modest and well-informed efforts at change; and despite its recent reorganization, Anspach remained a place of administrative control, even as united teams of teachers were mounting a growing challenge. Change can be scary, especially for schools with much to lose; conversely, the SDLC, an often stigmatized place of last resort, was also a school culture with an uncommon openness to risk-taking and tolerance for setbacks. In schools where frank, searching conversation runs freely, staff can more readily identify the kinds of risks they are willing to assume, and work cooperatively to minimize dangers.

Provide Adequate Time

While these teachers agree that substantive collaboration is impossible where schools fail to provide adequate time, their situations complicate the issue of adequacy. As Bird and Little (1986) attest, collaboration takes time on multiple levels: time for teachers to reflect on their practices, time for interactions among administrators and teachers, and time for whole faculties to explore schoolwide norms of collegiality and instruction. As noted earlier, administrators and teachers may define "making use of time" rather differently, the former imagining flow charts, the latter the multiple, simultaneous demands of students and relationships (Hargreaves, 1994).

What it means to have "enough" time for collaboration is a relative question, inevitably entwined in the concerns discussed above. Available time can be used in a focused, efficient manner where teachers have clear reasons for their joint work, and feel empowered and safe. Having had many lengthy, often contentious conversations in the past, having moved together through a host of school crises, Max and Bill found that their well-established relationship allowed a mumbled phrase or two to serve as useful communication. They had a clear understanding of what they were trying to do together and how it fit into a bigger picture; and while this, too, was always open for reevaluation, these were not dangerously new discussions. The Dynamo team, on the other hand, was still testing the waters, still steering clear of differences that might disrupt their new-found solidarity, and needed considerably more time than their every-other-day planning period—not only to talk about kids and coordinate curricula, but to explore one another's thinking, to establish the sort of trust that makes open disagreement possible, and to find ways to lobby for a substantially reduced student load.

When administrators speak of giving teachers time to collaborate, they usually mean meeting time, such as the Dynamo's every-other-day planning period, or the daily gatherings at Pioneer and Hamilton. Less seldom addressed are issues such as how long teams have been together, or alternative ways of spending time—if teachers have had a chance to visit one another's classrooms or team-teach, gone away to conferences or retreats, engaged in a range of substantive and mutually agreeable tasks, or had a chance to explore new scheduling options (Maeroff, 1993). A daily meeting time means little if teachers are perennially overloaded with too many students, excessive administrative demands, inadequate resources, or the challenge of juggling multiple attempts at reform. As Ada put it, teachers need "to be respected as professionals. And they need professional time— they should have *relaxed* time, not this *hectic* time."

Adjust Expectations to Fit the Situation

Max and Bill worked in a small school with a rich tradition of collaboration; Jo and Jane had known one another for years, sharing a sisterly sort of intimacy. These were people who could disagree without seeming unduly disagreeable, and their workplace contexts offered support and opportunity. All the conditions were right for collaboration that took risks, that ventured far, that eventually swept other colleagues into the flow. It would be unfair to compare their situations with the collegial landscapes of Anspach and Hamilton, to expect similar scenarios wherever teachers describe their work as collaborative. Ada and Lou were lucky to wedge in a half-hour's chat on days when chores and distractions could be held at bay. And Anspach's principal was right about the Dynamos' having "some growing to do"—but how much growing could be expected of teachers with their student load, their short and harried time together?

Collaborations cannot be evaluated as if all are situated on the same ground, nor can we expect to transplant programs across sites. What we can do is create promising conditions, and encourage teachers to explore what might work for them, what is possible here and now. A modest start, even if it stays modest for months or even years, might just be a beginning, like Ada and Lou's provocative experiment in de-tracking. Rapid changes come and go in schools, but little trickles sometimes turn ever so gradually into big rippling streams, carving the landscape in ways not so easily denied.

CONTINUING STORIES

Schools are beset by lots of forces and counterforces, and while collaborations hold power, one never really knows which current will prove stronger in the end. As this project comes to a close, the SDLC's future is much in doubt, its school district facing lean times and a need to cut programs. Central administration is reevaluating the role of the school, insisting that it develop curricula and procedures more consistent with districtwide practice. Teachers are still imagining new classes and activities together, but they say that the old days of trust and freedom are gone, a testimony to the fragility of even vibrantly collaborative school cultures.

Meanwhile, Ada and Lou are witnessing a slow erosion of Hamilton's tracking system. In addition to the unleveled courses they continue to offer each term, Ada and Lou have developed several new courses that also appeal to students with a wide range of backgrounds and interests. Several members of the department have retired since my time at Hamilton, and new, younger colleagues are teaching their own sections of the "integrated" course.

Anspach Middle School's principal has taken a job elsewhere, a post better suited to her talents and interests. The school is now led by a collaborative principalship composed of former teachers who share leadership duties. "They work hard as a team, are open, and spend hours with kids and parents," Steve tells me. "It doesn't get any better than this." A bond measure finally passed after teachers convinced community members to campaign door-to-door, and with their student load down to around 145, the Dynamos have begun developing interdisciplinary units. On most days they call themselves happy, and their school a much better place to teach and learn.

Jane has moved on, joining a collaborative seventh-grade team at a middle school near a major urban center. Jo has stayed at Pioneer, where she continues to assume local and state leadership roles, attending library science school in the evenings, still imagining murals beckoning kids to come browse a growing book collection. Both are doing well personally and professionally, weathering storms with sturdy persistence. They remain long-distance friends, but they miss the day-to-day contact, knowing they have lost something precious and rare.

The loss of a treasured colleague is ample cause for sadness, but like these others, Jo and Jane have developed a knack as well as a hunger for close partnerships. Each of these partnerships will be memorable for the people involved, but none will be their last. A teacher's work may be more commonly imagined in singular terms, but for these people a full professional life has everything to do with satisfying company. They may find its beginnings now and then, but like all of us, they will ultimately have to help create it, drawing on resources both individual and institutional, both pedagogic and emotional. These teachers have learned that opportunities are always out there, as long as one watches for the right people, places, and times. A loss here becomes an increase there, new common courses, people who help us work better, be better, and find our ways.

References

Applebee, A. N. (1974). *Tradition and reform in the teaching of English*. Urbana, IL: National Council of Teachers of English.

Applebee, A. N., & Langer, J. A. (1983). Instructional scaffolding: Reading and writing as natural language activities. *Language Arts, 60*, 168–175.

Ashton, P., & Webb, R. (1986). *Making a difference: Teachers' sense of efficacy and student achievement*. New York: Longman.

Atwell, N. (1987). *In the middle*. Portsmouth, NH: Heinemann.

Ayers, W. (1996). A teacher ain't nothing but a hero: Teachers and teaching in film. In W. Ayers & P. Ford (Eds.), *City kids, city teachers: Reports from the front row* (pp. 228–240). New York: The New Press.

Bakhtin, M. M. (1981). *The dialogic imagination: Four essays by M. M. Bakhtin* (M. Holquist, Ed., C. Emerson & M. Holquist, Trans.). Austin: University of Texas Press.

Bakhtin, M. M. (1986). *Speech genres and other late essays* (C. Emerson & M. Holquist, Ed., V. W. McGee, Trans.). Austin: University of Texas Press.

Baltes, P., & Smith, J. (1990). Toward a psychology of wisdom and its ontogenesis. In R. J. Sternberg (Ed.), *Wisdom: Its nature, origins, and development* (pp. 87–120). Cambridge: Cambridge University Press.

Bellah, R., Madsen, R., Sullivan, W., Swidler, A., & Tipton, S. (1985). *Habits of the heart: Individualism and commitment in American life*. New York: Harper & Row.

Bellah, R., Madsen, R., Sullivan, W., Swidler, A., & Tipton, S. (1991). *The good society*. New York: Vintage.

Bird, T., & Little, J. W. (1986). How schools organize the teaching occupation. *The Elementary School Journal, 86*, 493–511.

Birren, J., & Fisher, L. (1990). The elements of wisdom: Overview and integration. In R. J. Sternberg (Ed.), *Wisdom: Its nature, origins, and development* (pp. 317–332). Cambridge: Cambridge University Press.

Bogdan, R. C., & Biklen, S. K. (1982). *Qualitative research for education: An introduction to theory and methods*. Boston: Allyn & Bacon.

Bowles, S., & Gintis, H. (1976). *Schooling in capitalist America*. New York: Basic Books.

Brown, J. S., Collins, A., & Duguid, P. (1989). Situated cognition and the culture of learning. *Educational Researcher, 18*(1), 32–42.

Bruner, J. (1978). The role of dialogue in language acquisition. In A. Sinclair (Ed.), *The child's conception of language* (pp. 243–256). New York: Springer-Verlag.

Bruner, J. (1986). *Actual minds, possible worlds*. Cambridge, MA: Harvard University Press.

Bruner, J. (1990). *Acts of meaning*. Cambridge, MA: Harvard University Press.

Buber, M. (1965). *Between man and man*. New York: Macmillan.

Carnegie Council on Adolescent Development. (1989). *Turning points: Preparing American youth for the 21st century*. New York: Carnegie Corporation.

Cazden, C. (1988). *Classroom discourse: The language of teaching and learning*. Portsmouth, NH: Heinemann.

Cazden, C. (in press). Selective traditions: Readings of Vygotsky in writing pedagogy. In D. Hicks (Ed.), *Child discourse and social learning: An interdisciplinary perspective*. Cambridge: Cambridge University Press.

Chang-Wells, G., & Wells, G. (1993). Dynamics of discourse: Literacy and the construction of knowledge. In E. A. Forman, N. Minnick, & C. A. Stone (Eds.), *Contexts for learning: Sociocultural dynamics in children's development* (pp. 58–90). New York: Oxford University Press.

Clandinin, D. J. (1993). Teacher education as narrative inquiry. In D. J. Clandinin, A. Davies, P. Hogan, & B. Kennard (Eds.), *Learning to teach, teaching to learn: Stories of collaboration in teacher education* (pp. 1–15). New York: Teachers College Press.

Clandinin, D. J., & Connelly, F. M. (1995). *Teachers' professional knowledge landscapes*. New York: Teachers College Press.

Clift, R., Johnson, M., Holland, P., & Veal, M. (1992). Developing the potential for collaborative school leadership. *American Educational Research Journal, 28*, 877–908.

Clift, R., Veal, M., Holland, P., Johnson, M., & McCarthy, J. (1995). *Collaborative leadership and shared decision making: Teachers, principals, and university professors*. New York: Teachers College Press.

Coles, R. (1989). *The call of stories: Teaching and the moral imagination*. Boston: Houghton Mifflin.

Compton, J. (1994). *Ashpet: An Appalachian tale*. New York: Holiday House.

Cone, J. K. (1992). Untracking advanced placement English: Creating opportunity is not enough. *Phi Delta Kappan, 73*, 712–715.

Connelly, F. M. (1978). How shall we publish case studies of curriculum development? *Curriculum Inquiry, 8*, 78–82.

Connelly, F. M., & Clandinin, D. J. (1990). Stories of experience and narrative inquiry. *Educational Researcher, 19*, 2–14.

Cooper, M. (1988). Whose culture is it, anyway? In A. Lieberman (Ed.), *Building a professional culture in schools* (pp. 45–54). New York: Teachers College Press.

Covey, S. R. (1989). *The seven habits of highly effective people: Restoring the character ethic*. New York: Simon & Schuster.

Csikszentmihalyi, M. (1993). *The evolving self: A psychology for the third millennium*. New York: HarperCollins.

Csikszentmihalyi, M., & Rathunde, K. (1990). Psychology of wisdom: Evolutionary interpretation. In R. J. Sternberg (Ed.), *Wisdom: Its nature, origins, and development* (pp. 25–51). Cambridge: Cambridge University Press.

Datnow, A. (1997). Using gender to preserve tracking's status hierarchy: The defensive strategy of entrenched teachers. *Anthropology & Education Quarterly, 28*(2), 204–228.

Dewey, J. (1944). *Democracy and education.* New York: Macmillan. (Original work published 1916)

Dewey, J. (1963). *Experience and education.* New York: Macmillan. (Original work published 1938)

DiPardo, A. (1996). Seeking alternatives: The wisdom of collaborative teaching. *English Education, 28*, 109–126.

DiPardo, A. (1997). Of war, doom, and laughter: Images of collaboration in the public school workplace. *Teacher Education Quarterly, 24*, 89–104.

Eccles, J. S., & Midgley, C. (1988). Stage/environment fit: Developmentally appropriate classrooms for early adolescents. In R. E. Ames & C. Ames (Eds.), *Research on motivation in education, Vol. 3* (pp. 139–186). New York: Academic Press.

Eccles, J. S., Miller-Buchanan, C., Flanagan, C., Fuligni, A., Midgley, C., & Yee, D. (1991). Control versus autonomy during early adolescence. *Journal of Social Issues, 47*(4), 53–68.

Eccles, J. S., Wigfield, A., Midgley, C., Reuman, D., MacIver, D., & Feldlaufer, H. (1993). Negative effects of traditional middle schools on students' motivation. *The Elementary School Journal, 93*, 553–574.

Egan, K. (1992). *Imagination in teaching and learning: The middle school years.* Chicago: University of Chicago Press.

Eichhorn, D. H. (1966). *The middle school.* New York: Center for Applied Research in Education, Inc.

Emecheta, B. (1980). *The wrestling match.* New York: Oxford University Press.

Erickson, F. (1986). Qualitative methods in research on teaching. In M. C. Wittrock (Ed.), *Handbook of research on teaching* (3rd ed., pp. 119–161). New York: Macmillan.

Etzioni, A. (1993). *The spirit of community.* New York: Touchstone.

Farber, P., & Holm, G. (1994). A brotherhood of heroes: The charismatic educator in recent American movies. In P. Farber & G. Holm (Eds.), *Schooling in the light of popular culture* (pp. 153–172). Albany, NY: SUNY Press.

Finley, M. (1984). Teachers and tracking in a comprehensive high school *Sociology of Education, 57*, 233–243.

Finney, J. (1995). *From time to time.* New York: Simon & Schuster.

Fisher-Staples, S. (1989). *Shabanu: Daughter of the wind.* New York: Random House.

Forman, E. A., Minick, N., & Stone, C. A. (1993). Introduction: Integration of individual, social, and institutional processes in accounts of children's learning and development. In E. A. Forman, N. Minick, & C. A. Stone (Eds.), *Contexts for learning: Sociocultural dynamics in children's development* (pp. 3–16). New York: Oxford University Press.

Freedman, S. W. (1994a). Crossing the bridge to practice: Rethinking the theories of Vygotsky and Bakhtin. *Written Communication, 12*, 74–92.

Freedman, S. W. (1994b). *Exchanging writing, exchanging cultures.* Urbana, IL, and

Cambridge, MA: National Council of Teachers of English and Harvard University Press.

Freire, P. (1988). *Pedagogy of the oppressed* (M. B. Ramos, Trans.). New York: Continuum. (Original work published 1970)

Fullan, M., & Hargreaves, A. (1996). *What's worth fighting for in your school?* New York: Teachers College Press.

Gamoran, A., & Berends, M. (1987). The effects of stratification in secondary schools: Synthesis of survey and ethnographic research. *Review of Education Research, 57*(4), 415–435.

Gamoran, A., & Mare, R. (1989). Secondary school tracking and educational inequality: Compensation, reinforcement, or neutrality? *American Journal of Sociology, 94,* 1146–1183.

Gardner, H. (1983). *Frames of mind: The theory of multiple intelligences.* New York: Basic Books.

Gates, H. L. (1992). *Loose canons.* New York: Oxford University Press.

George, P., & Oldaker, L. (1986). A national survey of middle school effectiveness. *Educational Leadership, 43*(4), 79–85.

Gilligan, C. (1982). *In a different voice.* Cambridge, MA: Harvard University Press.

Goetz, J. P., & LeCompte, M. D. (1984). *Ethnography and qualitative design in educational research.* Orlando, FL: Academic Press.

Golding, W. (1962). *Lord of the flies.* New York: Coward-McCann.

Goleman, D. (1995). *Emotional intelligence: Why it can matter more than IQ.* New York: Bantam.

Goodlad, J. (1984). *A place called school: Prospects for the future.* New York: McGraw-Hill.

Goodlad, J., & Oakes, J. (1988). We must offer equal access to knowledge. *Phi Delta Kappan, 70*(2), 16–22.

Graves, D. H. (1983). *Writing: Children and teachers at work.* Portsmouth, NH: Heinemann.

Greene, M. (1988). *The dialectic of freedom.* New York: Teachers College Press.

Greene, M. (1991). Teaching: The question of personal reality. In A. Lieberman & L. Miller (Eds.), *Staff development for education in the 90s: New demands, new realities, new perspectives* (2nd ed., pp. 3–14). New York: Teachers College Press.

Grimm Brothers. (1945). Cinderella. In E. V. Lucas, L. Crane, & M. Edwardes (Trans.), *Grimms' fairy tales* (pp. 153–161). New York: Grosset & Dunlap.

Grossman, P. L., & Stodolsky, S. S. (1994). Considerations of content and the circumstances of secondary school teaching. In L. Darling-Hammond (Ed.), *Review of Research in Education, 20,* 179–221.

Grossman, P. L., & Stodolsky, S. S. (1995). Content as context: The role of school subjects in secondary school teaching. *Educational Researcher, 24,* 5–11.

Guba, E. G., & Lincoln, Y. S. (1989). *Personal communication.* Beverly Hills: Sage.

Hallinan, M., & Sorensen, A. (1985). Ability grouping and student friendships. *American Educational Research Journal, 22,* 485–499.

Hallinan, M., & Williams, R. (1989). Interracial friendship choices in secondary schools. *American Sociological Review, 54,* 67–78.

Hargreaves, A. (1993). Individualism and individuality: Reinterpreting the teacher culture. In J. W. Little & M. McLaughlin (Eds.), *Teachers' work: Individuals, colleagues, and contexts* (pp. 51–76). New York: Teachers College Press.

Hargreaves, A. (1994). *Changing teachers, changing times: Teachers' work and culture in the postmodern age.* New York: Teachers College Press.

Hatano, G. (1993). Time to merge Vygotskian and constructivist conceptions of knowledge acquisition. In E. A. Forman, N. Minick, & C. A. Stone (Eds.), *Contexts for learning: Sociocultural dynamics in children's development* (pp. 153–166). New York: Oxford University Press.

Hendricks-Lee, M., & Yinger, R. (1995, April). *An ecological conception of teaching.* Paper presented at the American Educational Research Association, San Francisco.

Hirsch, E. D. (1987). *Cultural literacy: What every American needs to know.* Boston: Houghton Mifflin.

Ho, M. (1989). *Rice without rain.* Portsmouth, NH: Heinemann.

Hurston, Z. N. (1978). *Their eyes were watching God.* Urbana: University of Illinois Press.

Johnson, S. M. (1990). *Teachers at work: Achieving success in our schools.* New York: Basic Books.

Joyce, B., & Showers, B. (1982). The coaching of teaching. *Educational Leadership, 40*(1), 4–8.

Kierkegaard, S. (1962). *The present age* (A. Dru, Trans.). New York: Harper & Row. (Original work published 1846)

Kitchener, K. S., & Brenner, H. (1990). Wisdom and reflective judgment: Knowing in the face of uncertainty. In R. J. Sternberg (Ed.), *Wisdom: Its nature, origins, and development* (pp. 212–229). Cambridge: Cambridge University Press.

Knowles, J. (1960). *A separate peace.* New York: Macmillan.

Kohn, A. (1996). *Beyond discipline: From compliance to community.* Alexandria, VA: Association for Supervision and Curriculum Development.

Kramer, D. A. (1983). Postformal operations? A need for further conceptualization. *Human Development, 26,* 91–105.

Labouvie-Vief, G. (1982). Dynamic development and mature autonomy: A theoretical prologue. *Human Development, 25,* 161–191

Labouvie-Vief, G. (1990). Wisdom as integrated thought: Historical and developmental perspectives. In R. J. Sternberg (Ed.), *Wisdom: Its nature, origins, and development* (pp. 52–83). Cambridge: Cambridge University Press.

Lakoff, G., & Johnson, M. (1980). *Metaphors we live by.* Chicago: University of Chicago Press.

Lave, J. (1988). *Cognition in practice: Mind, mathematics, and culture in everyday life.* Cambridge: Cambridge University Press.

Lee, D. M. (1993). The place of wisdom in teaching. *Learning and individual differences, 5,* 301–317.

Lee, H. (1960). *To kill a mockingbird.* Philadelphia: Lippincott.

Levine, L. (1996). *The opening of the American mind: Canons, culture and history.* Boston: Beacon.

Lieberman, A. (1992). The meaning of scholarly activity and the building of community. *Educational Researcher, 21,* 5–12.

Lieberman, A. (Ed.). (1995). *The work of restructuring schools: Building from the ground up*. New York: Teachers College Press.

Lieberman, A., & Miller, L. (1984). *Teachers: Their world and their work*. Alexandria, VA: Association for Supervision and Curriculum Development.

Lieberman, A., & Miller, L. (1991). Revisiting the social realities of teaching. In A. Lieberman & L. Miller (Eds.), *Staff development for education in the '90s* (2nd ed.; pp. 92–109). New York: Teachers College Press.

Lightfoot, S. L. (1983). *The good high school*. New York: Basic Books.

Lightfoot, S. L. (1986). The lives of teachers. In L. Shulman & G. Sykes (Eds.), *Handbook of teaching policy* (pp. 241–260). New York: Longman.

Lincoln, Y. S., & Guba, E. G. (1985). *Naturalistic inquiry*. Beverly Hills: Sage.

Lipsitz, J. (1984). *Successful schools for young adolescents*. Washington, DC: National Institute of Education.

Little, J. W. (1987). Teachers as colleagues. In V. Richardson-Koehler (Ed.), *Educators' handbook: A research perspective* (pp. 491–518). New York: Longman.

Little, J. W. (1990). The persistence of privacy: Autonomy and initiative in teachers' professional relations. *Teachers College Record, 91*, 509–536.

Little, J. W. (1993a). Teachers' professional development in a climate of educational reform. *Educational Evaluation and Policy Analysis, 15*, 129–151.

Little, J. W. (1993b). Professional community in comprehensive high schools: The two worlds of academic and vocational teachers. In J. W. Little & M. McLaughlin (Eds.), *Teachers' work: Individuals, colleagues, and contexts* (pp. 137–163). New York: Teachers College Press.

Lloyd-Jones, R., & Lunsford, A. (1989). *The English coalition conference: Democracy through language*. Urbana, IL, and New York: National Council of Teachers of English and Modern Language Association.

Lobel, A. (1970). *Frog and toad are friends*. New York: Harper & Row.

Lortie, D. (1975). *Schoolteacher: A sociological study*. Chicago: University of Chicago Press.

Louie, A. L. (1982). *Yeh-shen: A Cinderella story from China*. New York: Philomel Books.

Lytle, S., & Fecho, R. (1991). Meeting strangers in familiar places: Teacher collaboration by cross-visitation. *English Education, 23*, 5–28.

Maeroff, G. I. (1993). *Team building for school change: Equipping teachers for new roles*. New York: Teachers College Press.

McCutcheon, G. (1981). On the interpretation of classroom observations. *Educational Researcher, 10*, 5–10.

McDonald, J. P. (1992). *Teaching: Making sense of an uncertain craft*. New York: Teachers College Press.

Meachem, J. A. (1990). The loss of wisdom. In R. J. Sternberg (Ed.), *Wisdom: Its nature, origins, and development* (pp. 181–211). Cambridge: Cambridge University Press.

Meier, D. (1995). *The power of their ideas: Lessons for America from a small school in Harlem*. Boston: Beacon Press.

Menchu, R. (1984). *I, Rigoberto Menchu* (A. Wright, Trans.). New York: Verso.

Merriam, S. B. (1988). *Case study research in education: A qualitative approach.* San Francisco: Jossey-Bass.

Merz, C., & Furman, G. (1997). *Community and schools: Promise & paradox.* New York: Teachers College Press.

Moll, L., & Whitmore, K. (1993). Vygotsky in classroom practice: Moving from individual transmission to social transaction. In E. A. Forman, N. Minick, & C. A. Stone (Eds.), *Contexts for learning: Sociocultural dynamics in children's development* (pp. 19–42). New York: Oxford University Press.

Myers, M. (1996). *Changing our minds: Negotiating English and literacy.* Urbana, IL: National Council of Teachers of English.

Narayan, R. K. (1972). *The Ramayana: A shortened modern prose version of the Indian epic.* New York: Viking.

National Board for Professional Teaching Standards. (1989). *Toward high and rigorous standards for the teaching profession: Initial policies and perspectives of the National Board for Professional Teaching Standards.* Detroit: Author.

National Council of Teachers of English. (1962). *Resolution on class size and teacher load in secondary schools.* Urbana, IL: Author.

National Council of Teachers of English. (1991). *Resolution on tracking.* Urbana, IL: Author.

New London Group. (1996). A pedagogy of multiliteracies: Designing social futures. *Harvard Educational Review, 66,* 60–92.

Noddings, N. (1988). An ethic of caring and its implications for instructional arrangements. *American Journal of Education, 96,* 215–230.

Noddings, N. (1992). *The challenge to care in schools.* New York: Teachers College Press.

Norris, K. (1993). *Dakota: A spiritual geography.* New York: Ticknor & Fields.

Oakes, J. (1985). *Keeping track: How schools structure inequality.* New Haven: Yale University Press.

Oakes, J. (1992). Can tracking research inform practice? Technical, normative, and political considerations. *Educational Researcher, 21,* 12–21.

Oakes, J., Gamoran, A., & Page, R. (1992). Curriculum differentiation: Opportunities, outcomes, and meanings. In P. Jackson (Ed.), *Handbook of research on curriculum* (pp. 570–608). New York: Macmillan.

Oakes, J., & Lipton, M. (1992). Detracking schools: Early lessons from the field. *Phi Delta Kappan, 73,* 448–454.

Pal, G. (Producer & Director). (1982). *Time machine* [Film]. New York: MGM/UA Home Video.

Palincsar, A. S., Brown, A. L., & Campione, J. C. (1993). First-grade dialogues for knowledge acquisition and use. In E. A. Forman, N. Minick, & C. A. Stone (Eds.), *Contexts for learning: Sociocultural dynamics in children's development* (pp. 43–57). New York: Oxford University Press.

Paton, A. (1948). *Cry, the beloved country.* New York: Scribner.

Peck, M. S. (1987). *The different drum: Community making and peace.* New York: Simon & Schuster.

Perrone, V., & Traver, R. (1996). Secondary education. In J. Sikula, T. Buttery, &

E. Guyton (Eds.), *Handbook of research on teacher education* (pp. 392–409). New York: Macmillan.

Purkey, S. C., & Smith, M. S. (1983). Effective schools: A review. *Elementary School Journal, 83*, 427–454.

Quellmalz, E., Shields, P., Knapp, M., & Bamburg, J. (1995). *School-based reform: Lessons from a national study.* Washington, DC: Planning and Evaluation Service, U.S. Department of Education.

Rief, L. (1992). *Seeking diversity: Language arts with adolescents.* Portsmouth, NH: Heinemann.

Rogoff, B. (1994). Developing understanding of the idea of communities of learners. *Mind, Culture, and Activity, 1*, 209–229.

Rosenholtz, S. (1985). Effective schools: Interpreting the evidence. *American Journal of Education, 93*, 352–388.

Rosenholtz, S. (1989). *Teachers' workplace: The social organization of schools.* New York: Longman.

Rudduck, J. (1988). The ownership of change as a basis for teachers' professional learning. In J. Calderhead (Ed.), *Teachers' professional learning* (pp. 205–222). London: Falmer.

Salomon, G. (1993). *Distributed cognitions: Psychological and educational considerations.* Cambridge: Cambridge University Press.

Salter, S. (1993, August 8). Between the coasts, a sense of community. *San Francisco Examiner*, p. A-13.

Sarason, S. B. (1972). *The creation of settings and the future societies.* San Francisco: Jossey-Bass.

Sarason, S. B. (1990). *The predictable failure of educational reform: Can we change course before it's too late?* San Francisco: Jossey-Bass.

Sarason, S. B. (1996). *Revisiting "The culture of the school and the problem of change."* New York: Teachers College Press. (Original work published 1971)

Schwartz, J. (1991). Developing an ethos for professional growth: Politics and programs. In A. Lieberman & L. Miller (Eds.), *Staff development for education in the '90s: New demands, new realities, new perspectives* (pp. 184–192). New York: Teachers College Press.

Sergiovanni, T. (1994). *Building community in schools.* San Francisco: Jossey-Bass.

Shuman, A. (1986). *Storytelling rights: The uses of oral and written texts by urban adolescents.* New York: Cambridge University Press.

Siegel, P., & Byrne, S. (1994). *Using quality to redesign school systems: The cutting edge of common sense.* San Francisco: Jossey-Bass.

Siskin, L. S. (1994). *Realms of knowledge: Academic departments in secondary schools.* Washington, DC: Falmer.

Siskin, L. S., & Little, J. W. (1995). *The subjects in question: Departmental organization and the high school.* New York: Teachers College Press.

Sizer, T. (1992). *Horace's school: Redesigning the American high school.* Boston: Houghton Mifflin.

Slavin, R. E. (1988). Synthesis of research on grouping in elementary and secondary schools. *Educational Leadership, 46*(1), 67–77.

Stone, C. A. (1993). What is missing in the metaphor of scaffolding? In E. A. Forman, N. Minick, & C. A. Stone (Eds.), *Contexts for learning: Sociocultural dynamics in children's development* (pp. 169–183). New York: Oxford University Press.

Sutton, J. H. (1991). *Time for a change: A report to the people of Iowa from the teachers of Iowa.* Des Moines: Iowa State Education Association.

Tharp, R. (1993). Institutional and social context of educational practice and reform. In E. A. Forman, N. Minick, & C. A. Stone (Eds.), *Contexts for learning: Sociocultural dynamics in children's development* (pp. 269–282). New York: Oxford University Press.

Thiessen, D. (1992). Classroom-based teacher development. In A. Hargreaves & M. G. Fullan (Eds.), *Understanding teacher development* (pp. 85–109). London: Cassell/New York: Teachers College Press.

Tönnies, F. (1957). *Community and society* (C. Loomis, Ed. & Trans.). East Lansing: Michigan State University Press. (Original work published as *Gemeinschaft und Gesellschaft*, 1887)

Tyack, D., & Cuban, L. (1995). *Tinkering toward Utopia: A century of public school reform.* Cambridge, MA: Harvard University Press.

Vygotsky, L. (1978). *Mind in society.* Cambridge, MA: Harvard University Press.

Vygotsky, L. (1986). *Thought and language.* Cambridge, MA: MIT Press.

Walker, R. (1980). The conduct of educational case studies: Ethics, theory and procedures. In W. B. Dockerell & D. Hamilton (Eds.), *Rethinking educational research* (pp. 30–63). London: Hodder & Stoughton.

Weaver, C. (1979). *Grammar for teachers: Perspectives and definitions.* Urbana, IL: National Council of Teachers of English.

Weaver, C. (1996). *Teaching grammar in context.* Portsmouth, NH: Boynton/Cook.

Weissbart, D. (Producer), & Ray, N. (Director). (1983). *Rebel without a cause* [Film]. Burbank: Warner Home Video. (Originally appeared in 1955)

Wells, A., & Serna, I. (1996). The politics of culture: Understanding local political resistance to detracking in racially mixed schools. *Harvard Educational Review, 66,* 93–118.

Wells, H. G. (1949). *The time machine: An invention.* Melbourne: W. Heinemann. (Original work published 1898)

Wertsch, J. (1991). *Voices of the mind: A sociocultural approach to mediated action.* Cambridge, MA: Harvard University Press.

Wilson, K. G., & Daviss, B. (1994). *Redesigning education.* New York: Henry Holt.

Wirth, A. G. (1992). *Education and work for the year 2000: Choices we face.* San Francisco: Jossey-Bass.

Yeager, C., & Leerhsen, C. (1990). *Press on! Further adventures in the good life.* New York: Bantam Books.

Index

About the Author

Anne DiPardo is an Associate Professor of English and Education at the University of Iowa. She taught for 10 years before receiving her doctorate in Language and Literacy education from the University of California at Berkeley in 1991. She is the author of *A Kind of Passport* (NCTE, 1993) and a number of articles and book chapters about classroom collaboration and literacy learning.